NEW DAWN
NEW DAY

New Reign

NEW DAWN NEW DAY

Awakening The Kingdom Within

COURTNEY DAWN SHAW

XULON PRESS

Xulon Press
2301 Lucien Way #415
Maitland, FL 32751
407.339.4217
www.xulonpress.com

© 2022 by Courtney Dawn Shaw

All rights reserved solely by the author. The author guarantees all contents are original and do not infringe upon the legal rights of any other person or work. No part of this book may be reproduced in any form without the permission of the author.

Due to the changing nature of the Internet, if there are any web addresses, links, or URLs included in this manuscript, these may have been altered and may no longer be accessible. The views and opinions shared in this book belong solely to the author and do not necessarily reflect those of the publisher. The publisher therefore disclaims responsibility for the views or opinions expressed within the work.

Unless otherwise indicated, Scripture quotations taken from the King James Version (KJV) – *public domain*.

Scripture quotations taken from the New King James Version (NKJV). Copyright © 1982 by Thomas Nelson, Inc. Used by permission. All rights reserved.

Scripture quotations taken from the Holy Bible, New International Version (NIV). Copyright © 1973, 1978, 1984, 2011 by Biblica, Inc.™ Used by permission. All rights reserved.

Paperback ISBN-13: 978-1-6628-4224-5
eBook ISBN-13: 978-1-6628-4225-2

DEDICATION

———◇———

Jeffrey Michael Shaw, the love of my life, my best friend, forever encouraging me to answer the high calling of God in Christ Jesus.

Kingston and Carrington Reigns Shaw, my greatest gifts that keep on giving every single day. You both bring me immense joy and deep gratitude for the opportunity to be your mom and help you nurture and cultivate your God-given purpose. You are the inspiration for this book and the reason for a new reign. P.S. Isn't it like God to write a new chapter in our family's story as I complete this book? Surprise! We're going to be a family of 5!

My incredible parents, Kerry and Debbie Phillips, Pa and Ma Bear. You have always been in my corner and have taught me the power of God's unconditional love. You make life special, memorable, and meaningful.

My Shaw brothers and sisters. So proud to call you my family. We've been on this healing journey together, and I adore the memories we're making. Thank you for standing in truth and having the courage to create a new legacy as a united front. My amazing nephews and nieces. There is a mighty path being blazed for your safe passage. Never take it for granted and know that you are loved unconditionally by your Creator, King, and family.

My ancestors in the faith who went before me to pave the way. My family is bearing fruit from your fortitude, grit, sacrifices, and prayers.

My Phillips, Shaw/Cooper, Barber family. Thank you for your unconditional love, prayers, and endless support through the years.

Friends and sisters in Christ, Suzie, Candi, Arlene, Anissa, Tracey, Angie, and Jennifer.

My daughter, Carrington Shaw, has a series coming soon, which you can follow on Instagram at @ReigningHisway. Follow this curly-haired girl with lots of grit and a heart of gold as she introduces you to friends who will help you earn your crowns. She also has Care's Creation Station: "Inspiring Kids to be Creative while caring for others." Follow her on Instagram at @CarringtonReignsShaw.

My son, Kingston Shaw, is an inspiration for his generation. Follow him on Instagram as well at @KingstonReigns.

ENDORSEMENTS

Courtney Shaw is a courageous woman of God. She is fierce in her faith and frank with her views. But, as Courtney points out, being courageous doesn't mean you are *fearless*; it just means that you walk by faith in spite of your fears, and as you do, you will fear *less*. As Courtney shares her and her husband Jeff's story of love, pain and redemption, I think many will relate to the authentic way she describes what it means to reign with Jesus, even in the ruins of this fallen world.

- Pastor John Hampton
  Journey Christian Church Apopka, FL

Courtney and I share a joint mission to empower others to live in the freedom of Christ by glorifying God in their bodies. She powerfully delivers in New Dawn, New Day, New Reign. Through real life stories, biblical truth, and thought provoking questions, she shows you how to defeat the lies that hold you back and reign over the very things in life you think you can't. This book equips you to reign over identity, worth, friendships and even fitness. I plan on buying a copy for all of the women in my life.

- Kim Dolan Leto Speaker, Author, Mom, and Coach
  Best Selling Christian Author- Strong Confident His Podcast- Creator of Faith Inspired Transformation Workout Series
  KimDolanLeto.com

Identity is the core of who we are, and often the root of why we struggle. The global pandemic magnified those struggles for millions, and led some to reinvent their lives based on what matters most. Courtney Dawn Shaw understands the struggle over identity and writes on how to move past the pressure to realize your potential in Christ. If you've been feeling overwhelmed by bad news, or discouraged and stuck in a rut, remember there is a new day dawning. Pick up this book to find direction to live out your God-given true identity in freedom and peace.

- Dwight Bain
  Nationally Certified Counselor and Founder of the LifeWorks Counseling Group

In this book, Courtney powerfully shares her most vulnerable moments of raw pain, disappointment and triumph she's experienced throughout her life. For anyone who desires to discover who you are in Christ and overcome the lies of the enemy...*this book is a must read!!*

- Martha Munnizi
  Award winning gospel artist, Pastor at Epic Life Church with her husband Dan Munnizi

"I could not have read this book at a more opportune time. Stuck in a rut? Bored with the same old routine? Read this book and get ready to Reign in a New Day!"

- James Sang Lee
  4x ISKA World Champion

As a close friend and sister in Christ for nearly a decade, I have watched Courtney overcome challenges and build productive habits to 'reign' in every area of her life. In her multifaceted role as mother, wife, public speaker, entrepreneur, life coach, and beauty queen, she manages the demands of each responsibility with grace and elegance. Like a warm hug, you will find that this book, "New Dawn, New Day, New Reign" Awakening the Kingdom within, embraces the soul and brings comfort to those who may be hurting and need a shimmer of motivation. Through great transparency, Courtney takes the reader on a journey of self-reflection and thought that helps them to understand the real meaning of walking into God's light and setting a better standard for living. With each inspiring page, Courtney uniquely explores the purpose of our daily battles and demonstrates how to find hope, encouragement, and strength. From the point of understanding who you are, to knowing the legacy that you would like to leave, Courtney offers support with strategies for 'reigning' in life and becoming a better YOU!

- Anissa King
  Founder of the Ms. And Mrs. Corporate America organization

Courtney's knowledge of the word, purity of heart and her willingness to be vulnerable in order to help the greater good is refreshing. *A New Dawn, New Day, New Reign* is a must read. Congrats Courtney on this phenomenal book!

- Dr. James "Butch" Rosser & Dana Rosser
  Author of Thru Thick & Thin

Courtney Dawn Shaw is a woman who will fight for you when you're down in the trenches, walk alongside you in your deepest pain and grab ahold of your hand when you feel like everyone else has turned on you. She is the definition of an authentic woman of God. From the minute that you meet Courtney you know without a shadow of a doubt that God has placed and anointing on her to speak and share the depth of her soul with the world. I feel truly blessed to call her friend and sister in Jesus. This is just the start of her journey, so I suggest you jump on board, devour these words and buckle up as God speaks through Courtney to shower you with freedom in Him.

- Jennifer Porrata
  Actress, Mrs. New Jersey 2014-15

I've known and worked with Courtney for over 10 years through My Christian Films, 24 Flix, ICFF (International Christian Film Festival), and her radio and TV show Authentic Living. I've seen her grow both spiritually and personally while serving in multiple media platforms. Her commitment to be a private and public servant of the King has helped set her apart in an industry that is primarily focused on the outward show. She is a warrior for Christ and I can't wait to see what she does next. Her book is an inspiration and one that everyone must read.

- Marty Jean-Louis Producer
  Founder of ICFF, and 24 Flix

There is no other way to describe this masterful work of heavenly insights than to say Courtney Shaw's book is a God given love letter to those who need hope. As I read each word, I could feel my thirsty soul being filled with powerful nourishment to revive a hopeless heart. Her book takes you on a journey of discovering who were designed to be and to help you unleash the power of your royal position in God's kingdom. I was blessed beyond measure and forever changed by Courtney's words, so intentionally placed on each page. I strongly believe that any person who reads this will experience a transformation, more into the likeness of their creator.

- Candi Bryan
  Mrs. Corporate America 2019-20

ENDORSEMENTS

CEO of C&J Media, Marketing & Public Relations, Breast Cancer Survivor, and Host of The Good Morning Show

New Dawn, New Day, New Reign "Awakening the "Kingdom Within" is a powerful tool to guide you through a noble journey of healing, wholeness, acceptance, and power in Christ. Your mental health is on the forefront of God's mind all the time. Philippians 2:5-11 says, "Let this mind be in you which was in Christ Jesus." The enemy is a liar and a deceiver. He would want nothing more for you to be a slave to your past trauma and debilitate you from embracing truth, healing, and freedom. It's time to wake up and walk out your divine calling and position in the kingdom as a son and daughter of God. There is no shame in seeking wise counsel and accountability. Reach out to a local Christian counselor and put in the work to break the toxic cycles in your life.

- Dr. Marcelline Girlie, DNP,FNP-BC,PMHNP-BC

If you are looking for a roadmap to kingdom living, then "New Dawn, New Day, New Reign" needs to be your guide to forgiveness and allowing God's love to provide freedom and wholeness. My favorite part of the book is the "Quest"ions section at the end of each chapter. She gives you next steps and points you in the direction for growth. The words in this book breathe the peace of God while facing insurmountable odds. We need more bold believers to speak their truth rooted in God's grace. Clearly these steps have paved the way for success in Courtney's own life and if it has worked for her then I'm ALL IN!

- Angela Doggett Speaker
  Consultant, Executive Director for DLI.
  www.doggettleadership.com

From the moment I met Courtney I could feel and see her love for God and her love for people. She lives her life with authenticity and encourages and helps those around her do the same. How she communicates in this book is no different. She brings her authentic self to God and invites us to go along with her on the journey. I have grown and been challenged by this book already. I appreciate how she takes one area at a time and looks at how we can live with purpose and freedom in each of those areas. Courtney, keep sharing the love and freedom of God everywhere you go! Love you!

- Jodi Garvin
  Convoy: Women's Event Coordinator at Convoy of Hope
  www.convoyofhope.org

For many, life can be operated in survival mode. This is a natural modality of wading through the tough stuff, and it comes from a place of protection. However, it will soon catch up with you and begin to spill over into many different facets of life (personal, occupational, and relational), eventually impeding your true progress and growth. Courtney has taken the challenges of her life and has peeled them back for the readers to see that survival mode is not the only option. Through liberation in Christ Jesus, she understood her value. Courtney's raw and real experiences will help all readers come to a point of wanting more and better for themselves. As you read each page, you will feel like she's having a conversation with you over a cup of coffee. This powerful book is written in a way where you get her, feel her, and connect with her in many ways. It is a great honor for us to endorse New Dawn, New Day, New Reign: Awakening the Kingdom Within. You will be blessed beyond measure from start to finish!

- Dominick Shaw
  MBA & Diana Shaw, Ed.S, LMHC

(Founder of Chaos Solutions Counseling, LLC)

"New Dawn, New Day, New Reign inspires, empowers, and equips you with keys to awaken the kingdom within and embrace who you've been divinely designed to be as a son or daughter of the King. Living legacy minded helps you maximize your moments, relationships, and be intentional about taking responsibility for how your choices affect others around you. I believe God has a divine design for the family as Courtney so beautifully expresses. There has never been a greater time to claim and declare God's promises for your family and to fight for your family with courage and grace."

- Michelle Gage
  Author, Speaker, Pastor at ReThink Church, Worship Leader, Wife, and Mom

New Dawn, New Day, New Reign is a powerful charge to all of God's people to walk in your royal calling! Courtney's words written within these pages will awaken this generation to live the life Jesus died for us to live. As I've experienced in my own life, nothing truly worthwhile in this life is easy but we are more than conquerors through Christ Jesus. We have authority over the enemies plans and by reading this book you will be equipped to change your perspective and embrace God's truth. These words will speak to your true identity in Christ despite your gifting, talents, and abilities. It will empower you to release the lies of the enemy. My sister Courtney is on a mission to help you take your rightful place within the kingdom. This book is an invitation to come into right relationship with a God who loves you unconditionally, wholly, and completely not based upon your performance but because of your position as His son or daughter. It's time to rise, shine, and reign in a new way.

- Jeannie Ortega Law
  Recording Artist, Author, Evangelist, Journalist

I've had the amazing experience of sharing some of Courtney's journey with her as a sister in Christ. I believe God gave us a divine friendship many years ago so we could encourage, strengthen, and offer support for each other as we walked out our faith. Courtney's story is one of inspiration, determination, and transformation that comes from surrendering your life to God's will. He will build a kingdom life out of the darkness we face. The light of Jesus shines bright in her story so others can understand that all we face in life; the good, bad, and ugly can be overcome and we can thrive as children of God. We can conquer any life's obstacles with His Spirit reigning through and within us. It's time for a new day to dawn!

- Suzanne Hunt
  Founder of New Life Farm

TABLE OF CONTENTS

Dedication v
Endorsements ix
A Note From the Author xix

Chapter One   Reign in Your Royal Identity 1
Chapter Two   Reign over Your Past 12
Chapter Three   Reign in Truth 41
Chapter Four   Reign in Faith 72
Chapter Five   Reign in New Territory 100
Chapter Six   Reign in the Day 141
Chapter Seven   Reign in Relationships 181
Chapter Eight   Reign in Legacy 259

About the Author 321
Bibliography Notes 323

A NOTE FROM THE AUTHOR

*Note: This book can be read individually or as an eight-week study for small groups. The book is broken down into eight chapters. I intentionally chose eight because the number eight represents new beginnings. At the end of each chapter, you can answer the questions, study the scriptures, then write and speak out loud your New Reign declarations. If you are reading this book in a small group, each week, have your tribe read a chapter, take notes, and answer the questions. When you schedule your weekly gathering, have someone open in prayer, then begin the discussion. Make sure to share answers to your questions, then close in prayer. Let your group know this is a safe place to share, release, cry, laugh, and be built up. Make it clear to your group that everything shared during your time remains confidential. Reigning together makes life even better! At the end of your eight week journey plan a "New Reign Celebration." You can make it big or small in a special location. Invite friends and family to be in attendance to witness your transformation. Have each person in your group share their New Reign declaration and story. Don't forget to record a 30 second video declaring what you're reigning over in your life and #CelebrateYourReign on Facebook and Instagram.

Visit: CourtneyDawnShaw.com for more resources

Proverbs 27:17 proclaims, **"As iron sharpens iron, so one person sharpens another."** This simple statement is a calling to help us understand that no one is alone. In order to make yourself better, there is a mutual benefit making others better through mentorship, follower-ship, and leading.

Chapter One

REIGN IN YOUR ROYAL IDENTITY

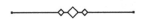

"You are a chosen race, a royal priesthood, a holy nation, a people for his own possession."

—1 Peter 2:9

DAWN

Tomorrow again the dawn will rise,
Always anticipated without surprise.
The day begins to grow more light
As the dawning appears to be in sight.

Many impressions dawn upon me
With the gift of a new day so free.
Darkness fades away during the daybreak
With a newfound strength you partake.

Up in the sky the sun begins to rise high,
Such a breathtaking beauty; you sigh.
This dawning of day stimulates the soul
To determine to attain a very definite goal.

Your soul awakens as the day begins,
To develop new beginnings; a message sends.
This whole transformation from night to day
Gives one sufficient reason to give thanks and pray.

It's a new dawn, it's a new day, it's a new reign when
you choose to let go of what was and embrace all
that God has called and created you to be.
So, receive your reign and let the truth make you free.

- Patricia A. Amburgey (My Mimi)
Award Winning Poet
Great Poets across America

Right now, we have a major identity crisis in our world. We are looking to politicians, celebrities, and influencers to tell us what we should wear, how we should vote, what type of house we should live in, and who we should marry. We measure our value by degrees, net worth, titles, accomplishments, and the amount of likes and followers we have. Although we have become more globally connected through the internet and social media platforms, we are more disconnected than ever before. When sitting at a table and eating a meal, we have a hard time engaging with the person in front of us because we are glued to a screen. With one quick scroll through Facebook, Instagram, or TikTok, our whole attitude can change from one of peace and confidence to one of insecurity, doubt, self-pity, and defeat. The average person spends nearly 2 hours a day using social media, which amounts to 5 years and 4 months of his/her lifetime. For teens, social media time spent could be up to 9 hours every day. Today, depression, low self-esteem, divorce, and suicide are at an all-time high.

There are seasons and times for everything under heaven, and there is a divine pace that allows us to walk in cadence with God's perfect will for our lives. However, our world is so fast paced that it feels like we are all on the verge of imploding. God never intended for His creation to live at this rapid speed.

Well, I believe a serious implosion took place in the spring of 2020. COVID-19 came on the scene, putting the entire world on pause. The hustle and bustle, social events, sports, activities, celebrations, and life as we knew it came to a screeching halt. Facing a global crisis, we were all forced to refocus on what really matters most. Many people lost family members, friends, and co-workers to this terrible virus. There is nothing like facing death head on that will awaken you to really living. In 2020, we were given a window of time in which we could take advantage of the silence and slower pace that came with the pandemic, allowing God to remind us of who we are and what His original plan for His creation was and still is.

So many of us have been forced to start over, feeling so devastated that we don't know where to begin. Let me start by telling you that there is nothing you did to deserve the pain, loss, or hurt you're experiencing. The Bible clearly tells us that in this world, we will have trouble, but we can be of good cheer because Christ has overcome the world (John 16:33).

My prayer is that as you read through these pages, you will find hope, encouragement, and strength, and that you will be equipped to activate your God-given authority to overcome life's obstacles. You are not powerless; you have access to resurrection power through the completed work of Jesus Christ on the cross over two thousand years ago. When you receive His gift of salvation, you are welcomed into a beautiful family where you are loved unconditionally, completely, and wholly. You did nothing to earn this birthright, for you were chosen and adopted into His family. You are now His beloved son or daughter. Because of this, the Bible says that nothing in all creation will be able to separate us from the love of God that is in Christ Jesus our Lord and King. All you need to do is believe it and receive it.

Your true identity, value, and worth are tied to an eternal God who loves you with an everlasting love. When someone knows that they are loved unconditionally, they feel safe, accepted, and protected, and they are empowered to take that first step, knowing that whether they win or lose doesn't change their position. You have nothing to lose and everything to gain by stepping into the unknown with courage and faith. So, I admonish you to take the first step of obedience and receive your reign.

Being a son or daughter of the King means that you have royal blood flowing through your veins. With all of heaven backing you, you now have access to walk in a place of authority over your past, present, and future. The kingdom of God reigns in you by the gift of salvation and through you by the transforming of your mind with the Word of God. You will ultimately reign with the King of kings for eternity. One glorious day, there will be no more pain, disappointment, devastation, heartache, discord, and chaos. All that was dark will come into the fullness of His marvelous light, and we will be made whole in the presence of our heavenly Father. 1 Corinthians 13:12 says, "For now we see in a mirror dimly, but then face to face. Now I know in part; then I shall know fully, even as I have been fully known." That is the hope we have as an anchor of our soul, firm and secure (Heb. 6:19).

If you have never accepted Jesus Christ as your Lord and Savior, now is the time to surrender. Maybe you've already said yes but find yourself walking in a place of defeat. Perhaps life is happening to you rather than through you. If so, now is a great time to re-dedicate your life and allow God's eternal peace, joy, and hope to reign in and through your life.

Pray with me:

Dear heavenly Father, I come to You right now and admit that I am lost without You. I recognize that You sent Your Son Jesus to die on the cross for my sins so that I might be reconciled to You. I receive forgiveness and release any hurt, anger, bitterness, trauma, and disappointment. I am now Your child and a part of Your royal family. I have full access to Your power and authority over anything that would come to weigh me down and rob me from all that You have to accomplish in my life. You love me unconditionally and perfectly, and that is more than enough to give me confidence to conquer my past, embrace the present, and look forward to the future. Your reign in my life begins today, _____ .

Happy spiritual birthday! (Make it "reign" confetti!) You are here to fulfill a divine purpose for such a time as this and to shine light into a very dark world. You are fearfully and wonderfully made, the head and not the tail, above and not beneath, more than a conqueror, and positioned for a beautiful new beginning. 2 Corinthians 5:17 says, "Old things pass away, behold all things become new."

Proverbs 18:21 tells us, "The power of death and life is in the tongue." If God created the world through His spoken words and you are now His child, then you've been given the same power in the words you speak. Words have weight and frame the world around you. There's an old rhyme that says, "Sticks and stones may break my bones, but words will never hurt me." That couldn't be more of a lie. Words can heal, uplift, build up, or tear down lives, families, generations, communities, and even countries. They can bring war or peace.

Declare out loud the following with me and feel every word as it leaves your tongue: "It's a new dawn, a new day, and a new reign in my life." Let's take a moment to break down the meaning of this powerful declaration.

> Words can heal, uplift, build up, or tear down lives, families, generations, communities, and even countries. They can bring war or peace.
>
> Declare out loud the following with me and feel every word as it leaves your tongue: "It's a new dawn, a new day, and a new reign in my life."

"A new dawn" is the period in a new day when light from the sun begins to appear in the sky, piercing through the darkness. It is also the time when something new begins, such as a new period in history.

"A new day" is day one in a journey or a period of time. It represents a clean slate, a fresh beginning, hope, a new opportunity, or a chance to begin again.

"A new reign" is the period during which a new sovereign occupies the throne. It represents a new dominating power or influence coming into control. Who or what is reigning in your life? How will you reign?[1]

It's time to embrace hope, healing, freedom, and wholeness in who you've been called and created to be. It's time to wipe the dust off of your broken dreams and allow the divine orchestrator to transform your life into a beautiful symphony. God wants to use your life to write an epic tale that will be told for generations to come. His pen is ready to record a gloriously grand redemption story in which His love transforms you and the world around you into something incredible.

God never intended for His crowning creation to walk around with her head held low, beaten down, and crushed by the cares of this world. Your decision to follow Christ will impact your family for generations to come. You can't control what happens to yourself in this life, but you can control how you will respond to all that comes your way. You can become better and not bitter. Your pain can either leave you paralyzed or propel you into a deeper level of purpose and dependence on your Lord and Savior.

How will you reign? Will you allow anger, envy, hurt, and regret to rob you of your God-given power, or will you allow unconditional love, compassion, wisdom, gratitude, and service toward others to drive you? God gave His creation free will. He wanted us to choose Him and in return receive His everlasting love that heals us, frees us, makes us whole, and empowers us to create lasting change for our good and His glory. We can allow the chains of our past to hold us prisoners or allow grace and truth to awaken the kingdom within and activate our birthright as a child of God.

So, what is the kingdom, and how do we activate it on a daily basis? In Luke 17:21, Jesus said, "For indeed the kingdom of God is within you." He was speaking of Himself. When you are under Jesus's lordship and give Him control of your life, you are filled with the kingdom of God. Romans 14:17 says that the kingdom of God is not rules and regulations, but righteousness, and peace, and joy in the Holy Spirit. It is not self-righteousness, such as being right to the detriment of others and breeding constant contention. Rather, the kingdom is the righteousness of God in Christ Jesus, which is having right standing with our heavenly Father through the sacrifice that Jesus made on the cross.

The peace that passes all understanding and the joy in the Holy Spirit are not luxuries but our royal birthright to access when the world is spinning in total chaos and uncertainty. The world tells us to seek after happiness, but it fails to inform us how fickle of an aspiration happiness is and how it is dependent on our external circumstances, which are always subject to change. True joy is an internal and eternal strength that does not come from this world. The Bible says that for the joy set before Jesus, He endured the cross. Jesus must have seen something so beautiful, breathtaking, and glorious that He mustered up the strength and fortitude to surrender to such agony during His crucifixion. He saw you and me totally redeemed and made free in His agape—unconditional—love for us. He saw the enemy defeated and under His and our feet forever. Love conquered all and continues to conquer all, both in this world and the one to come.

Join me on the most worthwhile journey of learning to reign over our past, activate our faith, and stand on the unchanging truth of God's promises. You will reign in your health, strength, and relationships, as well as conquer your day, embrace new territory, and live with your legacy in mind. I pray that you will be encouraged by my own journey and know without a shadow of a doubt that God is with you, for you, and not against you. At the end of each chapter, you will have a time of reflection in which you will go on a noble quest to answer questions, seek the truth, activate God's Word, and declare a new reign in different areas of your life.

Allow me to be your personal encourager and sister in arms. My mission is to remind you who you are in Jesus Christ and equip you to access total authority through Him. The battle is not yours; it is the Lord's. You, my friend, are not fighting for victory; you are fighting from victory! You are more than a conqueror and called to reign for such a time as this. God is Jehovah Nissi, the victory banner going before us into our daily battles.

Some years ago, a friend gave me a devotional called *My Utmost for His Highest* written by Oswald Chambers. In a devotion titled "The Doorway to the Kingdom," Chambers wrote these life-giving words that unlocked the mystery of the gospel to me: "Always remember the underlying foundation of Jesus Christ's kingdom is poverty, not possessions; not making decisions for Jesus, but having such a sense of absolute futility that we finally admit, 'Lord, I cannot even begin to do it.' Then Jesus says, 'Blessed are you...' (Matt. 5:11)." This is the doorway to the kingdom, and yet it takes us so long to believe that we are actually poor! The knowledge of our own poverty is what brings us to the proper place where Jesus Christ accomplishes His work.

KINGDOM (QUEST)IONS

1. What lies have you or someone else spoken over your life that you have believed?

   _____

   _____

   _____

2. What aspects of your life do you need to release to God?

   _____

   _____

   _____

3. What does a new reign look like in your life?

_____

_____

_____

4. Who can you ask to go on this journey with you?

_____

_____

_____

KINGDOM TRUTHS

"Behold, I am doing a new thing now it springs forth, do you not perceive it? I will make a way in the wilderness and rivers in the desert."–Isaiah 43:19

"For I know the plans I have for you, declares the Lord, plans for welfare and not for evil, to give you a future and a hope."–Jeremiah 29:11

"Fear not, for I am with you; be not dismayed, for I am your God; I will strengthen you, I will help you, I will uphold you with my righteous right hand."–Isaiah 41:10

"For nothing will be impossible with God."–Luke 1:37

"Therefore, if anyone is in Christ, he is a new creation. The old has passed away; behold, the new has come."–2 Corinthians 5:17

"And have put on the new self, which is being renewed in knowledge after the image of its creator."—Colossians 3:10

"For by grace you have been saved through faith. And this is not your own doing; it is the gift of God, not a result of works, so that no one may boast."—Ephesians 2:8-9

KINGDOM DECLARATION

Today, _____, I, _____, declare that it's a new dawn, a new day, and a new reign in my life. I choose to believe that I am fearfully and wonderfully made in God's image. I refuse to be imprisoned by the lies that have held me captive and will embrace the truth that I am a child of God, called to reign in Christ for such a time as this. I cast off fear and put on grace and truth in order to embark on this journey of total freedom. I will no longer limit myself by my words, actions, or deeds. I accept responsibility for my life and surrender all of my doubts, hurts, disappointments, and anger to my Creator and King. I choose to walk in righteousness, peace, and joy in the Holy Ghost and step into my royal calling.

In Jesus's name, amen.

Chapter Two

REIGN OVER YOUR PAST

"At the Break of Dawn"

"God is in the midst of her, she shall not be moved;
God shall help her, just at the break of dawn."

–Psalm 46:5

Here's the deal with the past: everyone has one, and anyone who has been on this planet for more than five minutes has gone through something. Even birth itself is a very traumatic experience. I mean, who really wants to leave the comfort, safety, and warmth of their mother's womb? If you haven't faced any adversity in your life, you will. That's not to put a damper on your reality; it just comes with the territory. We live in a fallen world where humans have been facing disappointment, hurt, rejection, loss, setbacks, failures, false accusations, abandonment, abuse, racism, and injustice since the beginning of time.

In this life, there are things that happen to us or our loved ones that are completely out of our control. We have an enemy whose mission is to steal, kill, and destroy (John 10:10). His battle to gain control over our souls begins early in our lives. The quicker the enemy can gain territory in our hearts and minds, keeping us in a state of defeat, the better his chances are to hold us captive as adults while blinding us of our royal identity and rightful authority over his plans. The devil would love nothing more than to have us all walking around wounded, ashamed, offended, and disillusioned, coaxing us to become skeptical of God's goodness, faithfulness, and perfect love. This deception began in the Garden of Eden, and the enemy's mission was to tempt God's creation to believe that God was holding back on them, keeping them in the dark. God's original plan was to give man dominion over the earth, but Satan came on the scene to destroy that plan.

Genesis 1:26-28 says, "And God blessed them, and God said unto them, Be fruitful, and multiply, and replenish the earth, and subdue it: and have dominion over the fish of the sea, and over the fowl of the air, and over every living thing that moveth upon the earth." Before the fall, Adam and Eve had free reign within the safety of God's protection. God had put these boundaries in place for their protection, not to block them out. However, when they succumbed to temptation and ate from the tree of the knowledge of good and evil, sin entered the world and the battle began.

Satan is a liar and deceiver, and the tactics he used in the garden are still the same in present day. His main aim is to convince us that we're not loved, not worthy, full of failures, unable to measure up, and without hope for eternity. The good news is that God had a redemption plan all along to reconcile and reinstate us back into our rightful place as sons and daughters of His kingdom. He sent His Son Jesus, the perfect sacrifice, to redeem all of humanity. God chose for His Son the most gruesome and dehumanizing death—death on the cross—which allowed Jesus to be a bridge of salvation, from death to life and bondage to freedom, for eternity.

There couldn't be a resurrection without the crucifixion. Sorrow and success are always interconnected. T.D. Jakes, one of my all-time favorite preachers and teachers of the Word, shared a powerful message called *Branded*, in which he discussed how after Jesus was resurrected and came back to visit the disciples, "Doubting" Thomas wanted to see Jesus's scars to know He was indeed his Lord and Savior. Thomas saw Jesus on the cross and desired proof and authentication of the resurrection. Why would God the Father not erase the visual of His greatest agony on earth? He wanted to show the world that He recognizes us through our scars.

Our wounds make us worthy of the call on our lives to reign with Him, both on earth and in glory. Our scars are our brand and what sets us apart. No one has gone through the exact circumstances as you, which is what makes you unique and authentically you! The Bible tells us that we are overcomers by the blood of the Lamb and the word of our testimony. We all have a story to tell, and once we invite Jesus into our story, He has the ability to deliver us, heal us, and set us completely free from the chains of our past, leaving us unashamed.

> Our wounds make us worthy of the call on our lives to reign with Him, both on earth and in glory. Our scars are our brand and what sets us apart. No one has gone through the exact circumstances as you, which is what makes you unique and authentically you!

I encourage you to invite this loving Savior to go with you on a journey to search your heart and confront all that has been holding you captive, preventing you from moving forward. When we take Jesus with us down this path, we don't have to be afraid of what we will find, for God has not given us a spirit of fear, but of love, power, and a sound mind (2 Tim. 1:7). God gave us a memory not to torment us but to help us recollect and learn from the past through the filter of His agape love.

You don't have to separate your pain from your power. They go hand in hand; you can't have one without the other. How would we have genuine compassion, empathy, wisdom, strength, grit, and fortitude if we had never gone through anything? How could we truly relate to or help others overcome their own challenges, pain, or trauma if our lives had remained untouched? What God has allowed you to go through and grow through was not for your destruction but for your construction, allowing you to be built up as a strong tower of hope and a beacon of light leading others to Christ, the Healer and Redeemer.

God always has in mind a greater purpose for our pain. He is sovereign and looks at our lives from a very different perspective. Isaiah 55:9 says, "For my thoughts are not your thoughts neither are your ways my ways,' declares the Lord. 'As the heavens are higher than the earth so are my ways higher than your ways, and my thoughts than your thoughts."

Your scars are like shimmering golden billboards for others to see God's glorious redemptive plan for His children. They are not something you have to cover up or be ashamed of. No amount of lying, denial, pride, makeup, or plastic surgery can ever hide the purpose in your pain. Until we make peace and own our war wounds, we will forever be prisoners never set free. So, put those babies proudly on display as reminders that you are branded, called, anointed, and set apart for such a time as this. The very thing you have been trying to hide is the very thing that will give you access to your greater purpose and fulfillment.

None of us can control the family into which we were born. Some of us even grew up as orphans, without a father or mother. Maybe you had parents but they were always consumed with work or had an angry and abusive nature. Perhaps you grew up in a loving home like mine but still felt an empty space within your heart that only God's love can fill. No other human being can match the endless love of our heavenly Father.

Whatever your childhood may have been, you are here, and God had a divine plan to bring you into the world through your specific lineage. There might be good things from your childhood that you can bring into the future, or you might have to start completely over. There are countless people that have suffered devastating loss from accidents, natural disasters, and abandonment. The one thing they all have in common is another chance to activate hope and start anew. Either way, you have the choice to take the good and leave the bad at the feet of Jesus.

My pastor John Hampton once said, "Jesus Himself was brought into the world in the most scandalous way. His mother was a 'pregnant virgin' and not yet married to her betrothed. He had murderers and adulterers in His bloodline. But, one thing is for sure. When He stepped in the family tree, everything was redeemed and forever changed. That gives all of us hope that we don't have to be defined by our past or upbringing." No matter how broken or sick our family tree may be, God can and will do a new thing starting with us. It's a new reign in your bloodline, and it begins with you.

Jesus says, "I am the vine and you are the branches. If you abide in Me you will bear much fruit. Apart from Me you can do nothing – John 15:5 God is the gardener, and He knows how to pluck and prune the painful spaces and places in our hearts so new life can spring forth and bloom. We can also look at Jesus as the Master Surgeon in our lives. He desires you to place your mangled, bruised, broken, and messed-up heart in His loving care and gentle hands. Allow Him to do exploratory surgery on your soul and walk down the halls of your heart that have been bruised, battered, and torn by the pain that you or others have inflicted. He wants to open up any areas where pain has formed and calloused blockage within you. Ezekiel 36:26 says, "I will give you a new heart and put a new spirit in you; I will remove from you your heart of stone and give you a heart of flesh." Jesus's mission is to open the blocked arteries so His precious blood can flow and restore life where there was death and decay. His blood that He shed on Calvary over two thousand years ago holds the same power today.

I can say all this with total conviction and confidence because He has done this deep work in my life. He is no respecter of persons (Acts 10:34). If Christ's love can heal, restore, and redeem me, His love can do the same for you. In order to receive from Him, you have to make a daily decision to care. This wasn't an easy decision for me, but it is one I choose to make every single day of my life. It's easy to stay prideful, jaded, skeptical, bitter, and hard-hearted, refusing to care, but it takes great courage, determination, and intentionality to cast off the lies you have been harboring and believe the truth that you are loved unconditionally. God gave His creation free will. He never wanted a bunch of robots walking around earth under His forceful control. Actually, His desire for us is the exact opposite. He wants His precious creation to freely choose Him and in return receive His unconditional love and never-ending restoration through His grace.

Courtney at 2 ½ years old A.K.A "Tough Cookie"

My story is one of growing up in a loving home with parents who not only loved each other but liked one another as well. In fact, they cleared the dinner table many nights with their "displays of affection." My parents were the definition of a team, and together they worked hard to make home a safe place where my brothers and I could take our armor off and be built up by their love. My dad treated my mom as his equal, and we knew that their love for one another was genuine.

I was in between two brothers and, from an early age, was nicknamed "Tough Cookie." I was fearless and tough yet sweet and tender, and I was all at once a talkative, adventurous, tom-boy and girly girl with a temper. My early years were consumed with training for the Junior Olympics, travel soccer, friends, dance, and celebrating life with family. I was confident in my parents' love for me, which gave me an unstoppable spirit to conquer in cross country, dance, and soccer. I grew up going to church on Sundays and knew Jesus loved me and I loved him back. My parents never beat me over the head with a Bible, and I believe that has something to do with my personal walk with God to this day. They always made it clear that a relationship with Jesus was something I would have to decide when I was ready to commit my life to Him.

My dad was and is an incredible cook, and during holidays, he always had something delicious on the table. My mom made every holiday special with decorations and set a fun, loving, and creative atmosphere in the home. We weren't wealthy, but my parents always made sure we had a safe home to live in and had all of our needs and many wants met.

I'm sharing all of this to explain that it wasn't until my teenage years when things started to shift for me. For many teens, these years are a time to break away from the safety of the family unit and test new boundaries. My friends and peers had great influence over my life during that time, and the pressure to be all things to all people became all consuming. During my freshman year of high school, I started dating a guy who was a senior, and our relationship became my main focus. I stayed with him through my junior year, when my world as I knew it would forever change.

Courtney in High School getting up to watch the sunrise at the beach

I can remember one day in the fall, when I was battling strep throat. Growing up, I always had big tonsils, and the doctors never wanted to remove them. They always told my parents that my tonsils were there to fight infection and should not be removed. However, they became my nemesis, as they caused me constant sickness. Looking back, I don't know how I competed in sports at the level I did while constantly fighting illness.

That day, I decided to stay after school and attend soccer practice so I could play in the game later that week. Despite running a fever and having trouble breathing, I pressed my way through. I remember coming home that evening and crawling up in my bed, shivering. My breathing was very labored and, feeling really weak, I passed out. Not too soon after, my parents came in to check on me and found me not breathing and incoherent. They immediately called 911, and the paramedics arrived promptly.

Thankfully, the fire station was just minutes away. The EMTs began to perform CPR and got me breathing again. Out of precaution, they decided to take me to the hospital to have me checked out. My mom rode in the front seat of the ambulance, and my dad followed behind us in the car. Halfway to the hospital, my mom heard the EMTs call out, "Code blue." I had stopped breathing again, and soon after, my heart stopped beating. The EMTs used the defibrillator to shock me back to life and finally got a pulse. Even to this day, as a mom of two, I can't imagine what was going through my mom's head while her daughter was flatlining in the back of an ambulance!

I don't recall anything that took place on the way to the hospital. The only thing I can remember is that I felt at peace. I woke up hearing my name called over and over again and finally came to awareness. There I was sitting in the ER, surrounded by my parents, the EMTs, and the doctors, all cheering that I was alive. That night, I was evaluated and finally had a doctor commit to getting my tonsils removed. The EMTs said my breathing passage was the size of the tip of a pencil. My tonsils had become so enlarged that there was literally no room to breathe out of my mouth. So, I had an emergency tonsillectomy and stayed in the ICU to recover. After the surgery, the doctor came into the room and told my parents and I that I had the largest tonsils he had ever removed in his career. Thank God those babies were finally out and I could breathe clearly for the first time in my life.

This event began the road to a recovery which led me down a path I would've never anticipated. After experiencing something so traumatic and facing death so closely, most people have "come to Jesus" moments. However, this would be a different journey for me. This experience stopped me in my tracks and opened me up to so many questions. *Why am I here? Why am I still alive? What is my purpose?* Life had become so much more than keeping up with the social circles, sports, and everyone's expectations or opinions of me.

During my time of recovery, I found myself starting to withdraw from my relationships with friends and losing interest in the activities I had once been so passionate about. I eventually gained the strength to return to school, but my school life wasn't the same. Nothing had changed in my external environment, but my near-death experience brought about an internal change. I went from being this bubbly, social, competitive, silly person to feeling heavy, sad, and depressed. I can remember walking the halls of my school and feeling like a zombie. The love for everything I had once known had faded away, as the world around me seemed so meaningless and shallow. I realized there had to be more to life than keeping up with the Joneses, partying, dating, and trying to figure out what my future after high school was going to look like.

In this season, I entered a dark place, and I couldn't find the light. Each day, I would go to school, go through the motions, then go home and lock myself in my room, shutting out everyone and everything. It even got to the point where I was shutting out my parents. In the evenings, I would cry uncontrollably and bury myself in my covers. I was losing my will to live. I didn't want to talk, and I sure didn't want a pep speech. Darkness and isolation became my plot, and I was tired of fighting for hope. It became very clear to my parents that they might be losing their daughter for a second time, so they did their best to seek medical help. But, I was not having it!

One day, my mom knocked on my door. "You don't have to talk, but I do have something for you," she said. I waited for her to leave, then I opened my door to find on the floor a journal with the poem "Footprints on the Sand" written on the cover. The poem shares a story about a man who had a dream that he was walking on the beach as moments from his life flashed across the sky. In most of the memories, there were two sets of footprints in the sand, but during the most difficult times, only one set of footprints appeared. The man called out to God and asked Him, "How can you be such a loving God if You weren't there during the darkest times of my life?" God called back to the man and said, "Son, that is when I carried you.", That poem sowed a seed into my heavy heart that would later blossom into joy and redemption. My mom gave me the best gift in the blank pages of the journal. She gave me a safe place to talk with God and begin emptying myself of the hurt, disappointment, regrets, and anger that I had toward myself, others, and Him. Even to this day, I get excited when I receive a journal or complete one and get to pick out a new one.

I also found the book *Battlefield of the Mind* by Joyce Meyer, which gave me such a clear understanding of how to start holding captive toxic thinking and start living from the inside out, not allowing emotions of external circumstances to dictate me. Soon after receiving the journal from my mom, I picked up my Bible and began to read it for myself. I had lots of questions, and the foundation of God's Word laid within my heart early on in life led me back to the source of my eternal hope. For the first time in my life, the Word of God started jumping off the pages. "For the word of God is alive and active. Sharper than any double-edged sword, it penetrates even to dividing soul and spirit, joints and marrow; it judges the thoughts and attitudes of the heart – Hebrews 4:12" I began learning about thousands of God's promises, which I would cling to as my lifeline. The Word was opening my eyes to the God of my childhood, who was now becoming the God of my more mature years. I needed Him in a way that I never had before, and I was holding onto every single word.

This is where the battle for my soul's deliverance, healing, and freedom began. You see, I had said yes to Jesus so many times in my childhood. I had gone to Sunday school, sung hymns, participated in vacation Bible school, and even "given my life" to the Lord at youth camps. The only thing I hadn't done in my younger years was truly surrender. Jesus was my Savior, but He was not yet Lord of my life. I was strong willed, bull headed, and a tough cookie, remember? Although I loved God, I still wanted to be in the driver's seat. That kind of stubbornness had led me to the very place I was in where I felt like a failure—defeated, down, not good enough, not worthy, and hopeless. How was life going to get better for me?

During this tussle with God, I was becoming weak. Ephesians 6:12 says, "For we wrestle not against flesh and blood, but against principalities, against powers, against the rulers of the darkness of this world, against spiritual wickedness in high places." For the majority of my life, everything had come so easy to me, but in that moment, I felt like I had lost all will power. Winning never took much effort for me, and I was used to it. I would show up at a race, lace up my sneakers, and run. For me, winning was easy, fun, and didn't take much training. I had been given natural talent and ability. Now, here I was having a hard time just getting out of bed and conquering the basic tasks of the day.

Then on a dreary day in November of 1998, I remember coming home from school again, locking myself in my bedroom, and deciding that I was ready to give up. I had read enough in my Bible to know that killing yourself was not the answer. I knew I had no right to take the life that God had brought into this world for a greater purpose. Yet, there was no other way of escape before me. The pain from the depression and hopelessness was too heavy of a weight to bear. I didn't want to live, let alone exist, like this anymore. Everything I had been reading in God's Word, every word I had written in my journal, and every prayer I had cried out to God had fallen on deaf ears. All hope was lost.

I remember looking in my closet and seeing a belt hanging there. A loud voice in my head told me to get it and wrap it around my neck. I did just that and stood on my bed, wrapped the belt around the top bar of my canopy bed, and whispered, "I don't want to live like this anymore!" I stepped off and hit the ground like a ton of bricks! The belt ripped off my neck, and I began to wail out to God. I wasn't dead; I was breathing and very much alive.

There on my bedroom floor, I told God, "If You save my soul and fill me with Your power, I will live for You. I will not be ashamed of

You. I want everyone around me to know You are real and Your love is more powerful than the pain of this world." At that moment, I felt God's presence like never before. I felt His peace that passes all understanding hover over me like a heavy, warm blanket. I felt comfort, I felt hope, and I felt salvation for my soul. I had finally surrendered and let go of my own will to receive God's. This experience was an ultimate act of faith that would change the trajectory of my life, taking me down a whole new path—one that I never would've imagined.

At that "break of dawn," God's kingdom could now reign in my heart and mind through Christ Jesus. He had given me a fresh start, a clean slate, and a beautiful new beginning for my life. If you are contemplating suicide please call the National Suicide Prevention Lifeline at 1-800-273-8255. The Lifeline provides 24/7, free and confidential support for people in distress, prevention and crisis support resources for you and your loved ones, and best practices for professionals in the United States.

From a young age, I can always remember liking the name my parents had given me. It just suited me. Courtney Dawn. My great grandmother even told my mom that she liked Dawn better for a first name. I believe that there is much meaning in a name. Dawn is the light that breaks forth into the darkness. It also represents the beginning of a new period of time. In my life, that moment with God in my bedroom was the beginning of a new reign over the plans of the enemy—a new reign over depression, low self-esteem, and hopelessness. It was a new dawn of freedom! I had tapped into a supernatural strength and power that can only come from above.

I kept that first journal from my mom that I had started back on December 31, 1998. Recently, I took some time to read through the pages within it, and I came across this poem wrote down toward the last page. Now, I want to share it with you.

Dawn in my darkness,
deep in my heart,
tell all the shadows to swiftly depart.
Send out Your love light,
dispelling despair;

Dawn in my darkness,
tell me You're there.
Dawn in my darkness of dreary days,
color my life with perpetual praise.

Paint with Your paintbrush
a heavenly view;
dawn in my darkness,
tell me it's You.

Dawn in my darkness,
Bring me new hope,
wake up my spirit,
Help me to cope.

Use me to tell others
Just who You are;
My Dayspring, My Sunrise, My Bright Morning Star.

Amen.

After graduating high school, I made the decision to stay home and attend community college. My fragile soul was not ready to take on the big world just yet, and my wings were newly clipped and just starting to grow back. I needed to be in a safe place where I could regain my strength to take on the unknown.

During this time, I became certified as a personal trainer and began working at Gold's Gym, which was the perfect mission field to share my newfound faith in Christ and help others get healthy. Growing up as an athlete, I always knew the value of physical activity and how it helped me channel stress and frustration while boosting my mood. There was nothing a good long run couldn't fix. Along with my love of fitness, I had a passion to empower others, so becoming a personal trainer was a natural fit.

God began to send me many clients who were battling with the very things I had recently experienced, which was confirmation that I was in the right place and was truly on a mission. I remember praying with my clients before we would train and watch them begin to transform from the inside out.

There was one client in particular I will never forget. Her name was Beatrice, and she came to me over 100 pounds overweight and crushed by an abusive relationship. She put her trust in me to walk her through the fragile process of rebuilding her sense of value and worth. Every workout, Beatrice and I would start with prayer. I would take her through various exercises to break her down physically and open her up emotionally. This helped her release not only the extra weight she was carrying but also the hurt, lies, and toxins. In time, Beatrice revealed that she had begun to eat to cover herself up in hopes that she would become unattractive to her abusive boyfriend. It didn't work. He grew more violent as she became unhealthier. Her lifestyle led to Type 2 diabetes and a decision to choose life or death.

Later in the book, I will share the process I took her through that became the *FIT 2B FREE Movement* curriculum that I co-authored with my husband. God was moving in so many ways during that time. In over a year and a half, Beatrice released over 120 pounds. By the grace of God, she was transformed from the inside out and rediscovered her confidence in Christ and went back to her passion for singing. Her journey forever impacted me and showed me that all things are possible with God. When we choose to confront our pain, deny the lies of the enemy, find accountability, and fight for life, a new beginning awaits us.

Even as a personal trainer, I was still quietly in a battle of my own behind the scenes. Although I was buff, blonde, and bubbly on the outside, I was still struggling with low self-esteem, body image issues, depression, and the makings of an eating disorder. The industry that God called me to work in was interesting, as so much of what I did was focused on external appearance. Everything was measured in inches, pounds, and achieving perfection, so the focus of internal beauty of the soul took a backseat to having ripped abs, a perky butt, and big biceps. This became a personal recipe for disaster because I was newly walking in Christ yet still bound to my old toxic behaviors, and I had not been completely delivered.

Like many new believers, I thought that when I finally surrendered, everything bad would just go away and I would be instantly set free and become this completely new creature in Christ. I mean, the Bible says that, right? "Old things pass away. Behold all things become new." Listen, in my life, I've heard many testimonies of people who were instantly set free from alcohol addiction, or the taste of nicotine left their mouth the moment they said yes to the Lord. In most cases, God takes us through a process to possess His promises in our lives. This is sometimes a moment-by-moment decision to surrender to the truth, love, and grace that gives us authority over strongholds.

Now is the time for God to begin training you to reign, which will take vulnerability, transparency, discipline, accountability, consistency, and equipping to activate truth in your life. It may have taken a while to create unhealthy, toxic, and distorted perspectives of your reality, but this process of divine training is not something that should be rushed but embraced as a lifelong journey. As we spend time in God's Word and presence and embrace His love for us, we become transformed into the image of His Son Jesus. Hindsight is always 20/20, and I wish

I knew back then what I know now. I really needed permission to invite God into my messy moments and know that He looked at me finished and still loved me in the process. He didn't want a perfect daughter; He wanted a willing and obedient child who would trust Him to do the deeper work.

As time went on and I was continuing my work in the fitness industry, I was encouraged to compete in the Ms. Fitness America competition. What a great idea...not! *Sure,* I thought, *I will weigh everything I put in my mouth, be a slave to the gym and scale, all while putting myself out there to be judged by my outer appearance.*

Prepping for the stage became an idol in my life that led me to an eating disorder, which began my love/hate relationship with food. Growing up, I ate whatever I wanted and would burn it off playing sports. If I wanted to eat some cookies, I did. Eating wasn't this all-consuming and monumental battle of whether or not to partake in it followed by overwhelming guilt. During the day, I would be militant with my eating and exercise regimen, train my clients, and go to school, only to come home exhausted, depleted, and starving. I would binge on whatever I could find and numb myself with comfort food. Right after eating, I would feel so guilty and immediately jump on the scale. If I had gained a pound, I would go straight to the gym and do cardio for over an hour to burn it off.

This went on for months and grew to be a major stronghold in my life. I was obsessed, stuck in a horrible cycle that I was too ashamed to tell anyone about. After all, I was the one helping others get healthy and break free from their battles with the bulge. I felt like such a hypocrite, suffering in silence. I may have been preaching the gospel of hope, freedom, and health, but I felt like a total fraud. I would go visit churches and occasionally force myself into community and accountability, yet once anyone got close enough to me, I would retreat back to my binging and "functional depression."

I would define "functional depression" as still carrying on with every day activities and responsibilities even when you're still feeling blue. It's going through the motions and living life muted and dull. You're not fully alive, present, or experiencing any joy throughout your day. You can't wait to get home and crawl under your covers and hide from everything and everyone.

I can remember calling out to God in my personal time and asking Him why He hadn't yet delivered me. I was literally going insane trying to break through, as I was finding myself going from one high to the next low. Unlike all the promises I had clung to when I first surrendered, I felt torn and not totally free.

During this time, I was dating, but I was frustrated with the lack of spiritual depth and motive in the guys who were pursuing me. They had the looks and the drive, but they were missing the main ingredient: Jesus! These relationships led me to even greater frustration than what I was already experiencing. I soon realized I was not cut out for the dating scene. It was frustrating, unfulfilling, and seemed like a waste of precious time.

By this time, I was eighteen, and I knew what I wanted in a future husband. My good friend Suzie invited me to attend a Power of a Praying Wife Bible study, which consisted of married women who were older than me. Some were fighting for their marriages and facing possible divorce, and others had children and were trying to juggle family life. While in the study, I spent most of my time listening and praying for my future husband. I was young and single with no clue what value I would add to this group. The only thing I knew about marriage was from watching my parents and seeing their love, commitment, and true partnership. These ladies embraced me and came alongside me to pray for my future Mr., while I prayed diligently for their husbands. Looking back, I know exactly why God had me in that Bible study at such a young age. He was preparing me for a sudden season not too far down the road.

It was during this time that I really felt led to get baptized. I was ready to make my public declaration that Jesus is my Lord and Savior. I wanted to go all in and all under. After my baptism, my friend Suzie presented me with a very unique gift—a beautiful ring neck dove. I was so excited to release the dove as a symbol of my newfound freedom in Christ. Suzie then informed me that the dove's wings were clipped and I would have to wait for the big release. How indicative of the spiritual season I was in. What was I supposed to do with a bird? I ended up taking it home with me, and it became my pet. I named him Spirit, short for the Holy Spirit. He was the most tame and loving animal, filling the house with a sweet cooing sound, and a whole lot of bird poop, as my mom would say!

As I was working at Gold's gym one day, I saw a guy I recognized walk into the gym with his friend. I had gone to school with his younger brothers and knew he was a good guy and came from a wonderful family. He was an amazing quarterback, student, and leader on campus. His brother Dominick happened to be working out at the gym that day as well and introduced me to his oldest brother, Jeffrey. One night after I was done training my clients, Jeffrey and I ended up working out together. The whole time, we talked about the Lord, family, and life, and we instantly connected. To be honest, he was the first guy I had spoken to who was mature in his walk with God and had his act together. He was handsome, loved Jesus, and had his life established. Jeff had been a pre-med biology and chemistry major in college while playing quarterback, had just bought his first home, and was working in the pharmaceutical industry while serving as youth pastor in his parents' church. The guy had his act together.

The natural next step was for him to ask me out. Well, he ended up asking me out on a date three separate times. Each time, when the big day arrived, I would call him up at the last minute and give him some lame excuse as to why I couldn't go. I cancelled on this "perfect guy" who could have been the one I was praying for in my women's

Bible study. It wasn't that there was anything wrong with him…it was me. *What would he think if he really got to know the real me?* I was too ashamed of what I was battling behind closed doors. What did I even have to offer this guy who had his act together? I was still living at home with my parents, studying in community college, and struggling with depression and an eating disorder.

The third and final time Jeff asked me out after graciously rescheduling, I cancelled on him again! That day, my best friend was back in town from college, and she had asked me to do her a huge favor and go with her to a club to see this guy she liked who had a friend. I would do anything for my best friend, so I said yes, although reluctantly. I felt horrible explaining this to Jeff, but at the same time, I was relieved that I wouldn't have to open up to him about my struggles.

Wouldn't you know, that same day was Jeff's best friend's birthday, and he had asked Jeff to go out to celebrate. Where did they go? The exact place my friend and I ended up. I will never forget walking into the club and seeing Jeff standing at the bar. What was this good guy doing in a club? There was no hiding. I saw him and he saw me. I immediately walked up to him and asked what he was doing there, and I'm sure he was wondering the same thing about me. I felt horrible and honestly would've preferred to leave with him and just get out of there. After our brief encounter, I said goodbye to him and walked upstairs to meet my friend.

I walked to the edge of the balcony of the club and looked out at everyone below. It seemed like everything was moving in slow motion. I started thinking to myself, *What am I even doing here? This place is like Sodom and Gomorrah.* I hadn't been in a club for a long time, and that environment felt so dark. I was a child of the light, not a child of the night. At that moment, a total stranger walked up to me and said, "What do you see?" Before I could respond, he disappeared. The Bible says that we must be aware of entertaining strangers, for we could be entertaining angels unaware –Hebrews 13:12 At that moment, I was ready to get out of there. I grabbed my friend. "Let's go," I told her. That was the last time I would step foot in that kind of atmosphere as a single woman.

Three whole years passed before I would reconnect with Jeff. I would occasionally see him at the gym, and he kindly encouraged me without even knowing it. I was still deep in my internal battle and at my wit's end. I heard from a friend that Jeff's brother Jonathan was dating someone I had been friends with since elementary school. Out of curiosity, I picked up the phone to call Jeff to confirm this information. When he didn't answer, I left him a message, and he ended up calling me back. Little did I know that Jeff was out of town meeting the family of a girl he was about to propose to. Thankfully, it the meeting turned out to be a hot mess, and that closed door made it possible for another one to open. God's sovereignty never ceases to amaze me.

I ended up speaking with Jeff for a while on the phone, and he confirmed that my friend was not only dating his brother but attending his parents' church in town. I was excited to hear this news because I had prayed for my friend to accept Christ as her Savior. This was the time for me to come clean with Jeff and share about my battles. I told him that I would come to his church's midweek worship service and see him there. I'm sure he wasn't holding his breath, since I had a reputation of cancelling at the last minute.

However, I did attend, and I ended up meeting my friend and walked in with her. The music was playing, and there were Jeff and his brothers front and center, singing and leading worship. The service was powerful. I closed my eyes and allowed God's presence to fill my heart and mind.

After the service, Jeff introduced me to his dad and mom. "So, you're the infamous Ms. Gold's!" they said. *What?* Well, after I had cancelled on Jeff for the third time, his family came up with a nickname for me. Since I was a personal trainer at Gold's Gym, that was how I earned this name. They had started to think I was a figment of

Jeff's imagination. Later, I discovered that Jeff had bought me a dozen roses for every date that we had scheduled, and each time I cancelled at the last minute, he ended up giving the roses to his mom. Well, that was embarrassing, but they laughed it off and seemed happy to finally meet me.

Jeff walked me to my car, and that was my opportunity to apologize to him. I told him that he hadn't done anything wrong but that I was too ashamed to share what I had been battling. He didn't make me feel bad. He just told me that he would've been there for me. I told him that I wasn't interested in dating anyone at the time but what I really needed was a friend. I asked him what he was doing that Friday. He said, "I will go to dinner with you, but I'm picking you up." By this time, he didn't want to risk me cancelling on him again.

Friday came, and Jeff picked me up at my parents' home. He met my mom and dad, and as we left, he opened the door to his red Navigator for me. On the passenger seat were a dozen red roses. I was overwhelmed by the beautiful gesture. Although, I did tell him that I didn't want to date and just needed him to be my friend. "Friends can give friends roses," he said.

That night, he took me out to dinner for sushi, which happened to be both of our favorite meals. We talked the whole dinner, and it felt like time stood still. It was the best "non-date" I had ever been on in my life. That was September 13th of 2002. From that moment on, we were inseparable.

One night, I brought all of my journals over to Jeff's house and laid them on the floor. I told him, "If you want to be in a relationship with me, then here I am. The good, bad, and ugly, and in the process of being made whole and free." It was absolutely terrifying to open myself up to someone else. *What if I get hurt? What if he doesn't want me? What if he finds me unlovable?* It was a huge leap of faith to put my fragile heart in someone else's hands. The more I shared with him, the closer we became, and the more he would affirm me in who God called me to be. I was twenty-one years old and ready to have accountability in my life. I was tired of feeling alone, vulnerable, and under constant attack from the enemy.

By October, Jeff and I knew that we wanted to get married. Our courtship process consisted of me spending much of my time in church, releasing a lot of tears and the lies I had believed for years. I was finally feeling loved, safe, empowered, and ready to begin my life with my best friend.

I not only fell in love with this man but with his family as well. I will never forget one night after a church service, walking into the bathroom to clean up my face from the snot facial that occurred while I was crying out to God. Jeff's mom, Pam, embraced me with a warm hug, looked me in the eyes, and said, "Courtney, you are a mighty woman of God." I wondered to myself how she could say that with the way I looked. I was a hot mess and falling deeply in love with her eldest son. How was I even fit to be his wife, let alone a mighty woman in God's eyes? I felt vulnerable and undone. But, something inside of me said yes to those powerful words. Jeff's mom saw what was below the blonde and fit exterior. She saw who God had called and created me to be.

By November, our families were connecting for the holidays, and it had become evident that God's hand was on our relationship. It was now time for Jeff to ask for my parents' blessing. He and I made a really nice dinner and had my parents over to the house. After dinner, my dad and Jeff went to the family room to watch the NBA Magic game. As Jeff was getting up the nerve to ask my dad's permission to marry me, my dad looked at him and said, "Jeff, the answer is yes!" Wow! In my opinion, my dad made it way too easy for him.

Now, it was full steam ahead with our wedding planning. We were in love and had no reason to drag out a long engagement. Our focus was set on searching for the perfect ring to symbolize God's overwhelming love toward us. You see, Jeff later told me that the day he walked in the gym and saw me, he told his best friend, "That is my wife." He knew all those years ago. God clearly had some work to do on us both before He would bring us together as husband and wife in His sovereign timing.

One night, I had a dream about my ring. It was so vivid that I woke up and drew a sketch of the ring next to the scripture Haggai 2:23 in my Bible, which says, "I will take you, Zerubbabel My servant, the Son of Shalatiel, says the Lord, and will make you like a signet ring; for I have chosen you, says the Lord of hosts." This ring would represent God's stamp of approval and seal on our union. It would be a daily reminder that with God all things are possible. The ring would be crafted into two doves in flight, with their wings spread to form the band, with the diamond shaped into a heart. I got the idea from the movie *Independence Day* with Will Smith. In the movie, Will Smith's character proposes to Vivica Fox's character, who loves dolphins, and he has a ring made for her with two dolphins forming the band with a stone in the center.

I immediately shared this exciting dream with Jeff. I knew this request wouldn't be too crazy to him because he is an incredible and creative artist. He and I then began a month-long journey to find the right person to make this "signet ring." We came up with nothing. I honestly started to feel bad because the task was all-consuming. However, it wasn't about a ring; it was about Jeff and me joining our lives together as one.

Just when I was about to give up the search, Jeff's mom asked us if we had gone to see Pablo yet. He was a master jewelry designer who worked at a place she had gone to for years, and he had just launched his own business right down the street from where we lived. We grabbed our sketch and made our way to see him. Upon our arrival, Pablo walked to the counter, and I saw that he was wearing a necklace with a dove on a cross. I looked at Jeff and said, "I think we are in the right place!" We shared our vision with the man, and he began to sketch our ring in three different dimensions. Then he proceeded to ask us if we had ever seen the movie *Independence Day*. By this point, both of our knees were getting weak. Pablo told us that my ring reminded him of the one from the movie. He then explained to us that he was commissioned to make the dolphin ring for the movie! We were done. In that moment, time and eternity collided. We knew that dream was from God, and it was nothing for Him to make it a reality in our lives. God brought us right down the street and to the exact person for the job. Nothing is too hard for Him. In Psalm 37:4 it says,that if we delight ourselves in Him, He will give us the desires of our heart, and did He ever!

Jeffrey and Courtney's wedding day

On December 20, 2002, Jeffrey proposed to me in front of our family and friends. When he opened the ring box, the treasure inside took my breath away. I was presented with the most beautiful reminder of God's love for us. As a bride to be, I was on a mission to make our wedding a beautiful reflection of God's goodness toward Jeffrey and me. This was also a very emotional time for me, as I was closing a twenty-one-year chapter of being in my parents' care.

During our engagement, Jeff gave me the tough love I needed not to beat myself up with trying to make my physical appearance my main focus. His effort wasn't without resistance, but he wasn't going to let that battle take authority over our relationship and newfound freedom in Christ. I felt covered, protected, and always redirected to receive God's grace when I fought back. Through Jeff, God replaced my previous exhausting cycle of depression and obsession with consistent love, encouragement, and accountability in my direction. Jeff became a safe place for me to release the pain of my past and receive my new reign as a woman and wife.

I became Mrs. Courtney Dawn Shaw on April 26, 2003. It was a beautiful spring day surrounded by our family, friends, and church body. I walked down the aisle to a violin playing "Turn Your Eyes upon Jesus." The presence of God was so thick that it felt like a warm blanket covering our union. We sealed our covenant with a holy kiss, and we were soon off to St. Lucia for our honeymoon. It was a whirlwind romance blessed by our Creator and King.

God had an unexpected plot twist in my story: a beautiful new beginning. He didn't want me wandering around young, naive, and susceptible to the enemy's attacks. Even before time began, He had set in motion a plan for me. A best friend, partner, and man after His own heart. Jeffrey Michael Shaw. His name means peaceful king, and that is exactly what the enemy would be coming after. His peace and ours.

KINGDOM (QUEST)IONS

1. Are there parts of your past that are holding you captive? If so, what are they?

   _____

   _____

   _____

2. Have you confronted your past? If not, why?

   _____

   _____

   _____

3. Who can you reach out to who will walk with you through this journey of deliverance and healing? Is there a counselor, friend, or family member?

   _____

   _____

   _____

4. What is your "why" to focus on while confronting the past?

   _____

   _____

   _____

5. Who else in your life other than yourself is being affected by the pain of your past?

_____

_____

_____

KINGDOM TRUTHS

"He whom the Son sets free is free indeed."- John 8:36

"Behold, I am doing a new thing in your life. Do you not perceive it?"- Isaiah 43:19

"Old things pass away, behold all things become new." – 2 Corinthians 5:17

KINGDOM DECLARATION

The following is a declaration for a new reign over your past

> *Today is _____. I declare that I am no longer a slave to my past. I will not be haunted by past mistakes, failures, hurts, disappointments, or traumas. I release the hands of my accusers, abusers, manipulators, and liars. I am safe in my Father's arms and protected, valued, and secure. I commit to walk in the newness of life and receive accountability while choosing to confront and conquer my past through the power of the cross.*

In Jesus's name, amen.

Chapter Three

REIGN IN TRUTH

"Truth is like a lion. You don't have to defend it. Let it loose. It will defend itself.–St. Augustine

"You shall know the truth, and the truth shall make you free."–John 8:32

There is a popular saying that says, "Exposure brings closure." I believe that's partly true, for exposure is really just the beginning. To find closure and healing, one must be willing, open, and fully committed to confront the truth and get down to the seed of a situation no matter the consequences. Most of us become weary on this quest and even quit because we're afraid of what we will find. The journey is too terrifying, too much work, too painful, too shameful, too embarrassing, too time consuming, and flat-out exhausting.

Imagine that you have been told that you have a brain tumor and need emergency surgery to save your life. Before your operation, the surgeon lets you know that you will have partial sedation so they can interact with you during surgery and make sure they aren't damaging your functions. You won't be able to physically feel any pain, but you will be conscious. You agree to the surgery and have total confidence that the doctor will remove the tumor and save your life.

However, in the middle of the surgery, you panic, thinking, *Who will I be without this tumor? I've become so accustomed to living in pain and fear.* The surgeon was just about to remove the tumor, but you have demanded him to close you up. He complies, and you choose to walk out of the hospital knowing that a deadly tumor is still in your brain. You have just given in and given up fighting for your life! How crazy does that sound?

The reality is, denying spiritual deliverance in your life is no different than denying physical healing. I truly believe what is works on the inside of your spiritual life, good or bad will manifest on the outside. That is why getting down to the seed of your dis-ease will help you with a proper diagnosis and game plan for healing. Society approved band-aids only work for so long and are meant to cover up wounds not completely heal them. Jesus didn't die on the cross for you to stumble through life wounded, toxic, and paralyzed by your past trauma. God has placed gifts inside of you to unlock and awaken the kingdom within. 2 Corinthians 4:7 says, "But we have this treasure in earthen vessels, that the excellency of the power may be of God, and not of us."

> Jesus didn't die on the cross for you to stumble through life wounded, toxic, and paralyzed by your past trauma.

In order for these gifts to come to the surface, there has to be an excavation handled with the utmost care. You must begin a process of purging the pain of the past and accepting the truth no matter how ugly it may be. Denial only leads to death—perhaps not a physical death initially, but eventually it will seek you out, hold you hostage, and take you down. Remember, you have an enemy, and his mission remains the same: to steal, kill, and destroy. On this noble quest to find the truth, you might confront anger, jealousy, compromise, unfaithfulness, wicked plots, vial behavior, abuse, infidelity, and so much more. We have to deal with these issues so we can truly heal and walk in the newness of life in Christ. Unfortunately, the majority of people will go to their graves without tasting freedom and peace in Christ this side of heaven.

St. Augustine said, "Truth is like a lion. You don't have to defend it. Let it loose. It will defend itself."

Maybe you're reading this and you have suffered false accusations, gross injustice, or abuse at the hands of someone close to you. There is nothing more painful or damaging than to be hurt by a family member, mentor, coach, pastor, or so-called friend. I'm here to tell you there is still hope for your healing. First and foremost, healing begins when you receive forgiveness for your soul. When you've been forgiven much, it becomes possible to extend the same toward others. This doesn't necessarily mean that trust or a close relationship with someone who has hurt you will be restored. Is it possible? Of course. "With God all things are possible Matt. 19:26)." But, it takes both parties willing to walk through forgiveness and the restoration of trust. That was God's original intent and purpose of forgiveness—to flow like a mighty river. If forgiveness were to stop with you, it would become a stagnant pond. There has to be a continual release to receive the goodness of God in your life.

One of my favorite authors, Matt Heard, author of *Life with a Capital L,* used this simple yet powerful example: God made you to be like a pipe, not a bucket. So, it's time to let go and let it flow. You weren't made to be a bucket and become a cesspool with no outlet. What Christ did for us on the cross gave us access to receive His amazing grace. Remember, forgiveness is not earned; it is a precious gift that keeps flowing from Calvary. Holding unforgiveness toward your accuser or abuser is like drinking poison and waiting for them to die—it only hurts you! There is freedom in releasing control. You can't force someone to ask for your forgiveness, just as you can't force someone to see value in you.

There is an old saying that says, "Hurt people hurt people," and that is very true. Yet, let me share a much deeper and eternal truth: loved people love people. Love conquers all, and perfect love casts out all fear because fear involves torment. It is *not* God's will for you to be tormented by the chains of your past. There have been many cases where victims' abusers have died, left the earth, and are no longer physically walking around breathing air, but they are still haunting those victims' everyday moments. Enough!

Dr. Caroline Leaf, a neuroscientist and best-selling author, says, "Forgetting a past trauma is impossible even with forgiveness."[3] We can't just erase traumatic events from our memory, as they impact our brains and are stored in our bodies. We can, however, change how these memories are stored and how the past impacts the present. You can't change the past, but with mind management, you can change your understanding of the past and how you feel about it. Use the past to your benefit, to fuel your healing and mission to break toxic cycles, and even to end injustices for others.

Don't let someone else's inaction keep you from taking action. You can make breaking cycles your closure. The reason I can share this truth with the utmost confidence is because of my own journey to forgiveness and allowing the truth of God's unchanging and never-ending agape love to deliver me, free me, and make me whole.

The Honeymoon Is Over!

Now, let's go back to my honeymoon phase with Mr. Shaw. When we got back from our romantic and adventurous trip to St. Lucia, it was time to get settled in and make his semi-bachelor pad a home. We immediately started putting touches on our sanctuary. That is what we named our first home together. Sanctuary 1 was a place of safety, refuge, and the love to reign. Home throughout my life always represented a place where I could take off my armor and just be Courtney. Jeff and I bought new furniture together, and we began our adventure of enjoying the newfound freedom we had in Christ and one another. During this season, I felt beautiful, safe, strong, confident, and totally free.

Not long after moving into my new home with Jeff, I joined him in leading the youth ministry at our church and felt called to remind this generation of God's faithfulness. We had about fifty kids we were pouring into on a weekly basis. Marrying into a family in ministry was a big responsibility. It was awesome and overwhelming all at the same time. I felt like I had hit the jackpot in Jesus!

I had just turned twenty-two, and I wasn't yet ready to start a family of my own. Desiring to create a perfect environment, I was busy attending to my new domestic duties. I married someone who is very meticulous, tidy, and detailed. He cared about his personal appearance and tended to his home and belongings excellently. I loved that about him. He grew up in a home with five men under one roof. His mom might've been outnumbered by all that testosterone, but she kept a tidy home. Jeff's aunt Diane would say, "You never knew that four boys lived in that house by how clean their bathroom was and smelled."

I can remember cleaning like a crazy woman one day, trying to get the house ready to surprise Jeff when he got home from work. I was vacuuming in the office when, all of a sudden, a loud rumbling started coming from the belly of that beast. I kept pushing through my cleaning duties until boom! The vacuum erupted like Mount Vesuvius and left me and every single item in the office coated with dust and ashes. Of course, my mouth was wide open from the complete shock. After I puffed out the dust like a dragon, it was time to clean up that disaster. All I could do to keep from crying was laugh my butt off. This was a new housewife epic fail!

Before leaving my parents' house to move in with Jeff, I had totally forgotten to ask my mom how to change a vacuum bag, and this one was completely impacted with dust to the top of the bag. It was just a matter of time before that baby blew up! I personally felt like it was a setup because Jeff had this vacuum before we got married.

One thing I've learned while facing tough times in life is to find humor in difficult situations. If you can't laugh at yourself, you're taking life way too seriously! Proverbs 17.22 says, "Laughter does good like medicine." At that moment, little did I know how much medicine I was going to need to make it out alive, married, and not admitted into a crazy house in the coming months.

One day, I got a call from Jeff while he was working. His voice sounded very concerned, and he told me to get to his parents' house immediately and that he would meet me over there. I jumped in the car and pulled up to his childhood home. There was a police car parked out front, and the house was wide open. My heart sank into my stomach, not knowing what I was about to walk into. I took a deep breath and prayed for God to give me strength.

As I walked into the home, I saw two large men sweeping my mother-in-law's beautiful collectibles into an oversized clear garbage bag. Running over to them, I asked them to please stop and that I would handle the items with care. The first person I recognized in the house was my brother-in-law Dominick. After I asked him what the heck was going on, he told me his parents were being evicted from their home and had less than twenty-four hours to be out. They had lived there for over twenty years, and the thought of trying to clear out their home in that short amount of time was almost paralyzing.

All I can remember my father-in-law saying was, "The devil took our home!" I thought to myself, *This didn't just happen,* remembering that there had to have been multiple warnings before the enforcer thugs came in to kick them out. It was devastating, but as a family, we had a job to do. The whole time, my mother-in-law was gone trying "to figure out" what happened to their home and to stop the eviction process.

This season was exhausting, devastating, and confusing all at the same time. Where would they go? At this time, my brother-in-law was thirteen and still in their care. Where would he go to school? There were so many questions to be answered with so little time. Jeff and I came together to find a solution, and when we did, we didn't even think twice. His parents were going to move in with us until they figured out everything. We had the space in our home, and we wanted to help them fix the situation. Yes, we were newlyweds and only three months into our journey as husband and wife. The typical newlywed arguments over debates such as which way to squeeze the toothpaste tube became very minimal in light of this mountain we were now facing.

However, one aspect of life I was prepared for was tough times. Growing up, when the proverbial "stuff hit the fan," my family pulled together, confronted the truth head on, and stuck together. It wasn't easy, but it's what we did. I'm so thankful my parents had the foresight and courage to be transparent with their children.

You see, this issue with Jeff's parents wasn't my first rodeo. During the mortgage crisis of the eighties, my parents had it all and lost it all. The market crashed, and my family was hit hard like many others during that decade. My dad had built communities and entered into business with someone who wasn't handling things properly. He and my mom had to take on millions of dollars of debt and start all over with a very young family. We moved from Kansas to Colorado and finally settled in Florida. My dad ended up switching industries and went into banking.

One day, my parents sat my brothers and me down and let us know the truth about the journey of digging out of debt that was ahead of us. It wasn't until I was in middle school that I became fully aware of the weight they had been carrying. My family always lived in a beautiful home in a nice community. On the outside, we looked like we had it all together. I can vividly remember moving out of a four-thousand-square-foot home into a three-bedroom apartment. Those were humbling and tight times. Living in such close quarters as a family of five could've made us or broken us. My dad had job offers out of state, but it was important for my parents to keep us in the same school with our friends and continue in sports. It was the last big run to clear all of that debt they owed to the IRS. They ended up staying in that apartment for a decade until they paid off every last bit of their debt.

During that time, my parents had become involved with Crown Ministries and applied biblical principles to their money management. Their first big step was kicking the "Joneses" out of the neighborhood, accepting their reality, and making a plan of attack to get out from under the heavy weight of debt. Proverbs 22:7 says to not be a slave to your debtors, and as my parents applied this and other principles to their finances, it turned into a passion and mission to help others by sharing what they learned.

Now, back to my in-laws—and pastors—moving in with Jeff and me. We quickly went from honeymoon bliss to hearing arguments on the other side of the wall and my father-in-law snoring at night. The weekly tasks of ministry went on full-steam ahead, and the show went on, as they say. No one except for close family knew what had happened to them. We were all told to keep things quiet because we didn't want to jeopardize my in-laws' ministry. This was a heavy burden for us to carry because we felt like we had no one in the church in whom we could confide.

After the initial shock wore off and the smoke started to clear, it was time for questions. I can vividly remember sitting down as a family one night, and the more we asked basic questions about documentation, the more arguments would ensue. It became a blame game between my in-laws that led nowhere real fast. This moment was an opportunity for them to share the truth with us, but that opportunity was withheld.

Finally, I knew I had enough! This was the couple whom I put in the position of a spiritual mother and father in my life. For the last six months, I had sat under their ministry holding onto every word they preached from the pulpit. They would share God's pure and perfect love and how it delivers, heals, and frees, but now this same love seemed to have no power in their lives. They were the ones supposed to be giving us guidance, not the other way around.

Finally, as a twenty-two-year-old young woman, I looked both of them in the eyes and asked a question that sucked all of the oxygen out of the room: "Do you even love each other?"

I looked at my mother-in-law, who immediately said, "Yes, with all my heart," but my father-in-law couldn't even open his mouth. This crushed my heart. I felt an overwhelming sadness and was totally duped by the show he had put on for not only me but his entire church. I thought I was marrying into this beautiful, loving family of ministry, yet, with that one question, I had just ripped a Band-Aid off of a festering wound.

By this time, Jeff and I had done some research, and we found out that my in-laws' home was indeed foreclosed on. This information was on public record, available for anyone to find. The house wasn't "taken by the devil" in some supernatural act of thievery, as my father-in-law had insisted. They were just in over their heads trying to maintain a growing ministry, rent, and their affairs at home. That was a lot to juggle, and what happened to them could have happened to anyone. This was the moment of truth, yet my father-in-law chose denial. Now, my in-laws' issue was no longer just about financial devastation; it was exposing unaddressed trauma in their relationship and family.

I can remember taking many long walks with Jeff and having a million questions to ask him. Until this point, the challenges in our marriage were all about me and my past pain. Jeff hadn't opened up about the truth of his childhood and the scars that he had been covering. This time was when he really started to share with me about his upbringing and the toxic home environment in which he grew up.

On the outside, the Shaw family had the utmost respect from their church and community. All of their boys were excellent students, leaders, and athletes. However, Jeff's dad was a militant man and ran a very strict household. He demanded perfection from his sons and felt they had to be better than great to make it in this world.

You see, he was a black man who married a white woman in the seventies. In high school, he was the captain of the football team, and she was the captain of the cheerleading squad. Their relationship was highly frowned upon during those times, and my father-in-law had his life threatened on many occasions. He and my mother-in-law ended up eloping right after high school, and he soon joined the military. They moved to Germany, where they had some crazy experiences. That was where he got saved and committed his life to Christ. They moved back to the states, and their family grew with their four boys. I can only imagine the pressure of keeping that many mouths fed and supporting all of the boys' sports.

But, behind the scenes, hell was breaking loose. Jeff recalled one time in particular during his senior year of high school. When he came home one day, he heard his parents engaged in an argument, and he walked in on his dad physically harming his mom. This argument had erupted because Jeff's mom had been exposed to the fact that her husband was having an affair. In that moment, Jeff jumped in to protect his mom and called 911, which led to an even greater escalation between him and his dad. When the cops showed up, Jeff's mom denied that anything had happened, and they left. Looking back, I'm sure she did this out of fear and a desire to protect her family, not wanting to expose the truth of what had happened.

Out of anger, Jeff's dad gave him an ultimatum because he had called the cops. Jeff could either take a beating or have his father take away his car, leaving him without a way to go to college. Jeff's mom begged him to take the beating to "keep the peace." As an eighteen-year-old young man, this was a pivotal moment for Jeff in his relationship with his father. Jeff's respect for him as a husband and father was deeply tarnished. When he finally left for an out-of-state college, Jeff felt horrible leaving his mom and younger brothers behind. As the oldest son, he always felt responsible for looking out for his siblings and his mom.

The actions of Jeff's father became a cycle of dysfunction and abuse that would continue for years to come. Jeff's dad, mom, and brother ended up staying with us for eight long months. My father-in-law insisted this was a blessing for my husband and I and that God chose us to be like "Obed Idem in the Bible." After all, we were housing the Ark of the Covenant. He told us that he was the carrier of God's anointing and presence. You can't write this stuff! Yet, I am writing it now, exactly as he said it. I thought to myself, *This isn't a blessing; this is a curse!* My father-in-law always had a masterful way of manipulating the Scriptures to fit his distorted agenda of control.

Around Christmastime of that year, Jeff and I realized that we couldn't do it anymore. If our marriage was going to survive this first crazy year, we needed to draw clear boundaries and have space of our own. Genesis 2:24 says, "Therefore shall a man leave his father and his mother, and shall cleave unto his wife: and they shall be one flesh." God set these marriage boundaries in place for each generation to start fresh. He wanted us to learn from the past, leave the bad behind us, and perpetuate the good for generations to come.

> A generational curse describes the cumulative effect on a person of things that their ancestors did, believed, or practiced in the past, and a consequence of an ancestor's actions, beliefs, and sins being passed down. An example of a generational curse is abuse or divorce. Examples of generational blessings are unconditional love, faith, trust, and healthy communication.

All throughout the Bible, God speaks of generational curses and blessings. A generational curse describes the cumulative effect on a person of things that their ancestors did, believed, or practiced in the past, and a consequence of an ancestor's actions, beliefs, and sins being passed down. An example of a generational curse is abuse or divorce. Examples of generational blessings are unconditional love, faith, trust, and healthy communication. Jeff and I were trying to join our lives together while being torn apart by the weight of our extended family's crisis and the pressure to fix their own mess. The situation had become so bad that I would hide in our closet and bury my face underneath the clothes and cry out to God for help. I was 100 percent confident that I loved Jeff and wanted to remain married to him, but I hadn't signed up for this craziness!

By this time, Jeff and I had done everything possible to reach out for help. We went to the elders in the church to share in confidence what was going on, which only resulted in many of the elders leaving the church and refusing to step up to help. My parents even offered their help, but it was vehemently denied by my father in law. They had genuine concern and compassion for Jeff and I because of what they had gone through financially. They also knew that if our fledgling marriage was going to survive, it needed a plan of action.

My father-in-law's pride and denial were making it impossible for us to start anew and break his unhealthy cycle. For years, my mother-in-law had carried the weight of managing the family and ministry finances, and it was crushing her. This was my father-in-law's opportunity to help shoulder that burden, yet he placed it right back on his wife.

Finally, that Christmas, Jeff and I went away and came back with a plan of attack. We ended up finding a new home for ourselves and had Jeff's family stay in our previous home until they got back on their feet. This boundary represented a new beginning for us, but the pressure and weight of being involved in the family ministry didn't go away. We tried for years to encourage Jeff's parents to gain spiritual and financial accountability, but our efforts were to no avail. Jeff and I, along with Jeff's other siblings and their spouses, were financially invested in the ministry and had a true passion to create a lasting legacy. However, there was always some type of contention going on that was related to the family ministry, and it exhausted us. The tension was robbing us of the joy, peace, and safety God had intended for our family. All of the siblings and their wives weretrying their hardest to keep the ministry going, while allowing themselves to be drained financially, spiritually, and emotionally. It had become clear that things were not going to change under my father-in-law's leadership, and, if we stayed involved in the ministry, we would be putting ourselves and our family in spiritual, emotional, and financial jeopardy. We had given so much of our time, talents, and treasures that it was now impacting us in a very negative and toxic way.

The year after Jeff and I bought our new home, we received a devastating call from my mother-in-law. Jeff's dad was on his way to the hospital with extreme chest pain. We soon came to find out he had 99 percent blockage in all of his main arteries and was going to need emergency bypass surgery. His heart was literally hardened. What had been working on the inside of him was manifesting on the outside. When the body is not at ease, dis-ease manifests within it. The combination of pride, anger, control, stubbornness, and unhealthy habits, along with the stress of keeping the ministry going, had taken its toll on my father-in-law. Was this the wake-up call God would use to get his attention? As devastating as this news was for the family, we were praying for divine intervention.

He successfully made it out of his surgery and had been given another chance, a fresh start at life. I was so convinced that this could be the pivotal moment for my father-in-law to release control and receive help, but that did not happen. When he got out of the hospital, I even made a concrete stepping stone in the shape of a heart for him as a recovery gift. I had the scripture "I will take out your stony heart and give you a new soft one"-Ezekiel 36:26 engraved on it. I was believing in God for a physical and emotional healing in my father-in-law's heart.

I clearly remember one night when he had just been released from the hospital. Jeff and I came by to discuss plans for the rest of the family to step up and minister as he was recovering. He was sitting at the kitchen table with a massive wound on his leg that had been stapled together, which was where the heart surgeon had removed a main artery from his leg for the operation. It looked like a great white shark had attacked him.

It was getting late, and our son was a baby at the time. He had started crying, and it was time to go to bed. My father-in-law was so insistent on nailing down plans that he kept pulling on Jeff to stay. I finally asked Jeff if we could resume the conversation tomorrow so we could get our baby in bed. At that moment, my father-in-law sat up and started yelling at me. *You're not going to control this conversation!* I thought. I was done. I took our son and ran out of the door. How could a man who just went through life-saving heart surgery have the energy to be this angry? He hated the fact that he felt so vulnerable from his surgery, for he was so used to being in control of everything and everyone.

My mother-in-law soon ran out to find me. I was in tears and so over the way he treated me and everyone close to him. She apologized for him, as she always did. How was it possible for this man to become even more hardhearted and angrier after what he had been through? He clearly felt like he was losing control and had decided to fight back with whatever he could muster up.

During this season, Jeff's family stepped up, and things seemed to thrive while his dad was healing. Everyone was flowing in their passion for true ministry during the services without the pressure of my father-in-law's control and sabotage. There was so much back-and-forth communication about the next generation stepping up to lead the ministry. I can remember Jeff and his brothers being willing to enter roles of leadership and take the call seriously, as they did with everything they ever put their hearts and hands to.

Eventually, my father-in-law took the reins back, and everything returned to what it was before. His choice to take control once more was a fear-based decision, as releasing the reins would call for accountability and transparency that had never before been in place. It was almost an annual expectation for us to ask Jeff's parents, our pastors, to release us so we could move forward and they could run things according to their desires. They were big on protocol and being "properly released," which was more of a control mechanism than sound biblical doctrine.

My father-in-law felt that he was above accountability and that no one could speak into his life. Yet, he expected everyone around him to live up to his own high standards. He would always tell us to "talk to the satellite," meaning God, and say that God would relay the message to him if he saw fit. There was no amount of prayer, fasting, tithing, or support that could get through to him. He trusted no one—not even those who were most loyal and faithful to him.

Truth be told, Jeff's parents couldn't let any of their children go. They needed our money, resources, and influence to help keep their ministry going, which was their main concern—not our mental, emotional, spiritual, financial, and physical well-being. They would shove the family picture in our faces, saying, "How could you break up our family?" No pressure there! Our relationship with them was always based on obligation, guilt, condemnation, and duty to "God" and family. We were to "honor" Jeff's parents so our days would be long according to Ephesians 6:3 That was another scripture used frequently to infuse fear and gain control. They told us that if we ever left the ministry, we would be threatening our time here on earth and be stepping outside of God's blessing, covering, and protection. It started to feel like we were trying to break out of a cult or gang, and the only way out was death!

Sadly, we were not the only ones subject to this type of spiritual and emotional abuse. If anyone left the church at any point, Jeff's parents made an example of them. They were gossiped about, cursed, considered dishonorable, and turned over to the devil.

At this time, Jeff and I now had a family of our own. When our son, Kingston, came on the scene, he changed everything for us. I will share his eventful entry into the world later on. He gave us a great sense of purpose and hope for the future, and it was no longer just the two of us taking on this battle. How would this ministry affect our child in the long run? There was little peace, lots of frustration, hurt, division, and the carrying of a massive false burden. We wanted to be free, and we wanted out!

Finally, it came time for us to make a clear break. Jeff and I loved our extended family and our church family. We knew the weight of this decision and how it would affect those we were leading in different areas of the church. However, with the knowledge of what was happening behind the scenes and how things weren't being handled properly, we had no other choice. We couldn't publicly endorse a lack of transparency and spiritual and financial accountability. We didn't agree with the way people in the church were being treated, as it wasn't a reflection of our hearts. As a result, Jeff and I sought counsel, which was very hard to do. We didn't want to see the family ministry exposed or destroyed, knowing this was Jeff's parents' livelihood. We just wanted out!

Knowing we needed to leave the ministry, it was very difficult for us to go anywhere else in town to worship because people knew who we were and the word would get back to my in-laws. Finally, Jeff and I ended up visiting a large church in the area where we could just sit in the back and let the Word of God wash over us. We were tired, hurt, and burnt crispy, and we just needed Jesus. There was so much guilt involved in our decision to attend another congregation. We didn't feel the freedom of Christ, but rather felt stuck in emotional, spiritual, physical, and financial bondage. We might have been physically free, but we were still mentally imprisoned and not yet whole.

Eventually, we mustered up the courage to let Jeff's parents know of our decision. They were tired, and so were we. We couldn't keep going on like this. It was their ministry, and they were going to lead things as they saw fit. It wasn't our place, and they were not receiving our deep concerns, counsel, or encouragement. We were witnessing the dying of a dream, a releasing of our home church, and the potential dividing of a beautiful family.

Sharing the FIT 2B FREE message

The eight months leading up to this decision, Jeff and I had been writing a faith-based health and wellness curriculum called the *FIT 2B FREE Movement*. We had developed a strong passion for freedom in Christ manifested within the spirit, soul, and body. Even outside of the trauma within our own family, we saw how the enemy was bringing division, pain, disease, and devastation, and we wanted to help others find total freedom from a pure heart. Everything that we had gone through up until that point was fuel to help us fight the good fight. We asked God to restore unto us the joy of our salvation from when we first believed. God had done too much for us not to cling to His promises for our lives, yet fear was trying to grip us and rob us of our peace. We had almost been convinced that there wasn't life outside the cult of existence that was my in-laws' ministry. The truth of the matter was that God hadn't given us the spirit of fear but one of love and a sound mind.

Jeff and I were ready to confront this giant and share the truth we had come to embrace in our hearts. We asked Jeff's parents to endorse our books as a way to honor them and "properly" release us into the ministry to which God had called us. Jeff told his father and mother that we wanted an opportunity for them to be just that in our lives—a father and mother—because, based upon everything that went on, they could no longer be our spiritual father and mother. Trust had been broken and too much pain had occurred for them to be a safe space for us, spiritually or financially. This would release both Jeff and I of the false burden they had placed upon us.

Jeff told his dad, "I want you to prove me wrong. I want you to show us that you can just be dad with no other strings attached. We can no longer carry the burden to support you and advise you on how you should run your ministry. We had given so much to our detriment." After Jeff spoke, there was silence, followed by, "So be it...go on now, get out of here!"

I think that day, both Jeff and I knew it would be impossible for Jeff's father to just be dad. If he didn't have complete control, then he didn't want to have anything to do with us or his grandson. He preached the pure and perfect love of God, but he withheld that love from his own flesh and blood. He would often quote a scripture in Matthew 12:50 that said, "Who's my brother, who's my sister..." but that wasn't relevant to his situation. God had blessed him abundantly with a faithful wife, grown sons, daughters-in-law, and grandchildren who loved the Lord and stood by him, yet he chose to sabotage and hurt the ones closest to him. In our hearts, Jeff and I knew that this wasn't his mom's desire. All she wanted was for her family to be together. That is what brought her true joy, but the ministry always took precedence over the family, which should always be the first ministry.

Now, we were finally "free" and on our way to recovery while embarking on a divine mission to help others. During this season, we were speaking, teaching, and training Freedom Ambassadors who led groups through the 12 week journey across the nation. We became members of the Presidential Council on Sports, Fitness, and Nutrition and were feeling a deep sense of purpose. Our curriculum was recognized as the hands and feet of our First Lady's Let's Move Initiative.

This time was bittersweet because although we were seeing God move in the lives of many, our own family was still disenfranchised. Jeff and I genuinely loved and cared for them and wanted them to succeed in all they did, so we would have sporadic interactions with them. We were taking baby steps to build trust and set a new foundation built on unconditional love.

One night, we let our guard down and asked Jeff's parents to watch our son while we went to do a television interview for our book. When we returned around 11:00 p.m., Kingston, who was two and a half years old at this time, was still awake, even though it was way past his bedtime. He had made a Lego tower that was sitting on the floor. He was trying to get our attention to show us his amazing creation that he had worked so hard on. My father-in-law told him to stop interrupting, and King became upset, kicked down his Lego tower, and started crying. Jeff immediately went to pick him up and comfort him. I said, "He's tired and just wanted to show us his project," to which my father-in-law responded, "Stop making excuses for his behavior," grabbing him from Jeff. "I will put him to bed," he said.

Everything inside of me wanted to stop him, but I was again trying to appease his controlling ways and yielded. He took our son back to the master bedroom and was gone for a little while, trying to get him to sleep. When he finally came back to continue the conversation, silence filled the room. I had this feeling in my gut that I couldn't shake—you could call it mother's intuition—but I also knew whose house I was in and how things were "handled" there.

I asked my father-in-law if he had taken King to the bathroom before he put him in the bed. He hesitated for a moment, then said no. We were potty training King at night, and I knew that there was a potential for him to pee in the bed. "I will be right back," I said, excusing myself from the conversation. "I'm going to take him to the potty." I could tell this made my father-in-law very uneasy.

I started walking very quickly toward the master bedroom and opened the door. It was dark, and I could barely see Kingston lying on their bed. I picked him up, and sure enough, he was soaking wet, having peed clear up to his neck. As I turned him toward the hallway light, I looked down at his face. His lip had been busted open and was bleeding, with snot running down his face. Everything inside of me began to shake and tremble with pure rage!

Jeff had gotten up and followed me down the hall. I turned around and looked at him, with our son in our hands. "Look what he did to our child!" I shouted. I will never forget the look on my husband's face as he saw his son's face covered in blood. It was already horrific for Jeff's dad to be abusive toward him, his wife, and his mom, but far worse his child! If this man had the audacity to handle our son with such aggression and violence while we were in the next room, what was he possibly capable of if we weren't there?

Jeff scooped King up and sped toward the door. His dad and mom walked in after us and saw Kingston's face. "What have you done?!" my mother-in-law yelled at my father-in-law. He immediately started saying that Kingston was out of control and did this to himself. He was crazy, and for the first time in my saved life, I wanted to kill him! That man had caused so much hurt and devastation in our lives, and this was crossing the line.

Jeff turned and walked out the door as fast as he could. As we were putting King in the car, he finally came to, and we asked him what had happened. With terror in his eyes, he said, "Grandad hit me." He sure did—he knocked him out! We sped out of the driveway, so overwhelmed with anger, disgust, and rage. Only the grace of God was keeping Jeff from retaliating. He had dealt with this abuse growing up, and it was now visiting the next generation. This was the final straw. In that single moment, the olive branch of trust we had extended to Jeff's parents had been obliterated.

We finally made it home, but we couldn't sleep that night. Any ounce of trust we had been trying to build with Jeff's parents was gone. What would we do? The issue was no longer about covering this sick man and saving the family ministry. Were we to call the police? At that moment, I couldn't tell my parents about what Jeff's dad had done to King. I could only imagine what my father would do to the man who hurt his cubby bear.

The next morning, Jeff had received a phone message from his dad begging for forgiveness while still holding on to the lie that King had hurt himself. There was no way a toddler was capable of doing that kind of damage to his own face. My father-in-law had lost control and physically abused his own grandson. We told him that we would not press charges or call the police. Instead, we chose to forgive him because we didn't want to carry the weight of hatred and bitterness toward him. After that night, trusting our child or future children in his care would never be possible. He had broken that, not us. In an effort of damage control, my father-in-law called family members to play down what he had done. Many believed him, but Jeff, his mom, God, and I knew the truth. We were willing to stand on that no matter the consequence. God was holding us responsible for the safety and care of our child and one another.

That horrible incident only brought confirmation that this man was still bound and not free from the bondage in his life. Anyone close to him would be a target of his deep insecurity, anger, and self-sabotage. He needed to get serious help not to be in a place of pastoring others. We had to accept the truth that this man was not changing and that God wasn't holding us responsible to fix him.

The crazy thing about injustice happening in your life in any way, shape, or form is that it makes you feel helpless, vulnerable, dismissed, and not protected. But, we serve a God who always sides with justice. It may not come in the timing we would desire or need, but it will be served. Everyone has to come to their day of reckoning before the King of kings and Lord of lords. 2 Corinthians 5:10 says, "For we must all appear before the judgment seat of Christ; that every one may receive the things done in his body, according to that he hath done, whether it be good or bad." Everything on earth that has been in the dark will be brought into the fullness of light. Where there was no justice on this side of heaven, there will be in eternity. If that doesn't put the fear of God in you, I don't know what will.

> The crazy thing about injustice happening in your life in any way, shape, or form is that it makes you feel helpless, vulnerable, dismissed, and not protected. But, we serve a God who always sides with justice. It may not come in the timing we would desire or need, but it will be served.

In Psalm 46:10, God tells us, "Be still and know that I am God." I always looked at that scripture as one to remind myself to literally sit, be still, don't move, and wait on God. Yet, I have read a different perspective of this verse, which explains that it means to literally be at peace, trusting God to fight your battles. He is the way, the truth, and the light. He is sovereign; He sees all and knows all. Nothing is secret or hidden in His sight. He will vindicate, He will redeem, and He will bring eternal justice to all that has been wronged in your life.

The years continued on after that devastating event. Some of Jeff's siblings were still faithfully serving in the church and hadn't broken free yet. Everyone had their own journey and their process to find freedom. Thankfully, Jeff and I were in a newfound place of freedom and operating in God's unconditional love, where everything that we had left had stayed exactly the same. We had established new healthy boundaries for ourselves, but it was looked at as if we were better than the rest of Jeff's family, which couldn't have been further from the truth. We had embraced grace to the fullest and were allowing God's truth to wash over our hearts and minds. We no longer thought less than ourselves to subject ourselves to any kind of abusive behavior.

We were still trying to work on the family relationships on our end. Believe it or not, we even came around Jeff's family for different holidays and special occasions. Without fail, there would always be some type of blow up at a family gathering. There was always an invitation extended for a birthday, sporting event, or holiday, which would be followed by a no-show or even worse—some type of sabotage. We had come to accept the truth that a family divided was our sad reality. We longed for unity, brotherhood and sisterhood, and we never stopped believing for and praying for God to move mountains.

There was so much underlying tension among Jeff's siblings because of their parents that relationships between them had become increasingly unhealthy. Lies were told to fuel and justify their anger toward us, and it was bringing division and lost memories between brothers, sisters, and cousins. We chose to love, forgive, and maintain our boundaries. Every time we would extend a bridge of reconciliation to members of Jeff's family, there would be a bomb detonating underneath it. A wise man once told us that a stable bridge has to have two solid footers to cross. If a bridge is one-sided, it's bound to crumble underneath you, and that couldn't be more true. We were healed and ready to move forward with realistic expectations. Our concerns for Jeff's family and our overwhelming desire for restoration ran so deep. I think all of the siblings had the same desire, but my in-laws' version of that desire was for every aspect of their ministry to return to what it once was.

One day, Jeff and I agreed to meet with his parents for brunch because they were open to communication and wanted to try to find some resolve. Our conversations with them always started out civil until genuine concerns were brought up. The problem was that Jeff and I had been forever changed, and there was no returning to the conditional love and toxic interactions that we once had with them. That was not our norm anymore, for we had been shown a new way of life in Christ. If we ever brought up anything from the past, our only motive was to bring to light that this type of toxic behavior was still going on. We had forgiven the past, but we hadn't forgotten. Many times, people will say to forgive is to forget. I don't agree with that statement. If that was true, why would God give us a memory? It's there for our protection, not to torment us or to hang things over the heads of those who have truly repented and changed their ways.

In our brunch conversation with Jeff's parents, they began claiming that we were keeping their grandson from them. That wasn't true at all. They were more than welcome to be in his life. We just made it clear that trust had been broken the night my father-in-law mishandled our son. We told them that we had forgiven them, and still forgave them, but that didn't mean we would trust them. My father-in-law had broken our trust in that act of rage, and it was something that only time, genuine repentance, and changed behavior could possibly earn back. Trust is not something you demand of others.

At that moment, my father-in-law said so clearly, with fire in his eyes and a deep, gravelly voice, "I did it, and I would do it again!" Oh, Lord! For all those years, he had denied actually physically harming our son, and now he was taking full responsibility for it, even bragging about how he would harm him again.

We were sitting in a restaurant, and here I was visualizing myself launching across the table strangling this psychopath! Jeff and I were waiting for my mother-in-law to say something, but for the first time, she just sat there quietly. She would normally be quick to bring correction and accountability, but she chose to do and say nothing. Not a word! In that sobering moment, I thought to myself, *Dear God, she's lost her voice. She is so tired, worn out, and over battling him to do what's good, godly, and right. This is the very same woman that called me a mighty woman of God and spent her time reminding so many other women of their priceless value in the kingdom.*

Jeff looked at his dad with such deep concern. He asked him if he truly had a personal relationship with Jesus Christ as his Lord and Savior. How can you preach God's love and the Father's heart yet be fueled by so much anger and hatred in your heart toward your own family? I told my father-in-law that I had been praying for his deliverance and healing since his heart surgery. I even reminded him of the stepping stone I had made for him that illustrated God's promise to give him a new heart. He stood up from his chair and yelled from across the table, "Shut up, woman! You don't have a voice!" It was as if Satan himself, with everything he had, was screaming at me, "Don't you speak life into this soul. He's mine and you can't have him." It was evident that the truth spoken in pure form was tormenting the enemy.

By this time, I was no longer naive or a people pleaser. I was a confident woman of God. I had found my voice. I hadn't allowed hatred in my heart to take root, and I was free from the opinion of this tormented soul. I wasn't afraid of him. He had lost his grip on me, my husband, and our child. We were FIT 2B FREE! We were free, on the other side of his empty threats and curses. We were not dead; we were very much alive.

In that moment, it was as if I could hear all of my female ancestors who had gone before me standing up cheering. I had been raised in a home where women's voices were valued, respected, and celebrated. I had come from a long line of women who were journalists, commodity brokers, poets, teachers, mothers, and ministers. They all had been married and honored their husbands and served their families while heeding the call of God on their lives.

My husband said to his father, "Don't you ever disrespect my wife like that ever again. This is the twenty-first century, and women have a voice that matters and is valued. God has given her a powerful voice, and she has fought hard to love you while you've chosen to reject that love and project hatred toward her."

We stood up from the table and left, completely disheartened by the gross display of bitterness, anger, and loss of total control we had witnessed. We were deeply concerned for my mother-in-law. She didn't look well, and we then knew completely that she was losing her strength to keep defending her husband and making excuses for his horrible behavior. He wasn't taking her desires for unity, peace, and healing into consideration.

We had finally come to the point of accepting the truth: Jeff's dad wasn't going to change, and although life had moved on for us, there were many we loved who still remained under the grips of his psychological, spiritual, and physical control. We knew the only thing we could do was pray and love him from a distance. We hadn't lost faith, but we had to get out of the way and let God move.

Ecclesiastes 1:18 says, "For with much wisdom comes much sorrow; to increase knowledge in the increase of sorrow." Our hearts were deeply burdened and heavy, yet very hopeful of what God's love could still do. In time, truth would be revealed to the hearts of our loved ones, and they too would begin to experience healing and freedom for their souls. The battle was truly the Lord's, and we had to put our trust in the God who had brought us out of darkness and into His marvelous light. There would be a new dawn, a new day, and a new reign for the Shaw family.

So, how do you discern whether someone is manipulating you with wrong motives and lies, or communicating with you from a genuine heart? Trust me, when the enemy is using someone close to you whom you love, it's very easy to be confused. It's a form of friendly fire. When you are in close proximity to that person, you become an easy target of their hatred. They would never think to display such careless behavior around other acquaintances outside of the family. They are too prideful to show who they really are because they've convinced themselves that they are always in the right, even when they are causing harm. In any situation, one thing you can always be certain of is that God is not the author of confusion but the author of peace (1 Cor. 14:33). He also says in Psalm 37:37, "Mark the perfect man, and behold the upright; for the end of that man is peace."

In order to know the genuine root of a person's motives and whether they are speaking from a place of truth or deceit, you must look at the fruit in their lives. I call this the spiritual litmus test. It's God's tool of accountability for us to decipher a situation and whether we are reacting in our fleshly, adamic nature or our redeemed, divine nature as a son or daughter of God. This is a tool not just for times of deep crisis but for our everyday battles of the mind on the road to healing and redemption. Romans 12:12 says, "Do not conform to the pattern of this world, but be transformed by the renewing of your mind. Then you will be able to test and approve what God's will is—his good, pleasing and perfect will." This discipline is not a one-time act. It's a lifestyle of intentionality, obedience, and action to embrace the truth of what God says about us in His holy Word and cast off the gross lies of the enemy.

Galatians 5:22-23 tells us, "But, the fruit of the spirit is love, joy, peace, patience, kindness, goodness, faithfulness, gentleness, self-control, against such things there is no law." So, no matter what weapon of destruction the enemy is throwing at you, you can access the absolute authority in Christ to stop, take a pause for the cause, and line it up with the Word. No matter how painful, paralyzing, or real that venom feels, you can grab hold of the sword of the Spirit, which is the Word

> In order to know the genuine root of a person's motives and whether they are speaking from a place of truth or deceit, you must look at the fruit in their lives. I call this the spiritual litmus test.

of God, and cut it off before it penetrates your heart and mind, leaving you wounded on the battlefield.

In John 8:32, Jesus states, "You shall know the truth, and the truth shall make you free." To know someone means that you are intimate and close with that person. You've invested the time to get to know their likes and dislikes and the smallest of details about them. They have shared things in confidence that they only entrusted to you. Numerous people know of you, but how many actually know you personally and intimately? That is a closeness reserved for a faithful few. Our frail humanity only has so much capacity for that kind of intimacy.

However, we all have the privilege of entering into and cultivating an intimate relationship with the Creator of the Universe. He is omnipotent, omniscient, and omnipresent. He is all powerful, all present, and all knowing. He can be everywhere at the same time yet give His sons and daughters intimate and individual counsel, attention, and guidance.

There is a saying that says, "When someone shows you the first time who they are, believe them." Nine times out of ten, that is very true. There is always room for grace to change. None of us would be here if that wasn't true. But, you can always watch someone's behavioral patterns and what they carelessly allow to flow from their lips. Luke 6:45 says, "Out of the abundance of the heart, the mouth speaks." So, what's in someone will eventually come out of them, especially when you put a boundary in place. Saying no can be the most revealing statement in toxic relationships. Whether someone has allowed truth or lies to take root in the garden of their heart will be revealed by the fruit of the spirit. Time, pressure, and circumstances will always bring to the surface what's lying deep below.

KINGDOM (QUEST)IONS

1. What lies have you chosen to believe?

   _____

   _____

   _____

2. What truths are you afraid of exposing and confronting?

   _____

   _____

   _____

3. Have you sought out wise counsel to hold you accountable to walk in the truth?

   _____

   _____

   _____

4. How are the lies affecting your life (health, relationships, finances, etc.)?

   _____

   _____

   _____

KINGDOM TRUTHS

"You shall know the truth, and the truth shall make you free."–John 8:32

"Guide me in your truth and teach me, for You are God My Savior, and my hope is in you all day long."–Psalm 25:5

"For the word of God is living and active sharper than any two edged sword, piercing to the division of the soul and the spirit, of joints and of the marrow, and discerning the thoughts and intentions of the heart."–Hebrews 4:12

"Love does not delight in evil, but rejoices with the truth. It always protects, always trusts, always hopes, always perseveres."–1 Corinthians 13:6-7

"Trust in the Lord with all of your heart, lean not to your own understanding. In all of your ways acknowledge Him and He will direct your paths."–Proverbs 3:5

"God is not a man that he should lie but all of His promises are yes and amen."–Numbers 23:19

KINGDOM DECLARATION

I declare and decree that the enemy can no longer lie to me. No weapon that's formed against me shall prosper. As a son/daughter of the King, I will choose to be on a lifelong quest to stand on and for the truth. I am a freedom fighter and no longer a slave to the lies the enemy has spoken over my life. I cancel every lie, curse, and demonic force trying to steal my joy, peace, and divine destiny.

In Jesus's name, amen.

Chapter Four

REIGN IN FAITH

◦◇◦

"Now, faith is the substance of things hoped for and the evidence of things not seen."–Hebrews 11:1

For Jeff and I, the big question now was, how do we move forward in full faith without having closure in a major area of our lives? God had called us out, very much like Abraham. We didn't know where the heck we were going, but we knew we couldn't stay where we were anymore. No longer could we drown out the voice of God. It was full steam ahead! If we didn't fully commit, step out in faith, and walk into a new environment, nothing would change. We couldn't fully heal and move forward in the environment that had caused us so much harm. After all, insanity is doing the same thing over and over again expecting a different result.

2 Timothy 1:7 says, "God hasn't given us a spirit of fear, but of love, power, and a sound mind." We weren't crazy after all. We had flipped that pancake of a situation every which way, and it was only coming up burnt, crispy, done, fried, baked, and bitter! We couldn't have one foot in the past and the other in the future. In James 1:8, the Bible says that a double-minded man is unstable in all of his ways. God's Word also tells us that if you're lukewarm, He will spew you out of His mouth (Rev. 3:16). I know that sounds a little harsh, but we serve an all-in kind of God. What if He just partially created the sun or the moon and set them in space closer to the earth? It would throw the whole world into

complete chaos. The shorelines would be flooded, and the earth and all of its inhabitants would be incinerated—just to name a few of the natural disasters that would occur. He is so precise and a God of order.

1 Corinthians 14:40 says, "God does everything decently and in order." This includes the orchestration of seasons in our lives. Ecclesiastes 3:1 tells us that there is a time and purpose to everything under heaven. There is a time to release and a time to receive. A time to grip tight and a time to let go. There is no such thing as partially putting your faith in God. It's amazing what happens when you finally decide to step out in obedience and trust God at His word. Authentic peace, joy, and freedom in Him will follow. You will look back and realize that the overwhelming fear that had paralyzed you for so long was like a hologram; it appeared very real, but there was no actual substance to it. When you expose the source of the projected image, it becomes less scary and loses power over your life.

Did you ever watch *Scooby Doo* when you were a kid? The team was always on a mission to uncover some scary, menacing, and haunting figures. When they finally caught the suspect and uncovered the disguise, they usually discovered the villain was someone who, without the smoke and sound effects making them appear larger than life, was not intimidating at all. That is much like the spirit of fear.

Many years ago, I heard a message preached on conquering your fear. The preacher gave an acronym for the word FEAR: False Evidence Appearing Real. That sounds like a hologram to me. Fear can appear so real that it can trick our minds into a state of paralysis. That's why it's so important to stop, take a pause

> Fear can appear so real that it can trick our minds into a state of paralysis. That's why it's so important to stop, take a pause for the cause, and look deeper than what we see with our natural eyes. Don't be afraid to ask questions, search out, and clarify.

for the cause, and look deeper than what we see with our natural eyes. Don't be afraid to ask questions, search out, and clarify. That's what Mystery Incorporated did. They searched for clues to unveil the source of the destruction. They worked together and investigated every angle to capture the criminal and bring them to justice.

Our faith journey was never meant to be travelled alone. Ecclesiastes 4:9-10 says, "Two are better than one, because they have a good reward for their toil. For if they fall, one will lift up his fellow. But woe to him who is alone when he falls and has not another to lift him up." Proverbs 27:17 tells us that iron sharpens iron, and one man sharpens another. God never created us to be an island to ourselves. One of the enemy's favorite tactics is isolating us so all that we hear is his loud, lying voice. In the midst of uncertainty or times of transition, we need our brothers and sisters in Christ to remind us of God's faithfulness and promises. My pastor once said that hearing the testimonies of what God did in the lives of others is a way for us to borrow some faith for ourselves. Romans 2:11 states, "God is no respecter of persons." In other words, if God worked a miracle for someone else, He can surely do it in your life.

Not only do the testimonies of others have power, our own testimonies do as well. Revelation 12:11 says, "And they overcame by the blood of the lamb and the word of their testimony." The more we share with others about what God brought us through, the more we have power over the bad things that happened in our lives. We don't have to be ashamed, embarrassed, or paralyzed by our past mistakes or the horrible things that have happened to us by no fault of our own.

I know that someone reading this may be thinking, *I don't even have the strength, much less the courage to take the leap of faith in my life.* If that is you, let me encourage you that sometimes faith is just about taking that first step. God isn't requiring you to have it all figured out to follow after Him. As a matter of fact, He's already worked it out. Revelation 1:8 says, "He is the Alpha and the Omega, who is and was and is to come." God already had the end in mind while creating the beginning. He is faithful to fulfill His promises in your life, and He will not take you somewhere that He won't protect, provide, and guide you into safety and fulfillment in Him.

Proverbs 3:5 says, "Trust in the Lord with all of your heart, lean not to your own understanding. In all of your ways acknowledge Him and He will direct your paths." Consistency over time builds trust. Trust is something that takes time to build and only seconds to destroy. God wants to show Himself faithful in our lives. As we learn to let go, cast all of our cares upon the Lord, and trust Him, He can carry us through some of the darkest and most uncertain seasons of transition. He wants us to get up, show up, sit at His feet, and give Him full permission to walk with us and talk with us.

I've been told many times, "You are just so brave!" Well, the truth is, I'm not brave at all. I didn't have some sort of superhuman strength to leap, trust, and go. I don't have that kind of faith and courage. Sometimes choosing to be courageous means you're moving in action even when you feel terrified. I honestly had gotten to the point that I was so sick and tired of being sick and tired that I had no other option but to trust Him. It was life or death. I also had a decision to make. I was going to trust God at His word and really activate my faith in what He said was true or try to prove Him to be a liar.

In Numbers 23:19, the Bible very clearly says that God isn't a mere human. He can't lie. He isn't a human being. He doesn't change His mind. He speaks, and then He acts. He makes a promise, and then He keeps it. When I realized that, I thought, *Okay, so what You're trying to say here is that it is impossible for You to lie. It's not in Your character.* Once I got that settled in my heart, mind, and spirit, there was no turning back to a life of fear, hesitation, or constant doubt.

Hebrews 11:1 tells us, "Now, faith is the substance of things hoped for and the evidence of things not seen." Faith requires immediate action. Like, right now! God wants us to have faith right where we are. He wants to take us from the "safe zone" to the "faith zone." The only way we can make that transition is by completely surrendering our hurts, fears, hesitations, and doubts over to God's loving care. Breaking free from analysis paralysis is always activated in a moment rather than an hour or a day. Have you ever had someone tell you, "Just take it one day at a time"? Well, when you are overcome with anxiety, fear, grief, or depression, it's almost impossible to wrap your mind around making it through the day. I can remember times when I didn't even have the strength to get out of my bed. The depression I was experiencing was like being a paraplegic mentally, and it was affecting my physical ability to respond. The physical weight of this depression was literally so heavy that I didn't have the strength or will to sit up. I had to ask for God's help one move at a time. *Father, help me sit up...Father help me move my legs to the side of the bed...Father, help me put my feet on the floor...Father, help me wash my face and get dressed.*

> Breaking free from analysis paralysis is always activated in a moment rather than an hour or a day.

If we don't ask for help, the spirit of fear has a way of making time stand still and grip us in complacency. Society has indoctrinated us with the belief that we must be the "boss man" or "boss babe." We can do it all and have it all in our own power. You don't need help. You're in control of your destiny. Do whatever it takes to get to the top—work hard, sacrifice, be cutthroat, be selfish, and even cheat. As a matter of fact, if you ask for help, you are weak, stupid, and incapable. We compare ourselves to self-help gurus and completely rule out any help from *the* Source of it all. In His own words, Jesus made it so clear that He is the only Source of help. "My grace is sufficient for you, for My strength is made perfect in weakness" (2 Cor. 12:7-10). You can't tell me the mind isn't powerful, especially when it's under the control of the King of kings.

Have you ever watched the documentary *7 Yards: The Chris Norton Story*? It's about a high school football player who got paralyzed during a game. His first big goal was to walk across the stage for his college graduation. To accomplish that goal, he went through grueling physical therapy for a year. He found his "why" and, with lots of help and support, put his will to the test. He says that there were countless times when he wanted to quit when his body wasn't responding and he was in excruciating pain. He kept going back to his original why, and that's what kept him going. Right before the graduation ceremony, he ended up proposing to his girlfriend. She adjusted her whole life to join in on his vision and was even the one who drove him to physical therapy that whole year prior. Later, his next big goal was to walk down the aisle on their wedding day, together as husband and wife. With God all things are possible, but we also need to find someone who can bear our burdens and help us activate our faith when the temptation to quit comes...because it will!

One of my favorite scriptures in the Bible comes from Zechariah 4:6: "It's not by might, nor by my power, but by my spirit says the Lord." This verse became a key to activating my faith and releasing myself from the pressure to figure everything out before I took the first step. It was and is my spiritual parachute for exiting the space of comfort and soaring into new horizons.

When I was eighteen years old, I made the crazy decision to go skydiving. I went with a group of people I worked with at the gym. Everyone had a very different experience of the adventure. Some were so excited, but most were completely terrified to jump! I chose to be the last one to jump out of the plane. I thought it would allow me to take in everyone else's perspectives before I jumped and help make the experience feel more real. After all, my hubby, Jeff, always says, "What sound-minded individual would jump out of a perfectly good airplane?" I watched as most jumped while shaking with fear, and others were pumped to take the big leap of faith.

Now, it was finally time for me to go. The professional I was diving with asked me if I wanted to go out backwards, and I immediately said yes. It made sense to me. I wouldn't have to face the abyss and could close my eyes and just let go. That's exactly what I did! We flipped backwards multiple times, and then we were straight free falling at 100-plus mph. For a split second, I thought to myself, *When is this parachute going to open?* Boom! It released and jerked me up in the sky so fast that my guts went all the way up into my throat. The parachute finally opened and caught the wind, and I was flying! Here I was above the noise, the hustle and bustle, among the birds, just soaring. It was so peaceful and beautiful. I was seeing everything from a very different perspective.

In order to see our trials, obstacles, and setbacks with clarity, we sometimes have to get above the chaos and enter calmness. If I had allowed fear to grip me, I would never have had this story to tell and a fresh perspective on how God sees our lives. Now, I'm not saying you need to jump out of an airplane to gain this perspective, but you do need to make an intentional decision to shift your atmosphere. You might gain this by just going for a walk on the beach or even around your neighborhood. When I first started walking with the Lord many years ago, I read the following poem. It was as if I could hear God calling directly out to me, telling me that I was created for more. He was beckoning me to a faith-filled adventure in Him where I would be free and safe to follow His lead into the unknown.

> Come to the edge.
> We might fall.
> Come to the edge.
> It's too high!
> COME TO THE EDGE!
> And they came,
> And He pushed,

> And they flew.
> Come, let us fly together.[4]

Sometimes we need to be pushed in love and reminded that we are called out and set apart to soar above our circumstances and situations. God really wants us to see our lives from a higher perspective. Dr. Caroline Leaf, best-selling author and neuroscientist, says, "He wants us to face our past and present fears head on, reconceptualize our pain, break toxic cycles, and use it to end injustice towards others."[5] That is often the best form of closure we can have when trying to move forward in faith while someone else doesn't want to take action.

So, how do we grow in our faith? Romans 10:17 says, "Faith comes by hearing and hearing by the word of God." Faith is much like our natural muscles. We only gain strength through resistance. It's easy to trust God when everything seems to be going smoothly, but trials, obstacles, devastations, disappointments, and life in general create resistance to activate our faith in God. The more opposition we face, the more we need to lean into God's unchanging promises. This builds our "faith muscles" and strength in Him. Ephesians 6:10 says, "Be strong in the Lord and in the power of His might." The Word of God is fuel that nourishes, strengthens, and builds our faith muscles.

> **The more opposition we face, the more we need to lean into God's unchanging promises. This builds our "faith muscles" and strength in Him.**

In the natural, physical resistance training actually puts micro tears in the muscle. So, when you work out, you're actually taking time to break down the muscle. When we rest and refuel, the muscle fibers start recruiting more and interlocking fibers, creating a stronger and much more fortified bond. That is called muscle growth. Recovery time, which consists of rest and refueling with nutrition, is just as important of a building process as weight training. After exercises are performed, lactic acid starts to build up in the body. If it's not properly flushed with water and stretching, it can cause extreme soreness, fatigue, and slower recovery time in between workouts. This is very similar to allowing life's disappointments and setbacks to come in and choke out our joy. Nehemiah 8:10 says, "The joy of the Lord is our strength."

The enemy wants us to grow weary and make us willing to give up and eventually quit when things get tough. It's so important to be reminded that God never promised that we would have a life of happiness or access to an easy button. That is a lie the world wants us to believe. We often think that if we're not "happy," then something is wrong with our lives, marriages, or jobs. We should just resign, redirect, and find something better. However, the truth is, happiness is a fickle and fleeting emotion dependent on our external circumstances being just right. Joy is an internal and eternal strength that only comes from the Lord.

Hebrews 12:2 says, "Let us fix our eyes on Jesus, the author and perfecter of our faith, who for the joy set before Him endured the cross, scorning its shame, and sat down at the right hand of the throne of God." We need joy to endure hard times. It gives us hope for the future and empowers us not to quit when things get tough or go wrong. We need Jesus as the very source of our joy.

During the Christmas season of 2019, right before the pandemic, I was driving around in preparation for a women's tea where I was going to serve as speaker. While driving, I kept passing this huge light-up yard sign with these three letters: JOY. God gave me the acronym for it: Jesus, Only You. Our true joy, our lasting joy, our strength can only be found in Jesus. We tend to believe the lie that happiness is the ultimate pursuit in life. But, let me reassure you that there is no greater pursuit than a personal relationship with your Lord and Savior Jesus Christ. To surrender to His love, safety, reassurance, and divine comfort is like nothing else on this earth. There is no house, car, vacation, job promotion, man, woman, or savings account that can provide deep fulfillment the way Jesus can. He really wants to be your all in all, the lover of your soul, and your everything. He wants to be the first thing you think about when you wake up and the last thing you think about before you go to bed.

Joy is like having high octane fuel to activate pure faith in our lives while empowering us to move forward into the unknown. Building our faith is a process not to be rushed or forced. Our modern-day society has turned the word "process" into a curse word. We want instant results and instant gratification. If I touch that button or ask Siri a question, then I get the answer. If I go through a drive-thru, then I should get an instant hot meal. The problem with these quick fixes is that there are missing problem-solving skills when I have answers given to me and missing key ingredients from fast food. Real life is quite the opposite. The best things in life that are strong, true, and lasting are built on a solid foundation and take time and pressure to fortify. Fad diets fade, and the latest exercise will be replaced with something new and improved. To experience lasting results requires a commitment to lifelong health that takes discipline, accountability, and consistency.

Creating an atmosphere of faith in times of transition is key to moving forward. If our faith comes by hearing, then we must be so intentional about who we're listening to, what we're watching, and who we're spending time with. For example, if you're always being a sounding board for a negative friend eventually it will wear off on you and weigh you down. It will affect your ability to think, speak, and walk in faith and total trust in God's promises. Negativity sows seeds of doubt that will be reaped in hesitation or complacency.

There is no more dangerous transition than leaving the safety of our mother's womb and entering this fallen world. During birth, so much can go wrong in an instant, and it takes a team of knowledgeable professionals who are trained and equipped to assist in this miraculous process. I had a textbook healthy pregnancy with our firstborn, Kingston. I even worked out right up until the delivery. Around 3:00

in the morning, my contractions started, and they became closer and closer to the point where I walked into the kitchen to call our doctor and let him know it was time. My water broke on the tile floor, and I started going into a split. I yelled for Jeff to come, and he bolted around the corner in a panic. I told him it was time! We rushed to the hospital... after I showered, did my hair, and put on makeup and bronzer. Listen, I wasn't about to have pictures of me looking crazy holding my beautiful newborn baby all over Facebook!

When we arrived at the hospital, I was brought into my room and continued laboring on an exercise ball. It was the only thing giving me some relief to press through the insanely painful contractions. Then a nurse walked in, looked at me, and said nonchalantly, "Oh, you have meconium in your water." *I have what?* In all of the books, blogs, and posts I read on labor, I had never come across that word. Finally, the nurse explained that when my water broke, my baby released its first bowel movement, and there was a major concern that he may have swallowed it. She proceeded to tell me how dangerous and potentially deadly it could be for my baby. She then told Jeff and I that they would be monitoring Kingston's vitals very closely and have a respiratory team standing by at delivery. All I could do was pray and ask God to keep King safe and give me the peace and strength to get through the labor.

I went without the epidural until eight centimeters, and I was already so tired with much longer to go. After fifteen hours in labor, I went ahead and got the epidural. It was now 6:30 p.m. and time to push. I became super quiet and really focused on pushing. After three big pushes, Kingston was out and totally limp. There was no sound of crying—just silence! The respiratory team was right there and took him from me; they immediately started pumping out his lungs. He had indeed swallowed a lot of meconium and wasn't breathing. All eight pounds, six ounces of our baby boy was lifeless.

This was the moment not to panic but to pray in total faith and confidence. I could hear my mom and mother-in-law, Pam, praying out loud, speaking life over Kingston. As the doctor was working on me, I was laser-beam focused on my promise from God. He had given us this child. This was His promise to Jeff and me. He had even given us his name, Kingston Reigns Shaw. It came from the scripture Proverbs 8:15: "By me kings reign, and rulers degree justice." It was a big name but one day our son would grow into knowing that the King of kings rules and reigns in his heart and mind. He would know from a young age the unconditional love of His heavenly Father and his family. He would be confident and kind, walking in his God-given authority over all of the enemy's plans. *Surely God didn't bring us this far to take that precious promise back,* I thought.

The team worked on Kingston for at least five minutes, but it felt like an eternity. The next thing I saw was this giant fist pumping to the sky, followed by the sweetest cry. It was my son's voice resounding through the room. We all finally exhaled and rejoiced in Kingston's birth, welcoming him with loud cheers and praises to God. The doctor brought him back to me, and I was finally able to hold my amazing son. He was glowing with God's glory...and a bit of the bronzer I was wearing. We all watched God breathe the breath of life into Kingston and will forever remember not to take that miracle for granted. Genesis 2:7 says, "God formed man out of dust and breathed into his nostrils the breath of life; and man became a living being." Our faith in God grew in an unmeasurable way on March 4, 2008.

Kingston Reigns Shaw 8 lbs 6 ounces

Not too long after Kingston was born, I saw that someone I knew on social media had a baby boy that had passed away from inhaling meconium. I knew that it was only by the grace of God that King was with us, and that he was destined to fulfill a mighty purpose here on earth.

Five years later, God blessed us with a beautiful, strong, and sweet girl who we named Carrington Reigns Shaw. She was born on September 25, 2012, at 6:50 p.m., just like her big brother. However, her entrance into the world was much calmer and less dramatic. Unlike Kingston, Carrington made her voice known as soon as she was born, and she hasn't stopped talking since. God gave us a beautiful promise on the other side of our personal Egypt. Her life was a symbol of restoration, joy, faith, passion, relentlessness, and hope for the future. We decided to give her the same middle name as her big brother so they could always share the bond of knowing without a shadow of a doubt the authority they have to reign over the enemy in their lives. Carrington's name honors Jeff's grandmother, Carrie, and my father, Kerry.

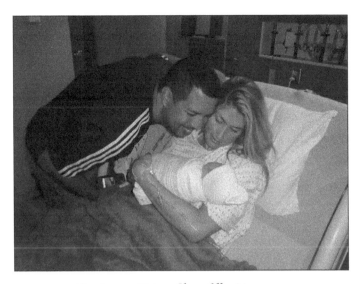

Carrington Reigns Shaw 6 lbs 11 ounces

Not long after Carrington was born, Jeff and I were asked to come on a local television show to share our *FIT 2B FREE* curriculum. We were excited to share our mission and passion to help others become healthy, whole, and free in Christ. The interview went great, and the studio called us back to be health experts on another show they were filming. We really connected with everyone there and loved their mission to bring faith into entertainment.

Shortly after, I was asked to sit in as a guest host on an inspirational women's show called *Let's Chat*. I had never done television, but the show went so well that the studio asked me if I would be interested in coming on as their main host for the show. *Me?* I had no formal education or training in broadcasting or TV. Our daughter was a newborn at the time, and I was still nursing her. Fear of failure and so many unknowns tried to grip me and prevent me from stepping into this great opportunity. I didn't even feel qualified for this position. Yet, someone once told me that God never calls the qualified, but He does qualify the called. Clearly, God was calling me out of my comfort zone.

After much prayer, I let go of any excuses—the largest one being that I had two little ones—and said yes! I was welcomed with open arms into a loving, family-friendly space to learn, grow, and gain new skillsets I didn't have before. The producers, crew, and onscreen talent became family to us. I would nurse my daughter in between shows and had the most incredible experience.

There was something so motivating about having a daughter. I felt a strong mandate on my life to pave the way for her. If mommy could do it, surely she could and then some. I never wanted our children to become an excuse for not pursuing a deeper purpose in Christ. I wanted them to be the reason to go through and grow through important moments together, and that's exactly what we did.

On set of Let's Chat at My Christian Films

At the station, I cultivated a passion for production, both behind the scenes and in front of the camera. After filming fourteen episodes, it became time for the season to wrap. One day, I went on a walk with two of the ladies who had mentored me on television, Dynell and Staci. We started talking about what we were all going to do during the break, now that the season was ending. They brought up the crazy idea about me competing in a pageant. I had mentioned that I really wanted to take *FIT 2B FREE* to the next level, but I wasn't sure what that looked like. We had groups going all across the nation and had spoken at several churches and businesses.

Walking with Staci & Dynell)

To be honest, I laughed at the idea of competing in a pageant. What was a married woman with two young children going to look like parading around in a gown? The idea also stirred up some old feelings about competing in the fitness arena. I was way beyond that stage in my life. *What would I really gain from putting myself and my young family through that gauntlet?* I thought to myself. *What grown woman of God would put herself in a position to be judged by random strangers who would determine if she was "worthy" to wear a crown and sash?* Dynell and Staci both encouraged me to look into it, sharing that I would be an amazing Mrs. Florida.

So, after the laughter wore off, the idea started to spark my curiosity, and I began my research. After searching on Facebook, I found a former Mrs. Florida America who went on to become Mrs. America, and then Mrs. World. April Lufriu was truly a mom on a mission, and I could relate to that. Her sister and children had been diagnosed with RP (retinitis pigmentosa) which leads to complete blindness. She used her platform of pageantry to draw attention to this personal cause and help get her family the care they needed.

Moved by her story, I took a "step of faith" and sent her a message. The worst that could happen was that she wouldn't respond, and I would take that as a confirmation not to proceed. Well, she responded right away and took my phone call. We chatted for over an hour, and I felt not only inspired but encouraged to run for Mrs. Florida. She even made herself available as a mentor and sounding board during my preparation. April told me that I had all of the main ingredients to win and make a huge impact during my reign. She shattered the mold of a "typical" beauty queen and showed me that there is so much more than physical beauty. She taught me that humility, servanthood, hard work, grace, grit, and determination are what made the crown and sash truly sparkle. The rhinestones, gowns, makeup, and pomp of pageantry would just be a megaphone to draw attention to my real mission.

My next step of faith was to attend to a meet and greet to connect in person with April, along with the founder of the pageant, Jackie Siegel, and the reigning Mrs. Florida, Deanna Silva. Jeff came with me, and we were welcomed with warmth, kindness, and open arms. Deanna was pregnant with twins at the time and totally shifted my perspective on pageantry as well. She was so helpful and encouraging during the whole process. She even let me borrow her heels to walk in during the pageant. Jeff and I were both pleasantly surprised. We left with 100 percent confirmation that the Mrs. Florida competition was a viable next step for not only myself but our family. We were in it together, sharing this mission to capture the crown in order to serve more people.

The day my journey to the crown began.
Mrs. Florida 2013 Deanna Silva, Mrs. World April Lufriu

It soon became time to put this plan into action by registering for the pageant. James 2:26 says, "Faith without works is dead," and I needed to put my money where my mouth was. The only problem was that pageantry can be really expensive. *Was this even a wise investment of our finances? What if I didn't win? Would we be willing to lose that money and time instead of investing it in more viable areas of return in our lives?*

After some discussion, Jeff and I came to the agreement that if I was going to do this and prove the validity of the pageant, then I would need to go out in the community and ask for sponsorship. This way, we could get all of the expenses paid without losing anything from our personal finances. It would also prove to be a training ground for me to learn the power of partnership and present the tremendous value my family and I were to local businesses as influencers and spokespersons. I then Googled, "How to make a sponsorship package," and I was off to the races.

> Any time you step out on faith to try something new, it's so important to ask for the right kind of help.

Any time you step out on faith to try something new, it's so important to ask for the right kind of help. I was so blessed to have my family from My Christian Films step up and help me with headshots, and they put together a fresh look for me for the pageant. I wanted to stay true to who I was, and the new "All-American" vibe they helped me channel went perfectly with my platform.

The next step was to draw up my first resume, documenting all of my previous experiences as author, speaker, TV host, and teacher. My hubby and I then put together a spreadsheet of all the expenses competing would involve. There were registration fees, program ads, the hotel stay for the competition, hair, makeup, gowns, shoes, interviews, a swimsuit, and the list went on. I also made a list of family, friends, and business acquaintances who would support me in this crazy endeavor.

I had my package ready to go and soon began making appointments to share my mission and vision for becoming Mrs. Florida America 2014. This was way out of my comfort zone, but I was clear on what I wanted to accomplish through this experience. I could serve in a greater capacity and leverage my future title to help more families become healthy and share the gospel outside the four walls of the church.

The first appointment I scheduled was with a friend named Merritt, who Jeff and I called "Car Dad." Merritt had taken care of us for many years at Central Florida Lincoln. He had been with us through the ups and downs, the births of our kids, and the expansions of our vehicles. I was nervous to share the idea with him, but he was excited and encouraged me to meet with the sales manager. He couldn't write me the check, but he could get me in the room with the man who could. I was "Mrs. Central Florida," after all. It just made sense for the dealership to partner with me.

On the day of my meeting with the GM, I was so afraid during the whole drive to the dealership. Remember earlier, when I talked about courage? Well, I might've been shaking on the inside, but my "why" was so much bigger than the fear of rejection. The worst thing this guy could say was no. I wasn't a salesperson. I didn't have any formal training or education in sales. I loved Jesus and had no problem sharing His goodness with boldness and confidence, but this challenge depended on my ability to sell this crazy idea. *Would he laugh in my face? Would he tell me I was out of my mind?* So many thoughts ran through my head.

When I arrived, I took a huge, deep breath, asked God to go with me in the room, and put on my big girl pants. When I sat down, all I could see was this stoic look on the manager's face. Had Merritt even prepped him? "How can I help you?" he asked. I went right in to sharing our long-term relationship as loyal customers with Lincoln, the impact we've made with our curriculum, and how it would be a win-win partnership to sponsor me for the Mrs. Florida pageant.

I stopped and waited for his response. He then proceeded to finally smile and say, "We would love to support you. How much do you need?" *What? Was it that easy?* All I had to do was ask. I showed him the breakdown of what I needed. "We can do this amount," he stated. *What?* That was more than what I needed to cover half of my expenses! I stood up and shook his hand, and he said he would have the check ready for me to pick up on Monday.

When I walked out of the office, I looked at Merritt and gave him the thumbs up. "That's my girl!" he said. He was such a big advocate for me and still is to this day. He not only pushed me out of my comfort zone to fly, but he also got me in front of the decision maker. That day, I learned so much about the importance of preparation and putting my faith in action. I could be confident in what God placed in me and who He surrounded me with, and go after my mission with boldness. We have not because we ask not. For so much of my life, I feared being rejected. I learned that on the other side of so many no's can be one powerful yes. Sometimes all we need is that one yes to keep us going.

After this wonderful experience, my heart was filled with gratitude and courage to go out and get the rest of the expenses covered. I was so excited to go home and tell my hubby what had happened. That was just another confirmation that this was the path God was leading us down for such a time as this.

I ended up getting all of the expenses covered, and my mom stepped up to be a pageant mom to a thirty-two-year-old woman with two young children. She helped me pull together my wardrobe, and God met us at every store. I know it sounds so silly, but I always ask God to go with me when I shop. I find the most incredible deals and pieces in a record amount of time. My mom has always had a passion for shopping and enjoys the hunt. She loves taking her time looking through things, while I like to get in, get what I need, and get on with my life. Together, we found the perfect gown, interview dress, swimsuit for my post-baby body, and heels to walk in.

I never liked walking in heels, and one of my biggest fears during the competition was not the interview portion but falling flat on my face in heels! I wanted a pair that was both beautiful and functional. After years of soccer, dance, and running, I had put my feet through so much. This mama needed comfort. I tried on so many pairs of heels, and I was not fit to walk in stripper heels—you know, the ones that are five inches high. I am 5'9 and flat-footed, so I didn't need super high heels. Unfortunately, about a week out from the pageant, we still had zero luck.

That week, our family decided to go to the beach for the weekend to relax and celebrate Mother's Day before the big pageant weekend. My daughter Care needed some beach sandals, so we decided to run into Payless and find something for her. The next thing I knew, my mom came walking toward me with a box. "I think I found your heels for the pageant," she said. I laughed at her, then opened the box. They were the exact same blue as my dress and even had bling on them to match the top part of my dress! Now to see if they fit and were comfortable.

It was a real Cinderella moment in the aisle at Payless, baby! They fit perfectly, and I could walk in them as confidently as I could in my Nike's. Thank you, Jesus! That was the last item I needed to purchase before the big weekend.

We went up to the register to check out, and the cashier rang up the heels. The cashier told us that this pair just happened to be on clearance, for $19.99. *Are you out of your mind?* I knew this would be a story to tell my grandchildren one day. It was just another reminder that God cares about the tiniest of details in our lives. As I put the card in the machine to pay, I glanced down at my ring. My signet ring was my daily reminder that nothing is too big or too small for God. He wanted my feet to feel comfortable, and He wanted me to walk in total confidence without breaking the bank or my ankle. Won't He do it (in my Pentecostal preacher voice)?!

I'm now going to take a dramatic pause for the cause and share the rest of the story that I began in the chapter, "Reigning in New Territory." Trust me, it will be worth the wait, I promise.

So, faith...Hebrews 11:6 says that "without faith it's impossible to please Him." Isn't our whole Christian walk about pleasing our heavenly Father? He really desires that we trust Him for every single detail in our lives. He wants us to invite Him into all of our moments, both the mundane and the mountaintops. He wants to help us get out of bed every day; do the massive piles of laundry; and go with us in the boardroom, the bedroom, or the classroom. He takes so much delight in seeing us loosen our grip of control and allow Him lead the way.

> He takes so much delight in seeing us loosen our grip of control and allow Him lead the way.

Have you ever heard of the story with the little girl and the pearls? It goes something like this. One day, a girl acquired a set of pearls from a vending machine. She wore them day and night, never taking them off. Her daddy noticed how much she loved those cheap pearls, and he decided that He wanted to do something extra special for his princess. One morning, he asked her if he could have her necklace. She looked at him like he was completely out of his mind. "I'm not going to give you these, Daddy," she said. "They are so special to me." He finally grew tired of asking her until one day, she came into his room and said, "Dad, you can have them." She had made a decision to release the tight grip of what was in her hand. Her dad then turned to the drawer by his bed and opened it. He pulled out a beautiful box and handed it to his daughter. She proceeded to open it to find inside a real Miki Moto pearl necklace—some of the most expensive and valued pearls in the world! This precious gift represented how priceless the little girl was in her father's life.

Just like the little girl, we can find ourselves gripping so tightly on the past, our fears, our regrets, and even our disappointments that we don't release them into our heavenly Father's loving hands. He so badly wants us to let go of what we are holding so that He can bring His very best in our lives, for we are His beloved sons and daughters. Don't find yourself settling for the imitation when you can have the real deal relationship with your Creator.

Luke 12:32 says, "It is His good pleasure to give us the kingdom." We can look at faith like making a deposit into an unlimited bank account in heaven. As we put our trust in God, we can then receive the desires of our heart. While trusting in God's timing and sovereignty, we will never have to fear the lack of anything in our lives. Philippians 4:19 says, "I will supply all of your needs according to my riches in glory." That sounds like an overabundance of replenishing resources to me. Release your faith to reign over any limitations, both seen and unseen, and watch God move so precisely and magnificently in your life!

God cares about the big problems in our world and the small daily details and stressors of life. We have to get out of the mindset of thinking that if something bad is happening in our lives, then God must be punishing us. That's garbage and some sick mentality that manipulative leaders use to control and suppress people they want to take advantage of.

We don't have a performance-based or guilt-based relationship with God; we have a grace-based and loving relationship with Him. In other words, God is for us, with us, and not against us no matter what. He doesn't turn His back on His children when things get tough. He is omni-present. He is our comforter, helper, way maker, and provider in times of lack. Cars break down, washing machines overflow, keys get lost, jobs come to abrupt ends, and friends turn their backs on you. Life just happens! When you experience hard times, you are not being punished or cursed because you didn't behave perfectly.

> We don't have a performance-based or guilt-based relationship with God; we have a grace-based and loving relationship with Him.

I can remember during a season when finances were tight that our air conditioner decided to break down. We live in Florida, and it was *the* hottest time of the year. When we walked in the house, the thermostat read 98 degrees, and the temperature was climbing fast. Jeff and I looked at each other and just wanted to cry and scream! *Really? Not the best time for this to happen.* It never is, right? Kingston was around three at the time, and he looked at both of us and, in his raspy voice, started singing a song from his favorite Disney show, *Handy Manny*. It was about a bilingual young boy who loved fixing things with his tools. "Dad, Mom, you gotta break it down. Wax it, wash it, and make it shine. When you take it one little step at a time. You gotta break it down!"[6]

My overwhelming desire to cry was replaced with a big smile and an "aha" moment. We knew just who to call! We have a family friend named George who Kingston used to call the "real life Handy Manny."

He could fix anything, and his specialty was fixing air conditioners. George took great care of us like he always did, and he didn't charge us an arm and a leg to replace the air conditioner unit.

In moments when we get hit with "life," our human nature wants to react in fear and anger, convincing us to feel overwhelmed. However, when we choose to stop, take a deep breath, and listen, God can give us the answer for the next step. That day, God spoke through our son, and He hasn't stopped doing so since. That sweet song comes to mind every time the "stuff hits the fan." Don't panic; put your faith in God for the next step.

When it comes to reigning in your faith, there are so many paths of discussion I could go down, but to summarize this aspect of reigning, I will start by sharing this truth: you will never "feel" like walking in faith. If we always allow our toxic emotions to dictate the next move in our lives, we most likely would remain in a state of paralysis or destruction. God gave us emotions as a beautiful way to process, express, and experience this journey called life. We have to ask for His power to reign over the bad emotions—as we learn from them—and teach us to embrace the good ones. He requires our obedience, which is the first step to walk by faith and not by sight.

If you are in a place where you feel cemented and stuck, then I would encourage you to ask God to reveal to you your last place of disobedience. Did He ask you to forgive, make that call, release that anger, or confront that lie? Go back and get it right, and I promise you, He will give you light for the next step of faith.

Have you seen the *Indiana Jones* movie where he has to cross a great divide to get to the treasure? In his natural sight, it looked impossible, and for the audience too. The clue Indiana Jones read told him that he had to take the first leap of faith. He mustered up the courage, and with sweat dripping from his forehead, he took the big step as we all gasped watching. Then suddenly, his foot hit a solid stepping stone, and as the camera panned out, it revealed from the side angle a clear path for him to cross to the other side of the canyon. It had been there all along! The illusion—the fear—in his mind was lying to him and holding him back from moving forward.

Isaiah 42:6 says, "I will lead the blind by a way they did not know; I will guide them on unfamiliar paths. I will turn darkness into light before them and rough places into level ground. These things I will do for them, and I will not forsake them." What a beautiful and powerful promise to cling to when God is calling us out into the unknown.

Faith gives us access to abide in peace that passes all understanding despite our external circumstances and uncertainty. So, take in a deep breath of Shalom and step out into the unknown! Shalom is a Hebrew word meaning peace, harmony, wholeness, completeness, prosperity, welfare, and tranquility. I always say, if you don't have peace, don't take the step. Be still and wait on the Lord to give you clarity, confirmation, and wisdom to move forward.

KINGDOM (QUEST)IONS

1. What is the greatest fear that you are facing right now?

___

___

___

2. What is something you would do if you knew that you couldn't fail?

___

___

___

3. Who can you reach out to and share your dreams and fears with?

_____

_____

4. What is your greatest reason—your "why"—to focus on while you conquer any fears and obstacles in your way?

_____

_____

KINGDOM TRUTHS

"God is working all things together for the good to them that love Him and are the called according to His purpose."–Romans 8:28

"I will show you the path of life; In Your presence is fullness of joy; At Your right hand are pleasures forevermore."–Psalm 16:11

"Looking unto Jesus, the author and finisher of our faith."–Hebrews 12:2

"Faith without works is dead."–James 2:17

"It is by faith through grace that we are saved, not by our works lest any man should boast."–Ephesians 2:8-9

"Therefore, since we have been justified through faith, we have peace with God through our Lord Jesus Christ."–Romans 5:1

"The only thing that counts is faith expressing itself through love." – Galatians 5:6

"I have fought the good fight, I have kept the faith. Now there is in store for me the crown of righteousness." – 2 Timothy 4:7-8

KINGDOM DECLARATION

I decree and declare, this _____ day of _____ 20_, that I will walk by faith and not by sight. I will fix my eyes on Jesus, the author and finisher of my faith. I will walk in obedience to You, God, asking You for help along the way. My heart is to be pleasing to You, and I know that without faith it's impossible to please You. I will have faith in Your sovereignty, timing, and direction for my life. God, give me the faith to believe for salvation, restoration, sanctification, and ultimately glorification.

In Jesus's name, amen.

Chapter Five

REIGN IN NEW TERRITORY

> "And Jabez called on the God of Israel, saying, Oh that thou wouldest bless me indeed, and enlarge my coast, and that thine hand might be with me, and that thou wouldest keep me from evil, that it may not grieve me! And God granted him that which he requested."–1 Chronicles 4:10

God is calling us all out into a deeper, broader, and more expansive place in Him. There is no height or depth that can separate us from the love of God. It can be either exciting or terrifying to try something new or to travel into unknown territory. So, what do we do in times of uncertainty, and how do we move forward without having reassurance of our safety, well-being, and expected outcome?

Psalm 139:7-10 is a beautiful reminder of God's promise to be with us in times of uncertainty. "Where can I go from Your Spirit? Or where can I flee from Your presence? If I ascend into heaven, You are there; If I make my bed in hell, behold, You are there. If I take the wings of the dawn, And dwell in the uttermost parts of the sea, Even there Your hand shall lead me, And Your right hand shall hold me." That's what I like to call blessed reassurance.

Well, one thing for sure is that if you never raise your anchor and launch out from the shore of comfort, you will never know the adventures and discoveries that await you. After all, a smooth sea never made a skilled sailor. You will never know what you're truly made of until you hoist your sails and venture out into the deep.

Reigning as a Real-Life Queen

Now, back to my Mrs. Florida America journey to the crown. A couple weeks before the pageant, I was invited to attend an orientation to prepare us for the big weekend. I can remember feeling so nervous on the drive there. This would be the first time that I would meet many of the women with whom I would be competing. The reality of the situation became super real, and I was ready to run in the opposite direction.

I walked into the room to find so many beautiful women who seemed to be put together so perfectly. I was confident in who I was on the inside and the mission I was on to even be there. However, I certainly didn't feel that same confidence on the outside. Our human nature is to immediately start comparing ourselves to others and sizing up one another, but God is very clear on what He thinks about that. 2 Corinthians 2:10 says it's foolish!

After a while, I began to introduce myself to everyone, and my nerves started to calm down. I was comforted by the former Mrs. Florida's who were in attendance, sharing their journeys and giving us some great tips in preparation for the pageant. I was focused and took plenty of notes. The next thing I knew, they were asking all of the contestants to stand up and get ready to work on walking across the stage. This was my biggest fear. Remember, I didn't want to fall flat on my face! Now, I had to practice in front of the same women I was competing against. No pressure there. I pushed my way through this moment and anxiety, but I couldn't help but watch how gracefully and confidently some of these women walked. Some even walked like professional runway models. That was it! I knew that I wasn't cut out for this. *I'm going to make a fool out of myself and embarrass my family and everyone who supported me to even get here,* I thought. It was now my turn. With a smile on my face, I bravely worked my way through it. I took a deep breath and remembered that my steps are literally ordered by the Lord according to Psalm 37:23. I can walk in confidence knowing that God goes before me. It wasn't as bad as I had built up in my mind. As a matter of fact everyone was really friendly and very encouraging. The reality was everyone competing in that room had similar insecurities and reservations. I still couldn't help but feel a bit overwhelmed by the thought of now walking in front of a live audience.

When the orientation finally ended, I drove home questioning my sanity for even saying yes to this crazy endeavor. Fear gripped me so tightly that I started to cry. I knew this fear was not coming from God, and I also knew that I needed to get this weight off my chest. So, I picked up the phone and called my friend Dynell. She calmed me down and reminded me of whose I was and who I was in Christ. She also reminded me that this mission was so much bigger than myself. She even offered to help me practice my walk. We laughed and then decided to get to work.

During our next Mrs. America workshop, the staff gave us the music that we would be walking to in the pageant so we could go home and practice our walks. Soon after, Dynell and Staci met me at a gym where I was training clients, and they helped me find my flow and confidence. The song I walked to in my evening gown was "Shine Bright Like a Diamond" by Rihanna. Man, had God ever taken me through a lot of pressure in life to present me as a polished diamond. After we practiced and practiced, I felt fortified, free, and flowing with ease in my walk. They both helped me feel settled, established, and strengthened in this new season, ready to go capture the crown.

The week leading up to the pageant was packed with a kindergarten graduation for Kingston and tons of running around acquiring all the last-minute necessities and making sure everything was in place. This time greatly reminded me of preparing for my wedding day.

The pageant weekend was now upon us. My family arrived at the resort, and it was off to the races. The first night, we had a meet and greet party with our spouses. It was so comforting to have Jeff by my side, helping me keep the whole process in perspective. We had a great time connecting with the other couples, dancing, and eating.

The next morning, I woke up early for the interview portion of the competition. This was 50 percent of my overall score and the part that I was looking forward to the most. I felt confident and at peace to share my vision and mission for my reign as the future Mrs. America. I loved connecting with all of my judges one on one and wouldn't have changed anything about that experience.

One of my judges was former Miss America Erica Dunlap, and she asked me what my first planned appearance on Monday after being crowned Mrs. Florida would be. I loved that question because it was based on my work and mission, not the title and prestige. With that question, she put me in the position even before I was crowned. Following the interview portion, we spent the rest of the day in rehearsals, learning choreography and preparing to take the stage that night. It was a marathon of physical, mental, and emotional proportions. Leading up to that weekend, I had never looked at pageantry like a sport, but it very much is! This time, I was exchanging my cleats for heels and going after a crown, not a trophy. With that mindset, I decided that I was going to present and enjoy the experience to the fullest.

Throughout the process, I loved getting to know all of the incredible women and hearing their stories. The competition was filled with women who had been competing in pageants their whole lives, as well as some, like me, who were doing this for the first time.

The day flew by, and it was finally time to get ready to take the stage. I'm forever thankful for my friend Jeshel, who did my hair and makeup and went to battle with me that weekend. If you've never been backstage at a pageant, it's a bit of a warzone. In between changes, hair, makeup, bling, heels, and gowns are flying everywhere.

The competitors went onstage for the opening number, followed by the swimsuit portion, and finally the evening gown moment. The closing part of the competition was an onstage interview question. I was excited about this because I felt confident sharing my voice and perspective on everyday issues. After randomly selecting a question, I answered it with conviction, clarity, and passion. The question I selected was: What should a teacher do if their student told them they were battling a drug problem? I said that they should communicate with the parents first, then get the counselor involved so they can come up with a game plan to walk alongside the student and get them the proper care. It's going to take consistency, time, and a village for the student to break free from addiction.

Now, it was time for the top ten finalists to be called. All of the ladies were brought back to the stage to wait in anticipation for their number to be called out. "Number Four, join the ladies!" *That's me! Wow!* I was relieved. The top ten ladies were ushered backstage while a performance took place, then we returned for our final evening gown walk. Next, they called the top five. "Number Four, join your place with the ladies!" I was so thankful, feeling even closer to the crown.

Then it was time for the final question. "If you were to be crowned the next Mrs. Florida America, what would you accomplish during your reign?" I knew exactly what I was going to do and what my mission was. I shared with boldness and confidence that my mission was to educate, empower, and equip Florida families toward a lifestyle of total health and wellness. That was it. There was nothing more for me to do but wait.

The time came for the host to call out the top three ladies. "Number Four, join your place with the ladies!" I was overwhelmed with gratitude. This was my first ever pageant, and there I was standing in the top three finalists!

Now, the moment we were all waiting for. Who would be crowned Mrs. Florida America 2014? My heart was pounding out of my chest. Once more, the host called my number, and now I was standing with the other remaining contestant. They then called our husbands on stage to join us. Having my hubby on stage next to me to share this moment was such an incredible feeling. I closed my eyes and grabbed the hands of the other lady, waiting during the long pause.

"Your Mrs. Florida America 2014 is...Mrs. Central Florida, Courtney Dawn Shaw!!!" The song "Happy" by Pharrell started playing, and Jeff and I danced, laughed, and celebrated over all of our trauma, defeats, disappointments, hurts, and setbacks. Very few people in the audience knew what we had been through up until this moment. Many of our family members and friends were there sharing this incredible experience with us. It was a pivotal moment for our family—so much more than a title, a crown, a sash, or prizes. It was a big win over so much devastation and a huge wink from God, confirming that He was leading and guiding us into new territory with new influence to serve in a greater capacity. He had given us beauty for ashes.

Jeff and I dancing as the new Mr. and Mrs. Florida

I'm so thankful that my grandmother was in the audience that night. At age eighty-nine, she had beaten breast cancer and moved to Florida to be with the family. She was now ninety-four and had macular degeneration, but that didn't stop her from being present. I will never forget the huge smile on her face. Later that year in November, she would pass, and I am so grateful she was there to witness that moment. Grannie Inez was such an incredible example in my life. I will share some of her story in the legacy chapter.

My mother-in-law, Pam, was also in the audience that night, supporting me, and that meant the world to Jeff and me, considering everything we had gone through. She even let me borrow her beautiful earrings and a bracelet to wear with my evening gown. My father-in-law chose not to be present and later said that no "woman of God" would ever compete in a pageant. That night, I wasn't going to allow his absence to steal a moment of joy.

Celebrating with my Shaw Squad Jeff, King, and Care

Celebrating with family

Soon after the crowning, Kingston and Carrington joined Jeff and me on stage to capture the moment as a family of four. Their little faces were beaming with pride. I am so thankful this happened while I was a wife and mom, for it made the victory even sweeter. That was the true beauty about being Mrs. Florida America. The pageant system's tagline is "We are family," and that couldn't be more true.

We celebrated as a family for the rest of the weekend, then we were off to the races once more. That following Monday, I already had an interview at a local television station scheduled to share our curriculum. Little did I know that this would be my first official appearance as Mrs. Florida. God was already opening doors and preparing the way for an unforgettable year ahead. My time at My Christian Films had prepared me to feel at home on a television set and comfortable in front of the camera. I had an incredible experience and was asked to come back on the show. During my reign, that station reached out to ask me if I would become their community outreach coordinator and on-air personality. Due to my busy schedule that year, it didn't seem like the right time to get locked in there yet. I also had to immediately start preparing to compete at Mrs. America in Tucson, Arizona, three months after being crowned Mrs. Florida!

To say that year was a whirlwind would be an understatement. I became a spokesperson for AmeriGroup and multiple businesses; filmed infomercials and television and radio interviews; and spoke at schools, churches, and businesses. I also met with our governor, competed at Mrs. America, helped launch a women's ministry, and brought my family along on this crazy ride.

State Costume pics

Jeff and I walking on stage

Picture in the Mrs. America program that won the Publishing Award

When it came time for my reign to come to an end, I felt ready to close this chapter as a beauty queen and begin the next in television. One of the previous Mrs. America's had asked me if I was sad about my reign coming to an end. I told her that I was not, because I had given it everything I had.

Throughout that year, I had placed my crown on the heads of so many individuals that it was about to fall apart. That crown now represented a year of servant leadership. I loved how this shiny object drew people in and I could remind them of their value in Christ. In life, we go after an intangible crown. I definitely felt God was saying, "Well done, thy good and faithful servant."

The night I crowned my successor, we played a video recapping my year. The biggest compliment someone gave me was that they were so blessed to see how my family attended so many events and appearances together. They were my reason, not my excuse. We did this together and will forever cherish all of the incredible experiences we shared.

To recap my year, you can check out "Mrs. Florida America 2014" on my Facebook page. It would take a whole book to share all of the experiences I had during that year. I never placed at the Mrs. America pageant. I won the publishing award and walked away with some incredible friendships that are still in my life today. One of my biggest blessings from that season was connecting with Mrs. New Jersey. Jennifer had a heart to empower women, and we joined forces with about fifteen other women to launch Our Life Songs Ministry. We blogged, came together for retreats, and served at women's conferences.

Reigning Queen on TV

A week before my reign ended, I met with the TV station and accepted their offer to come work for them. That decision began a new chapter for me, and I would learn so much over the next two and half years. While in my new position, I represented the station in the community and cultivated many relationships with individuals to share their life-changing stories on air. I also helped develop an inspirational women's talk show and tour in the community. I took my role seriously; to me, this was not just a job but a true calling.

On set

During my time at the station, I took my StrengthsFinder test. So much of our lives, we're reminded of our weaknesses. Truth be told, I think we all know what we suck at. This test helps you identify your natural strengths and how you can activate those gifts to serve in a greater capacity while being rewarded for it. The test narrows down your top five strengths. Mine are Achiever, Individualization, Relator, Positivity, and Communicator. I think those results were pretty spot on.

My work in television allowed me to grow greatly in my strengths. I was able to share my passion for Jesus and health, have my family on air with me, minister to millions of viewers, and open the door for many friends.

Ultimately, this experience taught me that I was meant to travel light. I know I brought tremendous value and elevated the atmosphere in a new place. I put my guts into this role, but I also knew my true worth and that I wasn't to be mistreated.

Although I originally signed a contract to be the community outreach coordinator and on-air personality, as time went on, there became a demand for me to transition into more of a sales role based on all of the relationships I was bringing into the station. One day, I was brought into the office and told that if I wanted to keep my position at the station, I would have to bring in a contract valued at a certain dollar amount. While I had zero desire to go into sales, I took on the challenge and brought in a substantial contract who had the potential to become a major partner for the station. By the way, there was no offer for commission on this new facet of my job. The reason people go into sales is not usually for the base salary but the potential commission they can earn.

From that point on, the way that relationship was handled was embarrassing and not a true reflection of how I would treat a client or a friend. I remember sitting in the production room with my client, and our producer at the time was complaining about not wanting to shoot these commercials. My superior said, "Isn't it amazing what you can accomplish when someone puts some fire under you?" That was such a manipulative comment and one of total disrespect. I didn't need to be threatened to perform or motivated by fear. I had brought countless valuable relationships to the station, and it was up to the leadership to turn them into paying clients if that was what they wanted.

Many times, we can find ourselves staying in a location or position past our season. When it's time to move on, God has a way of making things crystal clear. It's up to us to be obedient and ready to step out in faith, trusting Him for the next chapter. You see, my previous life experiences had prepared me to handle hidden agendas and corrupt leadership. I wasn't going to be enticed by the lights, camera, and action of the television industry. I cared about people and how they were treated and handled. Therefore, I could no longer remain connected to a place where that wasn't the standard. So, I gave everyone a handwritten Hallmark thank you card, packed up my office, and left, not knowing where God would take me next. When I closed that chapter, I felt the biggest weight leave my chest. Several people who had gone through that station had shared their experience with me and had given me a heads up about it. I appreciated those who cared enough to let me know. They also knew that I would gain great experience and skills by investing my time there.

So, here I was, almost three years later, stepping out into the unknown again. During that time of resting and regrouping, I received a call from a friend who had started a nonprofit to educate and empower women in the community. Arlene was planning the first annual Women on the Rise awards, which recognized the achievements of female leaders in our community, and she asked if I would be open to hosting the event. Little did she know how heavy my heart was from the abrupt closing of my chapter at the television station. I had felt like I had somewhat lost my voice and didn't have a clear direction for the next chapter of my life. However, I accepted her invitation.

I can remember showing up to the event with a new sense of purpose and excitement. Nothing brings me more joy than celebrating people and acknowledging their priceless value. The event was absolutely beautiful, and the time spent connecting with so many incredible people gave my spirit a much-needed boost.

Arlene had launched her nonprofit after the passing of her mom to pancreatic cancer. Arlene's mom had always been her number-one encourager and supporter. When she died, it left a huge gap in Arlene's life. Deciding to turn her pain into purpose, Arlene honored her mom's legacy while creating a safe space for women to learn and be equipped to excel in this crazy world. I've been so blessed by her friendship and the powerful community of female leaders we have cultivated over the years. Authentic female empowerment does not have space for comparison, cattiness, usury, or competition. It's founded on unconditional love, mutual respect, collaboration, diversity, and support.

After dedicating much of myself to this organization, God allowed it to renew my confidence, and I truly felt like I could stand on my own two feet with God's help and the proper support system. My value was not tied to a specific place or location but to my Creator and King. With this newfound strength, I decided to get myself out there again and do what I do—connect with others—and see what God had in store for my next move.

Hosting a Women on the Rise event

Not long after I was crowned Mrs. Florida, I was invited to an event honoring women in ministry. This event took place each year, and I had always been encouraged by the keynote speaker and worship. I also knew that there was a strong chance that if I went that year, I would run into a group of people I had worked with at the television station. While I was working there, I had made the connection with the station to promote and partner with this event. However, I wasn't going to allow my experience at the station to hold me back from attending.

When I arrived, the GM of the radio station who was hosting the event approached me to ask if I would pray after the keynote speaker finished. I said yes, knowing I would have to stand up and face the people who had turned their backs on me. I quickly went from a place of celebration to toleration. Instead of avoiding their table, I chose to walk straight over to everyone and say hello. I didn't leave things on bad terms, but the look on their faces was one of total shock that I was greeting them. These were supposed to be my sisters in Christ, yet they couldn't have felt colder.

As I got up to pray, I felt this huge release over my spirit. Psalm 23:5 talks about how God will prepare a table before you in the presence of your enemies, and that couldn't be more true. That day, the TV station was one of the main sponsors for the event, yet I was asked to close the event with prayer. The Bible talks so clearly about praying for your enemies and blessing those who curse you. In that moment, I made a decision to forgive those who had hurt me and move forward with my life. I knew the Lord had better for me. I just didn't know what that looked like.

I truly believe that God uses rejection for redirection in our lives. At the time of rejection, it may not feel good, but God promises to work all things together for our good according to Romans 8:28. After the event, the GM came up to me and asked if I would be available to meet the following week to catch up and discuss my future plans. I walked away with a renewed sense of hope and open to what God had in store for me next.

> I truly believe that God uses rejection for redirection in our lives. At the time of rejection, it may not feel good, but God promises to work all things together for our good according to Romans 8:28.

Reigning in Radio

Soon after, I met with the GM of the radio station and shared my experiences from the previous station. I let him know what I had learned and what I would never subject myself to again. I shared with him my vision for a show I wanted to develop called *Authentic Living* and how I desired to create a space where others could share their authentic voices with transparency and have no ulterior motive attached to their time as a guest. I had a true heart to support, celebrate, and promote the goodness of God in the lives of others.

The GM loved the concept and asked me if I would be open to having my show on their station. I had never thought about going into radio before. Again, here I was with zero experience in producing and hosting a radio show. There would be much to learn, but God always brings the right mentors in your life when you're ready to receive. The GM also asked me if I would be open to doing community outreach for the station and help with the annual event that I had just attended.

The best part about this opportunity was that I had 100 percent creative control and ownership of my show. It would be my responsibility to create content, oversee branding, promote the show, and generate revenue through sponsorships. I would run the show under my business and have full ownership of it. We arranged a contract that stated I would be compensated for time as an on-air personality and community outreach coordinator. If I brought any additional paying clients into the station, I would receive commission. This aspect of my contract specified that I was not required to sell anything; the commission was just a way to value my time if I chose to bring paying clients to the table. I felt at peace about this arrangement and was off to the races creating a new branding and promotional campaign for *Authentic Living*.

Authentic Living Branding photo shoot

In the studio with Angela Doggett, Martha Munizzi, & LaRue Howard

I'm forever grateful for my time in radio. I learned so much while I had my show at the radio station. I picked up right where I had left off at the television station and used this new platform to tell others' stories and promote all of the amazing things happening in the community. I was simultaneously wearing the hats of the producer, writer, and marketer, while booking guests and taking care of other important tasks. Putting an hour-long show together each week required a great amount of work, but I was loving the experience and the freedom I had to create again. I'm so thankful for my mentor Pete, who was my executive producer and taught me so much about radio.

During my show, I started filming the interviews with my friend Chris as well. We had previously worked together at My Christian Films, and he is also the co-founder of the International Christian Film festival. He helped me develop my YouTube channel and put a visual aspect to my radio show. I'm such a visual and animated person, so to bring that quality to life on radio behind a microphone was a big challenge for me. However, I took on that challenge, grateful that my voice was taking precedence over my appearance. When you're on TV, you are met with huge pressure to feel like you have to be physically polished all the time. Although my experience in radio taught me important lessons, at the end of the day, I knew that I would always go back to television. We live in such a visual world, and my desire was to show viewers how to live an authentic life in Christ.

During this season, I was greatly focusing on other people's stories and only sharing my life in areas that I felt comfortable with, as my husband and I were still battling with our family relationships and dealing with heavy toxicity and sabotage.

Reigning through Grief

One day in late August, we were doing our weekly grocery shopping when we ran into my mother-in-law by herself. By now, my family had to distance ourselves from the drama of Jeff's parents because of the hurt and disappointment it would always bring. We would invite them to the kids' sports events, but they would always make an excuse as to why they would not come. At one point, my father-in-law told my husband that he wouldn't support our son playing football until he was in high school because he didn't agree with him playing at that age. In the meantime, he would go to all of his other grandkids' activities, and evidence of it would be posted on social media right before our faces. Jeff's father always withheld his support as a way to control and manipulate. It was hurtful not only to us but to our children as well.

That is just one example of the games he would play, and my mother-in-law would have to go along with them. Otherwise, she would experience his wrath. If you weren't supporting his ministry financially or with your physical presence, then he would withhold "love" and support from you. This went on for years until Jeff and I had enough.

I will never forget when we ran into Jeff's mother on the business aisle at Sam's. We were standing in front of a big bold neon sign that said, "Open." We were always open to have a respectful and loving relationship with her and my father-in-law, even after all of the trauma that had occurred. We also knew our relationship with Jeff's parents couldn't look like it had in the past. There was no returning to that dead place, for it was abusive and destructive. We had fought too hard and too long to subject our marriage and family to that environment any longer.

We started chatting with my mother-in-law about surface things, but eventually we got right to the heart of the matter. Addressing the trauma and drama that went on in the family was never a comfortable conversation. It was never about being right but getting things right. Each time we brought it up, we would always hit the same wall and be left completely devastated and frustrated.

Forgiving is not forgetting! How would Jeff's parents truly learn from their past mistakes and bad behavior if they just kept sweeping the past under the rug? We all know what happens to the rug. It keeps getting bigger and bigger until the growth is undeniable and you're left with a massive mess to clean up. But, that's the crazy thing about denial. The truth can be staring us directly in the face and we can still choose to ignore it. In those moments, the spirit of strong delusion settles in and takes over.

The Bible talks about a reprobate mind, and I have come to understand how that can come to be. When we choose hardheartedness and pride and shun the truth over and over again, God's grace will lift from us. If this is an area of personal struggle for you or someone you know, I would recommend Dr. Caroline Leaf's teaching on the mind to gain clarity and understanding. Check out her latest book Cleaning up your Mental Mess. It's a culmination of her life's work studying the mind and how to reconceptualize and turn your trauma into purpose.

> But, that's the crazy thing about denial. The truth can be staring us directly in the face and we can still choose to ignore it. In those moments, the spirit of strong delusion settles in and takes over.

In that conversation with my mother-in-law, there was a moment when Jeff told his mom how important it was to guard his heart and his peace. She said, "Oh, so your peace is more important than having our family together?"

He answered, "Mom, my peace is everything. Jesus is our Prince of Peace and died for me to receive it and walk in it." I looked Jeff's mom in the eyes and told her that I loved her. She rolled her eyes back at me in total disbelief and disgust.

I realized something was way off with her. She didn't look well and had become completely cynical and hardhearted. Her eyes were filled with drowsiness, as if she was medicated. Pam was in a lot of pain from her knees. She had needed knee replacement surgery for years, but her health and well-being would always take second place to the needs of my father-in-law or the church.

She then said to me, "You don't know what I have to deal with at home." Jeff and I both told that her we had a really good idea of what she was experiencing and that she didn't deserve to be treated with such disregard. We knew that she loved her sons, daughters-in-law, and grandkids with her whole heart. Her family was her happy place, and her greatest source of joy was having her family united and making good memories together. Unfortunately, that was never my father-in-law's dream. He liked the optics of having a unified family, but he had zero interest in the investment of making that a reality.

Jeff and I told my mother-in-law that we had found life, peace, joy, and freedom outside of the abuse and that she could as well. We explained that we were there for her and that she was always welcome to spend quality time with us and her grandkids. We even added that she didn't even have to tell her husband if she was spending time with us, especially if he was going to give her hell about it. He was no longer welcome around any of us until he had a genuine heart of repentance and showed a real desire to be in our lives without an ulterior motive.

We asked her if she wanted to meet us for lunch that upcoming week, but instead of saying yes, she said, "I have to check my calendar." As the conversation continued, she began justifying my father-in-law's behavior and defending his actions and the current family dynamic. Ultimately, she grew very angered, and our talk ended with her walking away. She knew we weren't open to playing my father-in-law's game anymore. We had zero tolerance for the physical, verbal, mental, spiritual, and emotional abuse we had lived through for so many years. At this point, we had seen and experienced too much to be alright with the situation in order to have some resemblance of a relationship.

After that conversation of over three hours, word got back to our family of a story that was very different from what had actually happened—that Jeff and I had said all of these horrible things to his mother and that she would never go back to shop at that store again. She never even responded to us about having lunch together.

Well, the following Saturday, we were back doing our regular shopping at the same store, and there she was standing in an aisle. The kids immediately ran up to Memaw and gave her big hugs. Jeff and I hugged her and told her that we loved her. Clearly something was drawing her back to us, perhaps with the hope that she would run into us, and she did. We had a pleasant, warm, and loving interaction with her, and we didn't even bring up the previous conversation. We reminded her to check her calendar again so we could have lunch. I knew that meeting was a work of God's leading because that was the last time our family would see Jeff's mother alive. We would never again get one-on-one time with her. We are forever thankful for that last interaction, and we don't live with the regret of not telling her how much we loved her. We're also grateful that she was by herself and not with my father-in-law, who would have made the interaction all about himself.

Over the following months, family gatherings were planned without us receiving an invitation. We reached out to my mother-in-law, but there was no response.

In December 2017, we would receive the most devastating call at 2:00 a.m. Jeff's youngest brother called to let us know their mom was in the hospital and had died. There are no words to describe the wave of emotions that overcame both of us. Of course, Jeff immediately asked what the heck had happened. His brother told him that their mom had just left dinner at one of the brothers' houses and made a stop by the grocery store to pick up items for a family Christmas vacation in South Florida, to which we were not invited. As she walked the aisles of the store, her breathing became very labored.

My father-in-law was with her, and together they walked back to the car. She stood on the side of the car, coughing uncontrollably until she lost control of her bowels. She was having a massive heart attack! However, instead of calling 911, my father-in-law took her back to their home, which was twenty minutes away, to get showered. This was "supposedly" her request. What? When someone is having a heart attack, seconds matter. His delay in response cost her life. She passed out in the shower as the EMTs got to the door. They immediately went to help resuscitate her, but Pam was gone. She was only sixty-two years old. As I'm writing this, I just want to scream!

Jeff and I always thought my father-in-law would go first because of his health issues, but it became very apparent that his wife had lost her life under the crushing weight of family ministry. So many questions started flooding both of our minds at the same time, and we knew we would have to tread extremely lightly due to the damage to our reputation among the family. We had been portrayed as these evil villains who had abandoned the family and ministry. I was seen as the wicked witch who manipulated the oldest son away from his family. Jeff's family told everyone we thought we were better than them and too good for them and their ministry.

The truth was, we had finally come to fully understand and embrace our value in Christ. We never thought we were better than anyone else; we just didn't think we were less. We knew that Jesus didn't die on the cross for us to be imprisoned in the chains of religiosity. I was always Jeff's biggest advocate to fight for his family and to seek out healing if possible. I took so much mistreatment and abuse because I loved Jeff and wanted to believe in our extended family's restoration.

I never imagined my father-in-law and mother-in-law would treat me the way they did. There were so many times when they would try to bring division between Jeff and me. My father-in-law would make comments to Jeff like, "You really need to get your wife under control, Jeff. You really have your hands full." Jeff's parents would try to sow seeds of doubt in his mind to gain control and ultimately access to our bank account. I remember one time when my father-in-law actually came up with a list of things that he disliked about me—and shared it with us. My husband and I endured listening to this list of ridiculous items—the most childish, disrespectful, and concerning list—which he needed a weekend of alone time to come up with. He basically made it up in his mind that if he could crush my spirit, then he could gain some sort of control. Thank God I knew who I was in Christ! I was just doing what a godly wife should do and guard my husband's heart.

Finally, the situation came to the point where we had to accept that the old would literally have to pass away so God could do a new thing. The more we tried to fix things, the worse they would get. We had to let go and get out of the way so God could move.

I can still hear my mother-in-law's laughter filling the room when we had quality family time. Some of my cherished memories of Pam were when she was with her side of the family, entertaining them and just being herself. It's not that the Shaw side of the family was incapable of having fun or enjoying one another's company, but almost every gathering would be sabotaged by my father-in-law's wrong motives and hidden agenda.

Being a family in ministry comes with a huge price. Many years ago, Jeff and I had to make the decision that we didn't want to be a public success but a private failure. In other words, we didn't want to lose our souls, marriage, or family over a public platform of influence. Over the years, we had seen so many pastors and their wives get divorced because of infidelity or a lack of accountability, transparency, and vulnerability. We weren't drinking the have-it-all, do-it-all, be-it-all Kool Aid any longer.

There is a price to pay for everything. When we all stand alone before God at the end of our lives, we will have to give an account of every decision. God's grace is not a get-out-of-hell-free card to do whatever we want in this life. People are not our property but God's creation. Although slavery was abolished a long time ago, the spiritual, psychological, and emotional damage is still perpetuating through generations. We wanted answers and knew my mother-in-law's death was going to expose so much that had been covered up for years.

There was a point where Jeff had asked if the family could get an autopsy to find out what had really happened to Pam. My father-in-law insisted on not having one because he was "believing" for God to raise her from the dead. I truly believe the only reason he really wanted her back was to take care of him and all of their affairs. What was he going to do without her? The load from carrying all of that responsibility is what aided in her early departure. Now, she was finally free and at home with her Lord and Savior. So, Jeff and I treaded lightly and started asking more questions. It soon came to the surface that Jeff's mother had been taking some type of strong pain medication for her knees, given to her under the table from some doctor. Over time, we witnessed the exposure of several things that confirmed gross neglect and care for Pam's health and well-being.

Grief is a crazy monster. There is no timeline or specific way you're supposed to go through it. How do you reign through tragedy and overwhelming grief? Only by God's grace, mercy, and lovingkindness do we go through it one moment at a time. The key is you have to make the choice to go through it, not deny it, or be destroyed by it. I heard the most clear and powerful explanation of how to grieve from a remarkable woman by the name of Dr. Edith Eger. She was brought to Auschwitz as a 16 year old girl and survived the most horrific treatment by the Nazi's. She suffered trauma for years after enduring such horrific conditions. As the years went on she moved to America and became a psychotherapist. Dr. Eger talked about how the slightest thing could be a trigger for her and bring her right back into the concentration camp. She said that life is not what happens to you but what you do with it. She also learned over the years of practicing that you don't medicate grief. What comes out of your body doesn't make you ill, it's what you allow to stay in that will. So, cry, scream bloody murder, just get it out! Push it out or it will poison your whole body. You need to have surgery and be cut open for the deeper work to take place. Then, after you get to the root of your grief you can begin the healing process. You also can't heal what you don't allow yourself to feel. It's not an overnight process and can take a lifetime for many. But, it's a worthwhile journey to go on. In most cases victims end up becoming the victimizers if they don't make the decision to go through the grieving process and feel the suffering. Suffering is a part of life. No one wants to suffer but it instills in us wisdom, compassion, empathy, and a deeper appreciation for the human experience. Grieving helps you to never forget what happened but not run from or fight it.

The time to start planning Pam's celebration of life was finally upon us. Jeff immediately dove into piles of family pictures to help capture the life of his mom as a girl, woman, wife, mother, daughter, sister, and friend to many. Although she was Pastor Pam to numerous people, she was so much more at her core. Jeff wanted the story of his mother's life to be told in full, not just in her role as a pastor's wife.

For Jeff and me, the sobering truth was that we had started the grief process years before his mother's death. We knew that with the decision to draw healthy boundaries and fight for our freedom, our relationship with her was nearly impossible because of my father-in-law's grip and demands over her to gain access to our resources.

We will forever honor Pam's legacy, and we do everything in our power to give others a voice, value, and a place of safety. She tried to be that for so many people while privately battling with being devalued, used up, and diminished. We honor her by creating unity, peace, and joy among her children and grandchildren.

Later on, in the chapter on relationships, I will share how God healed our family and brought us back together for our good and His glory. Looking back, I don't even know how we got through the viewing and funeral. All of Pam's brothers, sons, and daughters-in-law shared such beautiful tributes to her life. When it was my father-in-law's turn to speak, he recapped the whole sequence of events that led to her death, explaining the experience as if he was trying to make himself look good and cover up any neglect on his part. I was sitting there so disturbed, angry, and embarrassed how he had no filter at such an important moment in time to honor his wife and mother of his children.

I will never forget watching as all of Pam's grandchildren lay a rose-shaped bouquet in her casket. Our kids were like a rock for Jeff during that time. Carrington didn't leave her daddy's side and would hug him and remind him of how Memaw is with Jesus now. I can vividly remember being at the cemetery, sitting and staring at the rose gold coffin where Pam was resting inside. So many years of memories flooded my mind. I could audibly hear her voice saying, "You're a mighty woman of God." As her coffin was being lowered into the ground, so much anger filled my heart and mind. Why was she there and not him? There would be no resurrection of Pam here on earth. She was gone, never to return here. That was it. The finality of that moment shook me to the core. I felt supernatural peace come over me, along with a huge relief, knowing that Pam was finally free and at home in her heavenly Father's arms.

2 Corinthians 5:8 says, "To be absent from the body is to be present with the Lord." In that moment, all of the hustle, burdens, sadness, and battles ceased to a deafening stillness. It would only be selfish to want Pam back on earth.

As I stared at her casket, I focused on her name, the year she was born, and the year she died. Suddenly, I heard these bold questions in my heart: "How will you reign? How will you live your life out here on earth? You know that dash between the day you were born and the day you die? Will you allow the chains of bitterness, unforgiveness, insecurity, strife, discontentment, or fear imprison you? Courtney, will you release the lies and embrace the truth for My kingdom to reign in and through your life?"

> "How will you reign? How will you live your life out here on earth?"

I remember whispering under my breath, "Let it reign." As I looked up to see my father-in-law, husband, and brothers-in-law singing over Pam, an overwhelming sense of sorrow and compassion came over me. *What was God's plan for my father-in-law?* I wondered. *Was this it?*

Would his wife's death be the wake-up call that would break his heart to win his soul? Would her death shatter his pride and open his eyes to see how truly blessed he was with his family? Would her death make way for true repentance and forgiveness to flow? Only time would reveal.

Surely, life as we all knew it would forever be changed. Pam's death ripped everything wide open, but it also left my father-in-law completely vulnerable and exposed. At the beginning of the new year, I went back to the studio, with so much on my heart that I wanted to share over the airways. However, I didn't feel released to open up that area of my life in full.

After Pam's passing, I felt this overwhelming pull to begin writing again. The radio station I worked for also had a publishing division, Xulon Press. My husband and I met with the team at Xulon, and we both knew it was time to take the first step toward putting my book in motion.

At the time, I wanted to write about finding your authentic voice and sharing it with the world. As time would pass, I would realize that in order to write from an authentic place myself, I would need to share my journey in full, not in part. After all, that would defeat the whole purpose. So much of the trauma we had gone through as a family in ministry played a huge role in fortifying my beliefs and who I had become as a woman of God, both at home and in a place of public service. It would take a couple of years and lots of restoration in our family, along with a ton of courage, to finally write what I am sharing now in these pages.

Later that year, I would close my chapter at the radio station and work alongside my friends Marty and Chris to film the *Authentic Living Show* on 24 Flix. I was excited to help them launch this new family-friendly platform that would be the new home for my show. We created a half-hour inspirational lifestyle show that brought faith into everyday life. One of our first episodes we filmed would be on the water sailing with my dad. Working with the team that helped me get started in television was a true full circle moment for me.

Perfect day on the water to film

Sailing into the Unknown

During this season, my dad, who was contemplating retirement, decided to revisit his passion for sailing. After many trips to and from St. Petersburg, Florida, he earned his captain's license, and on Father's Day weekend in 2018, we would embark on our first family sail. It was so exciting to experience and share in his passion for sailing.

You could say sailing is in our blood. When looking through old family pictures, my mom and I stumbled upon a picture of my grandfather sailing a small boat that he had built on a lake in Kansas. Years following my grandfather's passing, my dad bought his first sailboat and took my mom for their first date on the water. Three children, two moves, and many years spent on the soccer field later, my dad would begin a long hiatus of enjoying his love for sailing. He always put his family first, so during my childhood, he never missed a game, which didn't leave him much time on the weekends to hoist the sails and get away. Finally, his well-deserved retirement from the banking industry led him back to the sea.

Although we grew up hearing so many cool stories of his sailing adventures, we never witnessed our dad behind the helm. It was a true gift from God to get out on the water and let the winds and waves wash away years of heartache, trauma, and deep sadness.

I will never forget the night before our first family sail. We went to dinner at Stillwaters Tavern and toasted to the beginning of a beautiful new chapter for our family. Now, three years later, we've had so many amazing adventures at sea and many tales to tell. Some of our favorite trips have been sailing in the bay, down the Manatee river, and over to Clearwater, and our biggest adventures to date include sailing across the British Virgin Islands at the beginning of the global pandemic and to the Dry Tortugas.

Over the years, my dad earned the nickname Cap'n Crunch because of some of the crazy moments we would experience on the water and how he would react to them. After experiencing a "crunch moment" on the water with us, my brother-in-law Jonathan and sister-in-law Valentina sent my dad a Cap'n Crunch figurine. Soon after, I had crew shirts made, and the rest is history.

Here's the deal with sailing: every time you launch out from the safety of the harbor, it's never the same. Our motto for our crew is "life is boring without a little crunch." Listen, life happens to us all. We can either freak out, shut down, and quit, or respond with courage, conquer the obstacles set before us, and laugh our way through. "Sail or die" should be another motto for our crew. That's the beautiful part about sailing—it forces you to focus on the present and handle opposition as it comes. After all, if we didn't get into any "crunch moments" on the boat, we wouldn't have these epic tales to tell.

You can do your best to prepare the vessel, study destination and depth charts, and check the radar, but when you leave the dock, you never know what you're going to meet out on the open sea. I will never forget sailing through our first storm. It was Labor Day weekend, and we were having a wonderful day celebrating Jeff's birthday. The crew decided it was time to sail out past the Sky Bridge and check out Egmont Island. We grew curious and decided to change our route to sail around the backside of the island to explore more. This was once a military post guarding Tampa Bay, where many day boaters go to hang out on the white sandy beaches. It was a perfect day. We were all feeling so blessed to be together, taking in the fresh breezes and serenity.

After looking at the sky and radar, we knew it was time to head back to safe harbor to beat an afternoon storm that was supposedly on its way. As we were heading back, we couldn't help but notice a huge black wall moving very fast toward the bridge. Jeff, King, and I were looking out the back of the boat and witnessed an enormous amount of fish flying out of the water. We all looked at each other very concerned. It seemed like a biblical moment was about to go down, and we quickly found out we couldn't outrun a storm in a sailboat. An eerie feeling came over us, and the next thing we knew, lightning was striking all around our boat. Thankfully, Carrington had just fallen asleep on Jeff's chest. We took her below deck to keep her safe from the storm. Suddenly, the winds began blowing like crazy while rain was hurling at us sideways. My mom, King, and I went below to take shelter while the captain and co-captain worked together to ride out this wild storm.

The waves were tossing us around like wet noodles, and Kingston looked terrified. I told him, "Remember what Jesus did when the storm started raging on the boat? He fell asleep like your sister."

He looked at me and said, "Mom, Care is not Jesus!"

In this weather, the guys were sailing completely blind. The scary thing was that we weren't too far away from the bridge that was infamous for a large vessel running into it, killing several people. I was holding the radar, trying to keep it dry so we could see where we were.

All I could do was pray and ask God to shelter us from the storm and get us back safely.

Well, the storm lifted, and that was the quietest and most sobering five-hour ride back to the harbor. As soon as my mom saw land, she yelled, "Thank you, Lord, for terra firma," which means solid ground. Our family survived our first storm out at sea and lived to tell about it.

Remember the saying I shared earlier, "A smooth sea doesn't make a skilled sailor"? It couldn't be more true. When we face storms in life, we often find ourselves begging God to remove us from the storm, but in reality, He will usually take us through the storm. There is so much more to gain by depending on God in the midst of dark seasons in our lives. How would we know Him as our Protector, Provider, Guider, Comforter, or Healer if life was always easy?

That day, God calmed our hearts and empowered us to ride out the scariest storm we had ever experienced. From that point on, we checked our weather radar more frequently while out on the water because Florida storms can roll across the state very quickly and suddenly. It's also important to check your spiritual radar frequently which is the Word of God. It helps equip you with the proper perspective, truth, and tools to weather any obstacle that comes your way. It also reminds you throughout your journey to course correct, and at the end destination you will arrive home. The storms will come but we can always access hope as the anchor of our souls to hold of steady under turbulent weather.

> When we face storms in life, we often find ourselves begging God to remove us from the storm, but in reality, He will usually take us through the storm.

In December before the pandemic of 2020, my dad went to St. Thomas to get certified on a catamaran. Even in his seventies, he's still finding ways to stretch and grow, both personally and with his family. He had planned an epic legacy trip for our crew to sail across the British

Virgin Islands in March. He came back with the stamp of approval and an amazing experience that he couldn't wait to share with the crew.

Little did we know that the world would soon be hit with the biggest pandemic since the Spanish Flu. As the trip grew closer, the window for us to leave the country was closing fast, for each day, another country was closing its borders to contain this crazy virus that now had a name, COVID-19. After much discussion and prayer, our family decided to move forward with our plans. We didn't know how long it would be before we could ever do this again.

If you allow fear to paralyze you, it can rob you of some of the most incredible experiences. Thankfully, we didn't. The British Virgin Islands are truly the place where God kissed the earth. We arrived in St. Thomas USVI within three and half hours, then made our way to Red Hook, where we would take a water taxi to Scrub Island.

Our crew jumped on a speed boat for an unforgettable one-and-a-half-hour ride across the most vivid blue water I've ever seen in my life—not to mention the craziest ride we've ever taken on a smaller vessel. The waves were huge, and the Caribbean trade winds were intense. If this was a sneak peek of what we would be experiencing on the catamaran, we were in trouble. We were used to the much calmer waters of the Gulf of Mexico.

On Promithee 11 with our crew

Our family arrived safely at Scrub Island, where the catamaran was docked. We stayed there a couple days to get settled and prepare Promithee 11 a 46 foot catamaran to set sail across the islands. It was like we were in a dream, and I was doing everything I could to take in each moment. When the morning of our departure came, we were fully stocked with provisions, and our crew was briefed before we left for the most epic adventure of our lives.

However, so many thoughts of doubt and hesitation started flooding my mind, but I knew there was no turning back. I've always had a healthy respect for the ocean. It is one of the most powerful, beautiful, yet violent substances on the earth. Since we had our children on board with us, Jeff and I knew this experience would challenge them in a big way.

Once we got out of the harbor, there was a two-hour stretch to our first destination to moor for the night. The six-foot rollers started coming in from the Caribbean Sea and gave us the ride of our lives! Thankfully, the forty-six-foot catamaran we were on was able to straddle those big waves with ease. We also had on Dramamine bracelets to become adjusted to the waves and prevent sea sickness. Land ho! Finally, we were pulling into the Bitterend area and on the hunt for our mooring ball.

Although Jeff and I had attended the school of YouTube in preparation for our sail to learn how to tie our boat off, let me just say, there is nothing like real-life experience to prepare you for this task. A mooring ball is attached to a chain that is anchored to the bottom of the ocean. This is a more secure option than staying on anchor because when you set your anchor, there is always the possibility to drift. We attempted to pull the ball out of the water and attach it to the boat many times, all to no avail. The wind was pushing the boat away from it and making it difficult to give the captain direction. Jeff got ripped across his chest with wire, and I about took off my finger trying to hold the rope—you should never hold on to the rope. Getting this vessel secure was a lot of pressure. We didn't want to float back out to the crazy Caribbean in the dark. We were experiencing an epic YouTube fail!

We stopped for a second, and I prayed out loud, "God, please help us get this!" Not even two seconds later, a man who looked like Jesus began rowing over to us in his dinghy! He yelled out to us to throw him the rope, then he attached it through the loop and threw it back to us to secure the boat on both sides. Before we could properly thank him, he was rowing back to his vessel. Thank you for Jesus on a rowboat! Again, another reminder that God was with us on this journey and that we could trust Him to help us every step of the way

We have so many epic moments from that trip, and they are documented on my Facebook page for you to see. Our sailing adventures could fill up a book all by themselves.

Unforgettable views in BVI

The last story I will share from that adventure was when we had to return to harbor to get some help with our generator. As we were waiting for instructions on where to dock, we learned that the mooring balls were all taken. We decided to drop the anchor for a bit and have lunch while we waited. We could see the marina in our view and felt safe close to land. The anchor dropped, and we were set. The harbor master called us in, and when it came time to raise the anchor, it was stuck. Jeff attempted to raise it several times, but the remote that was pulling it up shorted. We had to call for help.

A team came over from the marina and checked it out. It wasn't coming up. What were we stuck on? One of the team members then proceeded to tell us that we were stuck on the powerline that powered the whole island! *What?! Umm, can we get electrocuted?* I wondered. *What if we shut the power down for all of Scrub Island?* The guy then asked my dad what kind of security deposit we had on the boat. You know that's not good! Then he proceeded to tell us he couldn't get a diver out until the next morning, so we would have to stay put for the night. *You've got to be kidding me!*

So, they drove off, and we were stuck. We decided to go ahead and make lunch and readdress our issue. As we were sitting there eating, my mom and I noticed the landscape starting to change a bit. *Wait, we're moving!* My dad immediately went to the helm and let the anchor drift a bit to give us some slack. Jeff returned to the anchor, and the motor started again on the remote. He was able to pull it up, and we were free!

The moral of the story is don't panic, have a picnic, and wait on the Lord to move on your behalf. When we get stuck in uncertain situations, our nature is to freak out rather than activate our faith. Our family decided to be still, take a pause for the cause, and take in the beautiful view. Our choices were either to do that or to expect the absolute worst scenario.

After we finished lunch, we pulled into the dock, and the guys who had come to help us looked at us in shock. We waved to them and told them that they didn't need to use our security deposit after all. Word had gotten around that this crazy family had gotten stuck on the powerline, but we had the last laugh because we were set free, with God's help, of course! All of the crunch moments in our sailing adventures made us appreciate safe harbor and the overwhelming beauty of the British Virgin Islands.

When stepping out into new territory, there are so many unknowns, but instead of being gripped by fear, I encourage you to let go and let it flow. God wants to take you on the ride of your life and show you spaces and places that give you a glimpse of His goodness and glory.

By the way, when we docked the boat after ten days at sea, the whole entire world shut down. We were the last people to whom they served a meal on the island. After barely arriving home, we walked up to our doorstep that had a cooler with four eggs, oat milk, and one-ply toilet paper! Thanks to our brother and sister Dom and Diana for getting us survival gear. Uncertain times were ahead, and everything would forever change.

> God wants to take you on the ride of your life and show you spaces and places that give you a glimpse of His goodness and glory.

That event turned into the longest spring break in history. I immediately became a homeschool mom to two, and although my husband was able to work from home, he didn't travel for a year. God kept us all healthy, and He provided an opportunity for the healing process for our Shaw family to begin. So many people lost their lives, jobs, homes, and any bit of normalcy, but the pandemic also slowed the world down, allowing us to refocus on what really matters most. We all learned how precious breath and life are and that things can suddenly change in an instant.

Even in the most dismal and uncertain times, God reigns and is sovereign through all and over all. If you wait until everything is "perfect," you will never go. Step out on faith and your feelings will follow. Trust the Lord for one step at a time and watch Him move on your behalf.

KINGDOM (QUEST)IONS

1. What is something you've always wanted to do or try but you have let fear prevent you from pursuing it?

   _____
   _____
   _____

2. When and how has God shown Himself faithful to you during life's storms?

   _____
   _____
   _____

3. What step can you take today to conquer new territory? Write down that step and commit to take it.

   _____
   _____
   _____

4. Who can hold you accountable to that step or even take it with you?

   _____
   _____
   _____

KINGDOM TRUTHS

"Do not fear, for I am with you; Do not anxiously look about you, for I am your God. I will strengthen you, surely I will help you, Surely I will uphold you with My righteous right hand."–Isaiah 41:10

"I can do all things through Christ who strengthens me."–Philippians 4:13

"Trust in the Lord with all of your heart, and do not lean to your own understanding."–Proverbs 3:5

"What shall we say then? If God is for us, who can be against us?"–Romans 8:31

KINGDOM DECLARATION

I declare, on this _____ day of _____, that I will choose to lift the anchor of fear and complacency in my life. I will hoist the sails of my hopes and dreams and ask God to fill them full with faith and trust in His plans. I thank you, Lord, for protection, provision, guidance, and direction as I let go and let You lead the way. I will allow the spirit of expectation to stir in my soul and fan the flame of my endeavors. Thank you for empowering me by Your Holy Spirit to take new territory for my good and Your glory. I will reign boldly in new spaces and places, all while enjoying the journey to get to my desired destination.

In Jesus's name, amen.

Chapter Six

REIGN IN THE DAY

"The steadfast love of the Lord never ceases. His mercies are new every morning."–Lamentations 3:22-23

A DAY

God gives us each a single day
To reverence and use as we may.
Attitude helps us to choose
How twenty-four hours we'll use.
A clock measures the time,
Seconds, minutes, and hours chime.
The period between dawn and nightfall,
From sunrise to sunset, you recall.
The earth completes a rotation on its axis,
A phenomenon our brain taxes.
An irreversible succession of time,
A day from the present to future sublime.
Choose to trust in the Lord with all of your might,
Don't allow anxiety, fear, and worry to paralyze you with fright.
Be present in every way,
Especially to those He's trusted in your care to this day.
Let His kingdom reign in each moment as you go
In righteousness, peace, and joy you will show.

> Surrender all of your what if's to the King of kings,
> Allowing His love and forgiveness to flow through everything
> So take a deep breath and inhale His shalom.
> You will find peace in His presence is like coming home.

Poem written by Patricia Amburgey (my Mimi) and published in *Poems: Mundane to Ridiculous*.

I can remember having a recurring nightmare as a young child. I would wake up in a cold sweat with my heart pounding in my chest. The next thing I knew, I would jump up out of my bed, start booking it down the hall, and run into my parents' room to find comfort and relief. There weren't defined locations or specific people involved in this dream. All I vividly recall is that it felt like time was speeding up so fast that I couldn't keep up, then suddenly, right before I woke up, it felt like it came to a screeching halt. Time's up! I could audibly hear the beating of my heart getting faster and faster. The overwhelming feeling of fear, anxiety, and regret would consume my mind and heart. I just felt like I needed more time to complete what I was here to do.

As a child, I hated this nightmare with a passion and didn't fully understand it. It wasn't until I grew up and came into the knowledge of my Lord and Savior that I would get an interpretation of the dream. In fact, during my teen years, that nightmare felt like it had become a reality when I was going through my darkest times of anxiety and depression. The days and nights seemed to blur into each other. I felt like time was my enemy and I was in a losing battle. Through His Word, God showed me that He is the author of time and holds my days here on earth in His hands. I don't have to be paralyzed by the crazy pace, expectations, or demands of this world.

We have often heard the following saying: "The days are long but the years are short." Don't blink, because time really does fly by. It's so true. In the grand scheme of eternity, this life is but a vapor.

The world operates on deadlines, timelines, and unrealistic expectations to outperform our latest accomplishments. Some people even refer to the "rat race" of life. Have you ever watched a rat running on a wheel? Their little legs are going ninety miles an hour just to realize that they are going nowhere real fast. The definition of insanity is doing the same thing over and over again expecting a different result. Maybe that's why I'm personally not a fan of running on treadmills. I need to see a change of scenery and feel the wind in my face. I know they make virtual exercise experiences now that seem like you're running in Paris, but I prefer the real thing. I want to smell the fresh baguettes wafting through the air and hear the sound of a beautiful romantic language spoken at sidewalk cafes as I'm jogging by. I don't want a fabricated experience. I want to touch, taste, feel, and smell change.

We can either choose to wake up and live in the goodness of God or just drown out His still, small voice with busyness and excuses. When we choose to let go of fear and enter into God's presence by intention and faith, we position ourselves to receive peace, joy, and clarity in Him, no matter the season of life we're in. We break the cycle of insanity and come into divine alignment with a kingdom cadence and pace for our lives. We begin to live life through the reality of His living Word and His promises rather than the lies of the enemy. John 10:10 tells us that the enemy's mission is to steal, kill, and destroy. Jesus's mission is to give us life, and life more abundantly in Him.

So, what does that look like in a day's time, and how do we steward and maximize our moments, seconds, minutes, and hours in Christ? I believe the answer to that question is found in our daily routine. We need to learn how to invite the Lord into our mundane moments, monotonous schedules, and sometimes overwhelming responsibilities. We need to allow Him to fill our moments with meaning and vibrancy. God does everything decently and in order (1 Cor. 14:40), and so should we.

We need to get back to the basics and consistently reign in our routine. Some of the most impactful people on this planet have learned to conquer the clock and break free from being a slave to the crazy tick-tocking pace and pressures we face.

Through the years, God began to give me a formula for this, and it slightly alters during different seasons of life.

Before I was married and became a mom, my days were completely mine. Even more so, I now have to be intentional about reigning in the routine so I can be fully present and appreciate the awesome roles of responsibility God has entrusted me to steward. I needed to live in a responsive, not reactive, way. It is so easy for me to tell when I'm operating from an empty cup versus a full one. Trust me, my husband and children can tell you when I'm off. I'm irritable, snappy, on edge, impatient, and frustrated. We all know the quote "too blessed to be stressed." But, the reality is, we need to be reminded daily that our strength is found in surrender, not just in quoting "Christian clichés" found on cute t-shirts or coffee mugs. Stress and pressure are parts of life that can crush us if we don't claim authority over them. We all need to take a pause for the cause in the midst of chaos, inhale a huge, deep breath of God's peace, and release the cares of the world at His feet.

My mother-in-law's favorite scripture was James 1:2-4, which says, "My brethren, count it all joy when ye fall into divers temptations; Knowing this, that the trying of your faith worketh patience. But let patience have her perfect work, that ye may be perfect and entire, wanting nothing." This verse is such a profound reminder that struggles will come, but in the midst of them, we can give God praise because we know there is always a greater purpose. We can be confident that He is working all things together for our good, according to Romans 8:28.

In our walk with God, there comes a time when we have to put away childish behavior and take responsibility for how we manage our emotions and treat those around us. There is no excuse for taking out our frustrations and anger on our loved ones. God wants us to abide in a state of surrender, where we respond with grace instead of reacting in constant anger, irritation, and frustration.

God showed me that the keys to unlock the kingdom within are found in how I start my day. He gave me Rise, Shine, and Reign™. Throughout the Bible, God reveals the importance of waking up early before the break of dawn. In fact, Jesus modeled this behavior as He rose early and went away from His disciples to be alone with His heavenly Father. Mark 1:35 says, "In the morning long before sunrise, Jesus went to a place where He could be alone to pray." Think about how many crazy situations Jesus came across in His days. Everywhere He walked, He would confront demons, sickness, dead situations (literally), and haters. Not to mention all of the ridiculous stuff His disciples put Him through!

It's no different with us. If Jesus needed an "adult time out" with His Father, how much more do we? There is something so powerful and impactful about entering into stillness with God. Before the chaos and the hustle and bustle of the day begins, there is a sacred space that few enter into.

> **If Jesus needed an "adult time out" with His Father, how much more do we?**

I know someone reading this might say, "I'm not a morning person." Trust me, I can relate. I wasn't always an early riser, but after having children and surviving the early years of sleep deprivation, I can recall that some of my sweetest moments with my babies took place during that early morning feeding hour. The house was quiet, and it was just me, God, and my precious miracle. There were no outside noises or distractions to pull me away from complete awe and adoration of God's incredible creation.

I can remember studying King and Care's faces and giving God praise for every little detail and feature He fearfully and wonderfully made. My heart would fill with so much gratitude that my body couldn't contain, and tears would begin to flow from my eyes, dripping down onto their tiny faces. All the feelings of insufficiency and insecurity as a new mom would fade away in the shadow of God's goodness and grace. In those moments, I knew I was loved completely and wholly. I also knew that if I did everything I could to stay connected to that source, my children would know that same love and feel safety and courage to conquer a new day.

What if we approached our heavenly Father like that every morning? With anticipation, we would long to meet Him in the stillness and sit at His feet.

"Therefore He says: 'Awake, you who sleep, Arise from the dead, And Christ will give you light'" (Eph. 5:14). I want to encourage you to set the atmosphere in your home and create an inviting space to **Rise** and start your day before the break of dawn. There's nothing like creating "shalom in the home." The word "shalom" in Hebrew means peace, harmony, wholeness, completeness, prosperity, welfare, and tranquility and can be used idiomatically to mean both hello and goodbye. After all, this is your sanctuary and a safe place in a crazy world. Put on some instrumental worship music, light a candle, open a daily devotional, and let the Word of God come alive to you.

> There's nothing like creating "shalom in the home." The word "shalom" in Hebrew means peace, harmony, wholeness, completeness, prosperity, welfare, and tranquility and can be used idiomatically to mean both hello and goodbye.

Remove the temptation to grab your phone first thing in the morning by putting your notifications on silent until you're done with your quiet time. The worst way to start your day is by scrolling through social media, filling your head with the thoughts of everyone else. Don't even open emails, read texts, or dare to turn on the news. The world, with all of its demands and distractions, will be waiting for you. Trust me, it's not going anywhere. Mark 4:19 explains, "And the cares of this world, and the deceitfulness of riches, and the lusts of other things entering in, choke the word, and it becometh unfruitful." When you give God the first fruits of your day, you will bring Him glory and fill your heart and mind with peace and clarity. You will be armed and ready to fight the good fight of faith.

During this quiet time with God, have a journal and pen ready to write down what you're thankful for and begin your day with a grateful heart. 1 Thessalonians 5:18 says, "In every thing give thanks: for this is the will of God in Christ Jesus concerning you." God is drawn to a thankful heart. Journaling gives you a safe space to release, receive, and dream. It's something women in my family have been doing for many generations. There's also something so powerful about putting pen to paper, for it allows us to become so much more intentional with our thoughts, desires, and hopes when we write them down. By doing so, we are taking ownership of our lives and documenting God's faithfulness. One of my favorite things to do is read back through old journals to see my growth and God's answers to my prayers and my heart's cry.

Open your ears to hear His still, small voice and let Him fill your cup until it overflows. Find a quiet place in your home to meet Him. In Psalm 46:10, He tells us, "Be still, and know that I am God: I will be exalted among the heathen, I will be exalted in the earth." The intentionality of entering into God's presence gives you access and authority over the clock and empowers you to enter into eternal moments with your Creator and King. This is the space and place where we can take off our armor and come before our heavenly Father as a child. We can strip ourselves of external toughness and allow ourselves to be vulnerable, open, and broken in His loving presence. As you receive His

> **The intentionality of entering into God's presence gives you access and authority over the clock and empowers you to enter into eternal moments with your Creator and King.**

unconditional love for you, His kingdom reigns in your heart and mind. You gain supernatural strength and a fresh perspective to see your day through His eyes and respond with grace, not angst.

This is our birthright as sons and daughters of God. When Jesus died on the cross, the veil in the temple, behind which only priests could enter into God's presence, was torn in two. This was a powerful message that God sent to all of creation, declaring that we now have direct access to the Creator of the Universe. Hebrews 4:16 says, "Let us therefore come boldly to the throne of grace, that we may obtain mercy and find grace to help in time of need."

Next, it's time to **Shine** God's truth into your heart and mind so your path can be lit before you. Psalm 119:05 says, "Your word is a lamp unto my feet and a light unto my path." In those moments when we don't have clarity on the next steps to take or our feet feel too heavy to move, the Word of God will lighten our burdens and give direction to our day. Sometimes approaching the Bible—the best-selling book of all time—can feel overwhelming. You may be thinking, *Where do I start? How do the stories in the Bible relate to my life and time?* The Word of God is alive and sharper than a two-edged sword; it can cut and heal at the same time. Here's the absolutely amazing thing about the Word of God: you can read a passage in one season of your life, and years later, that very same scripture can meet you right where you are. God is just that awesome, and His Word is just that powerful. It will not return void but will accomplish everything it says it will do.

A great way to get started reading and absorbing the truth is through a daily devotional. I have many laying around the house to keep everyone's cup filled and heart encouraged. I keep them at the kitchen table and in the bathrooms, where they are accessible for a quick and potent dose of God's goodness. Think of devotionals as "power snacks" for your spirit. Ooh, that's good, if I do say so myself! Snacks are meant to keep us fueled in between our main meals of the day. Similarly, our faith is activated through the hearing of God's Word;

this hearing is not a one-time act but a lifetime commitment of washing our minds with the Word and being transformed into the image and likeness of His Son Jesus.

Another powerful way to get fueled with the Word of God is through listening to messages. The Bible App has an audible feature where someone with a very distinguished voice will read the Word aloud to you. Here's another tip: personalize the Word of God directly to you by placing your name in front of His promises. This empowers you to take ownership of God's promises and activate the truth in your life. For example: "Courtney, you are fearfully and wonderfully made." Then, after you write down each promise, say it out loud. Now, you have made that promise personal in your life. There's nothing more powerful than putting God's precious promises into action. Proverbs 18:21 says, "The power of life and death is in the tongue." So, when the lies begin to scream in your head, stop, look, listen, and declare God's unchanging truth over your life.

Be intentional about keeping the Word of God in front of you. Write His promises on sticky notes and post them all throughout your home or office. Become a student of the Word. While studying for a major exam, my sister-in-law Diana placed sticky notes all over her bathroom mirror so she could have a visual reference in her head when it came time to take the test. Isn't life just a series of tests we need to pass? The weapons will be formed, but they don't have to prosper when we are equipped for the battle. I truly believe we are visual human beings. When we see someone's face, something happens in our brain. We might not remember their names, but we will definitely remember their faces. The same thing is true with the written Word of God. When it's hidden in our hearts, we can pull it out and conquer the enemy with its truth.

Throughout the Bible, the truth is referenced as a sword many times. It's the most powerful tool we have to defeat the unfruitful works of darkness. So, grab your sword and reign over this day with the infallible, unchangeable, and life-giving truth! Hebrews 4:12 tells us, "For the word of God *is* quick, and powerful, and sharper than any two-edged sword, piercing even to the dividing asunder of soul and spirit, and of the joints and marrow, and *is* a discerner of the thoughts and intents of the heart." In Isaiah 55:11, God states, "My word will not return void but accomplish everything it sets out to do!" In layman's terms: the Word works when we activate it with our faith.

Now, it's time to **Reign** and conquer the day ahead. Prayer is a powerful way to lean into God's presence. Listen to His promises, absorb them, then activate them in the atmosphere and over your loved ones, your situations, and the circumstances you are facing. One of my favorite things to do with our kids is to start our morning with prayer. Look at prayer like having a conversation with your best friend. We should come before God's throne of grace with a willing and open heart.

Prayer is not just about giving your Creator a laundry list of things you want from Him; it is more of a time to enter into His presence. Psalm 16:11 says that in His presence is fullness of joy. The Bible also tells us in Nehemiah 8:10 that the joy of the Lord is our strength. So, in order to be fueled up for the day, we need to come before our heavenly Father with a grateful heart. There's something so powerful about giving God praise and thanking Him for who He is. He wants us to have a heart and posture of awe and wonder. He is awesome, mighty, and everlasting! You can be real, raw, and unfiltered, all while feeling safe and not judged.

When my son, Kingston, was in elementary school, I started a morning time of prayer with him. We would listen to an audio devotional called *Keys for Kids,* discuss the Word, then pray our way around the carpool loop until the safety patrol opened our door to greet us. This brought him an overwhelming sense of peace, strength, and confidence to conquer the day. It also gave this mama's heart peace and confidence knowing my child was covered and protected in my physical absence. We were activating God's truth over the atmosphere and commanding our holy angels to go before us.

Today, I carry on the same routine with his little sister, Carrington. I love hearing her declare God's goodness over her school campus, her teachers, her classmates, and the day ahead. God's light shines so brightly through our kids, and I am so thankful they know without a shadow of a doubt that Emmanuel (which means God is with us) is with them in the classroom, on the playground, and when they interact with their peers. I pray that they are filled with wisdom, discernment, compassion, and kindness. They are carriers of the kingdom and are called to reign everywhere they go.

I think it's easy to fall into a monotonous routine in our prayer lives, but when we really wake up to the idea of the genuine power of prayer, we can become ambassadors of the kingdom everywhere our feet step. I can see the peace and joy all over my children when we start our day reigning in prayer. I encourage you to do the same for yourself and with your family. Prayer truly changes things and shifts the atmosphere from one of worry and fear to one of total trust.

Years ago, my husband and I attended a 5:00 a.m. prayer service, and a gentleman there shared this acronym for prayer: Power Rising Above You Early Riser. That has always been a good reminder for me to set the alarm clock early before the break of dawn and go before my Creator and King with prayer and thanksgiving. This doesn't have to become some religious routine but more of a call to enter into a place of rest and safety, where you can be filled with divine strength, wisdom, and clarity for the day ahead. There will be many days when focused quiet time won't be a reality. When that happens, you should not feel condemned or guilty but choose to invite God's presence with you through even the simplest of ways.

Sometimes prayer might look like taking a deep breath and whispering the name of Jesus. There is so much power in speaking His name and acknowledging your need for Him in that moment. He is I AM and Emmanuel. He is not some distant dictating God who sits on a throne of perfection, judgement, and entitlement. No, He is a loving Father who pursues us with an everlasting love and provides comfort whenever and wherever we need it throughout the day. He is present, kind, caring, and considerate, and He understands our human condition far greater than we ever could. He is our Prince of Peace, Provider, Guider, and Protector in the midst of uncertainty, exhaustion, and life's daily obstacles.

Worship is truly a lifestyle and not just meant for raising our hands, closing our eyes, and singing to the Lord. We worship our Creator and King through everything. It's how we do the laundry, drive our car, fulfill our work responsibilities, treat others, and move our bodies. We worship in the way we simply live each day.

Reigning Fit and Healthy

A huge part of reigning over your day has to do with how you fuel your body with proper nutrition, move it with exercise, and provide it with adequate rest. It's not God's will for you to be a slave to the scale or give up on His promise to empower you with divine health. He came to free you from the chains of obesity, diabetes, heart disease, sickness, and an obsession with your physical appearance.

Back in 2011, Jeffrey and I co-authored the *FIT 2B FREE Movement*, a curriculum that empowered others to enjoy their total health and liberty in Christ. It took participants through a twelve-week journey to activate God's promises in their lives while creating lasting healthy habits. We partnered with the Let's Move initiative and became members of the President's Council on Sports, Fitness, and Nutrition. We trained Freedom Ambassadors across the nation, which led groups to earn their President's Active Lifestyle Award and commit to honoring God with their bodies and habits. I'm going to share the fundamentals with you so you can begin to reign in your health and strength. This will help you maximize your moments and have more energy and vitality to be productive and reign over whatever the day throws your way.

God wants us to be whole—even holy—spirit, soul, and body. 1 Thessalonians 5:23 says, "And the very God of peace sanctify you wholly; and I pray God your whole spirit and soul and body be preserved blameless unto the coming of our Lord Jesus Christ." When you grab ahold of this truth and the powerful visual that it is, it can change your life. Joyce Meyer wrote a book called *Battlefield of the Mind,* and within it, she shares this concept on how God created us with this desire for wholeness for us. Her words empowered me to reign over my emotions and take responsibility for what I put in my body, which is God's temple, carefully considering how I moved it with daily exercise. I no longer felt trapped and imprisoned in my flesh but began to pursue wholeness in Christ and take authority over my choices.

Listen, the flesh is truly a hot mess. As you are blessed with the privilege of growing older, you begin to see the weird stuff your body does just through the process of normal aging. If you throw in years of neglect and unhealthy habits, your body will start reacting crazier and shutting down on you. We have to surrender to God's will and receive spirit-led self-control, discipline, intentionality, and consistency over the desires of the flesh. We will continue to be slaves to self-deprecation, yo-yo dieting, and unhealthy habits as long as we try to gain control over our bodies in our own power. The reality is, we will be in a battle against the desires of the flesh until the day we finish our race here on earth and reign with our King for eternity.

> The surrender and stewardship of the temple God gave you is truly a journey that lasts a lifetime. You only have one body, and God entrusted you with an incredible vessel that can take you to amazing spaces and places when you realize this simple yet profound truth.

The good news is that God did not leave us without help. He sent His Holy Spirit to be our helper and comforter, who empowers us with supernatural strength to overcome any temptations or obstacles set in our way. Galatians 5:17 tells us, "So I say, walk by the Spirit, and you will not gratify the desires of the flesh. For the flesh craves what is contrary to the Spirit, and the Spirit what is contrary to the flesh. They are opposed to each other, so that you do not do what you want." The surrender and stewardship of the temple God gave you is truly a journey that lasts a lifetime. You only have one body, and God entrusted you with an incredible vessel that can take you to amazing spaces and places when you realize this simple yet profound truth.

1 Corinthians 6:19 says, "Don't you know that your bodies are temples of the Holy Spirit? The Spirit is in you, and you have received the Spirit from God. You do not belong to yourselves." Think of your body as a vehicle—a Ferrari—that houses your spirit. Psalm 39 says, "You are fearfully and wonderfully made." In other words, God doesn't make junk or mistakes. He has placed you here during this dispensation of time on purpose and for a purpose. He chose to bring you through a specific lineage and gave you a certain model, make, shape, and size, along with unique features. Be thankful and celebrate what He's entrusted you with. There will never be another you.

Remember this truth of your purpose and don't covet what someone else has. Instead, choose to be the best you in Christ and embrace your uniqueness and the specific race that is set before you. You survived birth, a global pandemic, and many other things that tried to destroy you. You are a fighter and have the gift of life right now! Sure, there might be some wear and tear on your vehicle from the highway of life, but that just comes with travelling through all kinds of seasons and terrain. It's time for a pitstop and a visit to the body shop for some much-needed repairs, TLC, and tune-ups. He has a master plan to redeem anything that came to destroy you or take you out of the race of life. Ecclesiastes 9:11 states, "The race wasn't given to the swift nor to the strong, but to them that would endure until the end." Your life is a marathon, not a sprint. We often get so caught up in trying to reach our final destination that we forget to take in the joy of the journey and embrace the process to possess the promises of God in our lives.

Society has placed such misguided perspectives on beauty and health. Every day, thousands of images are thrown in our faces to influence our views on what our bodies should look like, what we should eat, and what we should wear. This can affect your distorted view of your body and your love/hate relationship with how to fuel it and move it. Let's lay all of that at the feet of Jesus and get back to the basics of caring for His priceless creation with intentionality, consistency, and gratitude. If you are breathing and reading this now, you've been given the opportunity to make the right choices that will bring you the desired results of health, strength, energy, and vitality.

Some of us feel too far gone and completely exhausted on our journey toward health. If you feel that way, I want to encourage you that it's never too late to surrender and make the daily decision to fight for your health. Think of your health journey as a marathon, not a sprint. Society offers so many false promises of instant gratification. "Take this pill and the fat will melt off." "Drink this shake and you will gain muscle." "Follow this Instagram fitness influencer and you will look just like her or him." The truth is, there is no one-size-fits-all plan. Our bodies are all different, our genetics are not the same, and we are all in different seasons of our lives.

As Americans, we have the most gyms, fitness programs, access to healthy food, and an overload of information at our fingertips, yet why are we still the sickest country in the world when we have the best healthcare system? It's because we live in an overly indulgent microwave society. We have fast food around every corner and have gotten sucked into a rapid pace of life that was never God's original plan for His creation. There's something so powerful about taking the time to be intentional about what you're putting in your body. There is thought that goes into the preparation with great anticipation and appreciation for the meal when it's served. You know the TLC that went into it and feel good about the ingredients you're putting into your body.

Before we get into nutrition and how to properly fuel your body, I want to give you a powerful visual to change your perspective on how God created you. First, let's break down who and what you are so you know how to reign from the inside out and embrace your journey toward wholeness and health in Christ.

You are a **spirit** that has a **soul,** which consists of your **mind** or **conscience, will** or **heart,** and **emotions,** and you live in a **body.** In order to walk in authority and reign and experience freedom over the flesh, we need to begin to live surrendered lives in Christ and take responsibility for our lives. Zechariah 4:6 says, "It's not by my might, nor by my power, but by My Spirit says the Lord."

HOW WILL YOU REIGN?

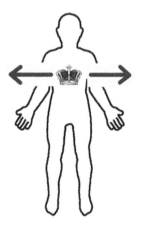

Reigning Inside Out

Spirit dictates to soul, body, and external circumstances

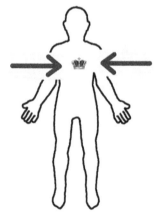

Reigning Outside In

Body, soul, and external circumstances dictate to the Spirit

The person on the left is living in peace, joy, and clarity in Christ. They know who they are and whose they are. They are a son or daughter of the King. They feel loved, safe, and secure. They know without a shadow of a doubt that they don't have to perform to be accepted, celebrated, or appreciated. They are focused on the bigger picture and living with their legacy in mind. They are doing the work to confront their past and find healing in God's promises. They are plugged into a local church and have someone speaking into their lives. They've chosen to become better and not bitter. They are dreaming again and believing God for deeper meaning in their life and relationships. They are not ashamed of their scars and the battles they've been through. They are ready to share God's faithfulness during their darkest times. They are grateful for where they are and excited about where they are headed. They are enjoying a new reign in life! They feed their spirit with the Word of God and prayer, and they have spiritual accountability in their life. They fuel their body with living foods, move daily with physical activity, get adequate rest, and activate their God-given authority over their daily circumstances.

The person on the right is overwhelmed, depressed, full of anxiety, and reacts with anger to life's obstacles. They feel stuck and hopeless, and they are consumed with worry and fear. They exist in a reactive state and blame everything that is going wrong in their life on God and others. They choose to be a prisoner of their past by rehearsing the trauma they endured and crave vengeance upon their abusers and users. They have low self-esteem and find themselves living vicariously through others on social media and television. They do everything they can to just go through the motions and crave empty solutions to fill the God-shaped space in their spirit. They believe in God but choose not to surrender all of their pain, disappointment, jealousy, and self-depreciation to Him. They stuff themselves with comfort foods that numb them and ultimately keep them a prisoner in their own bodies. They are hanging on by a thread and are a slave to the enemy's lies. They desire to break free but have lost the will and hope to get help and live.

The good news for the person on the right is that God gave His creation free will. He didn't want a bunch of religious robots roaming the earth, controlling them to fulfill His agenda and make us love Him and do whatever He wants. No, instead, He chose to give us free will so we would choose to receive His never-ending love and grace. God is not a dictator; He is a loving Father who wants to lead and guide us into a place of holiness and wholeness in His presence.

The news that is even better is that He didn't leave us powerless when He ascended to heaven. In John 14:6, Jesus says, "And I will ask the Father, and He will give you another Helper (Comforter, Advocate, Intercessor—Counselor, Strengthener, Standby), to be with you forever." We need a fresh indwelling of the supernatural power and grace to reign and make Spirit-led choices that will bring His kingdom in earth—us—as it is in heaven.

What does that look like in my daily life? It's accessing power and strength in my daily decisions and the obstacles I face. Will I choose to respond or react? Who is in control of my tongue, actions, and emotions? Our true Spirit-led power comes from inviting Jesus into every moment, allowing us to enter into a place of responsibility and maturity in Christ. It's about stewarding our moments and maximizing all that God has given us for our good and His glory. It's about getting out of the way one moment and one decision at a time. That is how He reigns in and through our lives.

Reigning as part of God's kingdom is not about perfectionism but keeping a tender heart toward correction. It's all about Christ's character being forged in our hearts and minds by receiving the truth of what He says about us and our situations. It is also about owning our bad behavior and being quick to genuinely repent. It doesn't mean just saying we're sorry then turning around and repeating the same toxic and damaging behavior. Consistency is key, and we're not always going to hit the mark.

So, now that we know we are empowered to make healthy choices, let's get back to nutrition and fueling our temples with that high-octane fuel. 3 John 1:2 says, "Beloved, I wish above all things that you would prosper and be in health even as your soul prospers."

Below I have provided foundational information on how to establish healthy habits and stick with them consistently. If you have any health issues, please consult your physician before making any major changes to your diet or exercise regimen.

> Reigning as part of God's kingdom is not about perfectionism but keeping a tender heart toward correction. It's all about Christ's character being forged in our hearts and minds by receiving the truth of what He says about us and our situations.

Over the years, I have frequently been asked what people can do on a daily and weekly basis to maintain their health and physique. I want to start off by saying there is no one-size-fits-all regimen. However, there are some very practical and fundamental things that every age, body type, and human living on this planet can benefit from. One thing I stopped doing a long time ago was jumping on the fad diet train. If you stop and look at the word "diet," you realize that it has "die" in it. I don't want to "die of starvation" trying to look good on the outside while feeling exhausted, irritable, and hangry on the inside. Yes, I said, "hangry"—it's when you get so hungry that you become angry. I have two men under my roof, and I do my best to not let them get to that point.

Fad diets don't work. Point blank. Period. In my personal opinion, they only lead to frustration, possible eating disorders, bondage, and disappointment. They can help establish boundaries, but they ultimately take away our freedom to enjoy a variety of life-giving foods. All fad diets are the foundation for developing unhealthy habits and a love-hate relationship with food.

I'm a firm believer that God created food for our enjoyment. With food, there are so many different colors, textures, flavors, cultures, and culinary delights to explore and enjoy. God wants us to savor the flavor and reign over our plates. Why else would He give us taste buds? He didn't make us with a built-in defect to torture and torment us. He had full intentions for His crowning creation to be able to savor the flavor of food. He also gave us a nose to inhale the amazing aromas, as well as a belly to be satisfied, not stuffed full. He wants us to eat to live, not live to eat. Nourishing food is supposed to satisfy our taste buds and give life, strength, health, and vitality to the body. Food can be healing to our bodies when sick and soothing when we are upset.

In the dieting world, there is a terminology called "cheat meals." I personally don't care for that way to describe giving yourself permission to enjoy something sweet or contrary to the daily healthy foods you consume. The word "cheat" has such a negative connotation to it that is usually associated with guilt, shame, and overwhelming regret. How about changing the phrase to "treat meal"? You're giving yourself guilt-free permission to enjoy something to the fullest, in moderation, of course. The crazy thing about sugary and salty food is that when you don't eat it on a regular basis, your body doesn't crave it as much. When eating "treat meals" in moderation, your taste buds will change and your stomach won't have an unlimited capacity to digest those certain foods. A little bit goes a long way. So, go ahead and add in a treat here and there. I personally don't keep a lot of processed foods and sweets in the house because they're just too easy to grab and make bad choices. As a family, we either decide to make something sweet or indulgent from scratch or go for a special outing.

Let's begin with portion control. When I was in personal training, I heard this tip, and I think it's the perfect reminder for us to "reign over our plate": eat breakfast like a king, lunch like a queen, and dinner like a prince. Breakfast is truly the most important meal of the day because it gets your engine revved and fueled up to conquer what's ahead. It helps kick-start your metabolism and sets the precedent for the level of energy you will have throughout the day. How well would your car perform on empty or even at a half tank? Your body is the same way. A proper breakfast "like a king" will give you mental stamina and physical energy to have authority over whatever comes your way. It should be your largest meal of the day. A balanced breakfast should consist of a variety of foods that offer a range of nutrients. When consumed together, they provide longer-lasting energy, satiety, and a greater chance of meeting daily nutrient requirements. Let's think about our food in groupings. We have our proteins, carbohydrates, vegetables and fruits, and sources of fat. A balanced breakfast would include foods from most, if not all, of these groupings in your meal.

> Eat breakfast like a king, lunch like a queen, and dinner like a prince.

Next up is lunch. Think of this as the midway pitstop through the race of your day. It's a vital moment to slow down, fuel up, and get the proper nourishment to finish strong. Your lunch portion should consist of a protein the size of your palm, a serving of carbohydrates the size of both palms, and an amount of veggies the size of both palms. The last meal of the day is dinner, where you'll want to eat like a prince. Think of this meal as lunch with half the portion of carbohydrates. For dinner, your protein serving should be the size of your palm, your carbohydrate serving should be the size of one palm, and your serving of veggies should be the size of both palms.

Consider the following if you're in a season where you're wanting to release weight—notice I didn't say "lose" weight? If you lose your keys, what do you immediately want to do? Find them! It's the same way with excess weight or unwanted pounds we're carrying around.

Our words have power, and when we are getting healthy, we have to re-train our brain and what we speak over our lives.

Hebrews 12:1 says, "Therefore we also, since we are surrounded by so great a cloud of witnesses, let us lay aside every weight, and the sin which so easily ensnares *us,* and let us run with endurance the race that is set before us." Some negative things in life aren't necessarily sin (which separates us from God), but they can become unnecessary weights and burdens that we carry around. I like to say, "Travel light." When something is no longer serving you, then it's time to release it into the hands of God.

When you feel better, you look better and act better. What's working on the inside manifests on the outside. When you steward your health and activate authority over your plate, you will see the glow in your skin and God's goodness radiating through your life.

When it comes to actually sitting down to dine, I want you to be intentional about eliminating any distractions that would keep you from being fully present and enjoying and taking the time to savor your food. Before each meal, stop, take a deep breath, and say grace. This is a moment to give thanks for the food God has provided and the opportunity to nourish your body and steward your health. In our modern-day society, families rarely sit down together to break bread and connect over a meal. During the week, I know this can feel almost impossible to accomplish, but I would encourage you to at least start planning family meals once a week. The table represents a place to unify, nourish, and encourage one another, where wisdom can be shared with the next generation. Listen, if Jesus thought it was important to gather His disciples around the table at the Last Supper, we should too. He knew that meal would be an opportunity for Him to have His disciples' undivided attention and give them instruction for what was to come in His kingdom.

Lastly, between your main meals, you'll want to add in a light snack. You should be eating a total of five to six times a day. A snack can be a meal replacement shake or smoothie consisting of plant-based protein, fresh fruit, veggies, or powdered greens. You can also find some healthy meal replacement bars for on the go. Fresh fruits, veggies, and nuts are also easy ways to snack healthily on the move. It's important to keep healthy snacks stocked in the pantry or at your workplace so that you can quickly grab something to fuel your body and keep your metabolism going strong throughout the day.

Let's discuss the difference between health and fitness. When we are healthy on the inside, we feel and look good. When we just focus on being fit on the outside, we could be suffering from a lack of internal health. Many can appear fit on the outside while being extremely sick on the inside. That's why committing to your total spiritual, emotional, nutritional, mental, and physical health will give you the vitality and strength for sustainability and longevity.

Even if we eat five to six small meals a day, we are still not getting all the necessary nutrition that our bodies need to function at their best. To overcome this reality, we can use supplements to fill the nutritional gaps so that we can function in an optimal state of wellness. I always encouraged my clients to take a high-quality daily **multivitamin.** You can get multivitamins for men, women, and children. In addition, you can include the following in your daily supplement routine:

Vitamin D: Without enough vitamin D circulating in your bloodstream, it's impossible to absorb all the calcium you need. Vitamin D also influences cell growth and immune function, which keeps inflammation in check and allows your nervous system to work properly.

Fish Oil: Fish oil supplements help support your heart health. Supportive but not conclusive research shows that consumption of EPA and DHA omega-3 fatty acids may reduce the risk of coronary heart disease.[7] The omega-3 fatty acids EPA and DHA are critical for normal brain function and development throughout all stages of life.

MCT Oil: I add MCT oil to my meal replacement shakes and smoothies. This important supplement is great for creating sustainable energy and brain health.

Collagen Powder: Collagen powder helps with the growth of hair, skin, nails, and healthy joints. This can also easily be added to shakes and smoothies.

Super Greens: These greens are like natural rocket fuel for your body. Even if we eat a ton of fruits and veggies throughout the day, we still don't get enough nourishment. Adding greens to your water or smoothie helps fill those gaps and build your immune system to fight off any foreign invaders.

Another vital element to add to your daily regimen is good ol' H_2O. Our bodies consists of 60 percent water, which is why it is so important to stay hydrated throughout the day. Proper hydration helps with mental clarity and flushing toxins out of the body. Experts recommend drinking eight eight-ounce glasses, which equals about two liters, or half a gallon, a day. This is called "The 8x8 Rule" and is very easy to remember. Rather than chugging water only when you're thirsty, it's best to sip on water throughout the day to stay hydrated and allow your body to absorb it.

Next, I want to talk about the importance of your gut health. God truly created a masterpiece in our digestive system. Remember earlier how I was sharing that we were created to be a pipe and not a bucket? I'm not just talking about our psychological, emotional, spiritual, and relational health, but our physical health as well. 70 percent of our immune system is in our gut. Sickness and disease like to thrive in an acidic and toxic environment, or "in-vironment." A simple way to tell if you're toxic is to measure your energy level. If you're tired all the time, irritable, and have low energy you might need to de-tox. This can be a good indicator of how healthy we are internally.

> **70 percent of our immune system is in our gut.**

The Complete Guide to Gut Health talks about how the digestive system works in many wonderful and mysterious ways. The digestive system is designed to break down what you put on your fork into nutrients that your body can use. Like a chop shop, whatever you put into your digestive system gets stripped down to various parts—carbohydrates, protein, fat, vitamins, minerals, and fiber.

Hormonal shifts, stress, allergens, nutrients, circadian rhythms, and more can all impact the gut and throw off the digestive process. A circadian rhythm is a natural, internal process that regulates sleep-wake cycle and repeats roughly every 24 hours. These factors may cause the signals between your brain and bowel to get disrupted, leading to constipation, abdominal pain, and more. Sleep deprived? When you are lacking sleep, the key hormones that control hunger may go haywire, prompting you to eat more and gain weight. When communication gets messed up, or the food you're eating isn't good quality, is overly processed, or contains ingredients you're sensitive to, this can trigger inflammation in the body where the system breaks down. The good news is that cleaning up your diet and lifestyle can lead to amazing and unexpected shifts in your health.

One of the most important questions a doctor can ask you is "How are you pooping?" You can tell a lot about someone's overall health by how they are using or not using the bathroom. Constipation is a major sign that your digestive tract is backed up, which can lead to serious health problems. Think about what happens to the pipes in your house when they get clogged up. You have to get liquid Drano to unclog the blockage and get things flowing again. If the clog is worse than expected, you might need to hire a plumber to take more aggressive measures. It's so important to get your colon checked at the age a doctor recommends. About one in twenty-three men and one in twenty-five women will be diagnosed with colon cancer.

In order to ensure a properly functioning digestive system, there are some key things to add into your daily regimen in addition to eating health:

Pro-biotics: Probiotics are made of good bacteria that help keep your body healthy and working well. The good bacteria benefit you in many ways, including fighting off excess bad bacteria, helping you feel better. Probiotics are part of a larger picture concerning your bacteria and your microbiome. Gut microbiota are the microorganisms including bacteria that live in the digestive tract of humans and animals. These all help in the breakdown and absorption of the good nutrients, as well as the elimination of the toxins in your body. Cleansing every sixty to ninety days can also help reboot and restore gut health. This can be done by juicing and fasting from too much caffeine, sugar, processed foods, and alcohol. This time of cleansing your body can help slow down and restore your gut health and overall wellness for your digestive system.

Checkups: Regular checkups with your physician are very important in your journey of self-care and stewarding your health. Prevention and early detection have saved millions of lives. Get your blood work done annually and know your numbers. A worthy health goal is to have a good report from the doctor. Listen, your numbers don't lie and are a great indicator of what is going on in your body and the adjustments you need to make. Denial leads to disease and, even worse, early departure. Take a day to get all of your appointments scheduled; place them on your calendar with a reminder to make sure you follow through. It's a lot cheaper to live a healthy, proactive, and preventative lifestyle than it is to become a regular at the hospital.

Meal Planning: Planning your meals is a great way to be intentional about creating a healthy lifestyle. There is a saying that goes, "If you don't plan, you plan to fail." Today, we have so many amazing tools at our fingertips to plan out our weekly grocery shopping. There are countless companies that provide healthy pre-packaged meals for you to cook or heat up. You can even go online to your local grocery store and create a shopping list with all of your foundational foods. The website will create a recurring list so all you have to do is go back and click on what you need. You can even have your groceries delivered or have someone bring them to your car, which helps you avoid impulse buying.

We all know to never go grocery shopping while we're hungry. When we do, we end up buying foods that will not be healthy for our bodies. If you do like to shop in person, then I would recommend making a solid list, sticking to it, and making sure to eat a healthy meal or snack before you go. Do a scan of your cart. Are there more living foods than processed foods? If so, then you are on the right track to a healthy lifestyle. Living foods are items that are grown and processed foods are items that are generally boxed or in a can. When you feel better, you do better, and you are setting yourself and your family up for a life-giving week ahead.

Take a day to do some meal prep. I like to grill, bake, and steam some key items to make our meals ahead of time. We are all so busy, so the reality of making meals from scratch daily is probably not going to happen. There are a variety of great tools that can help you cook a nutritious and delicious meal in less than thirty minutes. I love the Instant Pot, air fryer, and rice steamer. Convenience is key to reigning over your plate and making healthy choices more consistently.

Now, it's time to share some key fundamentals of fitness. The proper fuel—nutrition—will help supply your body with the energy you need to get moving. The saying "Move it or lose it" couldn't be more accurate when it comes to our bodies. God created us for movement. He created us with bones, tendons, ligaments, and muscles. If we don't stimulate our muscles and move them daily with physical activity, our bodies can turn into mush. Over one hundred years ago, you didn't see gyms on every street corner. The thought of going to a box to move and "work out" would be laughable. In the past, everyone walked everywhere and had to work to grow, harvest, clean, and cook their food. Days started before the sun came up in order to take care of the essentials of life. Now, we have grocery stores, restaurants, fast food joints, and Uber Eats to get access to feed ourselves and our families.

We have to be intentional about exercising our bodies as a way to take authority over stress, anxiety, disease, and excess weight. I like to look at exercise as stewardship and training for reigning—worship unto our Creator and King, not idol worship of ourselves. Something so powerful happens when you get the blood flowing in your body. You allow more oxygen to flow to your brain, the lump in your chest (from stress, anxiety, worry, or depression) seems to dissipate, and you can think more clearly. The lies of the enemy begin to fade away, and God's still, small voice begins to take precedence in your life.

> We have to be intentional about exercising our bodies as a way to take authority over stress, anxiety, disease, and excess weight.

I look at exercise as a way to wage war against the enemy, who only wants to steal, kill, and destroy your life and God's plans and purposes for you. James 4:7 says that we have to resist the devil and he will flee. We can't just sit down, quit, give up, and let him have his way with us. We need to rise up as sons and daughters of the King and reign over every tactic to destroy, delay, or sabotage God's goodness and faithfulness toward us.

1 Corinthians 9:26-27 says, "Therefore I run thus: not with uncertainty. Thus I fight: not as *one who* beats the air. But I discipline my body and bring *it* into subjection, lest, when I have preached to others, I myself should become disqualified." I truly feel that intentional physical exercise is a way to wage war against the spirits of depression, confusion, self-doubt, deprecation, and insecurity.

Earlier in the book, I spoke about how resistance training is so similar to how we grow our faith muscles. We can't grow closer to God and stronger in our faith without opposition; it's the same with our physical bodies. We were made to handle load-bearing exercises. After the age of thirty, the bone density in women begins to decrease. It's all a part of the natural aging process. But, in order to combat rapid deterioration and age with grace and strength, we need to do some type of load-bearing activity three to five times a week for a minimum of thirty minutes.

I've always looked at weight training as a way to put on our physical armor. Ephesians 6:11-18 says, "Put on the whole armour of God, that ye may be able to stand against the wiles of the devil." God created us with bones, tendons, ligaments, and muscles to hold all of our internal organs in place and give us the strength to move our bodies from place to place while doing miraculous things. The reality is, your muscles can only grow through a process of breaking down, which is what happens during resistance training. You are putting microtears in the muscle, and when you rest, your muscle fibers start recruiting more and build a fortified bond. My friends, that is called building muscle 101.

When it comes to any type of weight training, the most important advice is to practice proper form. It doesn't matter how much weight you're slinging or lifting. You don't want to injure yourself, because that will only lead to a deeper level of frustration. Not to mention coming back from an injury is difficult and time consuming. If you're interested in working out at a gym, invest in some sessions with a personal trainer or find someone you know who is knowledgeable to teach you proper form and use of equipment.

Also, there are literally thousands of ways you can work out with your own body weight. Remember back in PE in school, we would have to take the President's Fitness Test? It consisted of push-ups, pull-ups, sit-ups, sit and reach, running, and basic body movements.

> Use what you've got! Some of us have a little and some of us have a lot. The key is to just start and stay consistent.

Use what you've got! Some of us have a little and some of us have a lot. The key is to just start and stay consistent. That is why having an accountability partner or workout buddy is so vital to your long-term success. There will come days when you don't "feel" like exercising. Trust me, when you're sore, tired, or just too busy, you can give yourself a million justifiable excuses for why you don't to take care of yourself. Commit to be fit and faithful in your exercise routine by reigning over isolation and excuses, and don't be afraid to ask for help. If you know you have to meet someone at your workout, you're more likely to show up. You're even more likely to show up if you invest in some help to get you started. Once you learn the basics, then you're off to the races and feeling confident to conquer the gym without being intimidated or embarrassed.

There are fitness options for all ages, stages, and phases of life. The goal is to age with health, strength, and stamina so you can finish your race strong and hear the words "Well done, good and faithful servant" (Matt. 25:21). You can choose to rust out or wear out. I know trying to choose the best type of exercise for your fitness level and age can be overwhelming. I love this saying I heard some years back, and I share it often when asked what exercise is best: "The exercise you should do is the exercise you will do." Here's the truth: you are more likely to be consistent and committed to something you enjoy versus something you dread.

Most of the time, you are not going to "feel" like exercising. That is where discipline, accountability, commitment, and consistency come in. I can promise you that there has never been a time where I've regretted investing in my health. When I spend my time and energy on my health, I always feel lighter, less stressed, and more grateful. Fitness truly helps you build a new thing and find new strength, new joy, new focus, new direction, and new vision. It empowers you to live for something bigger than yourself.

Along with exercise, sweating and stretching are also valuable aspects of fitness. Breaking a sweat outdoors is a great way to get necessary vitamin D and release toxins from our bodies, which can be achieved by simply getting outside and taking a walk. Sitting in a sauna is another wonderful option for detoxifying through sweating. God created our bodies with multiple ways to release toxins. It restores health to the body and brings about a natural glow. In addition, take time to learn how to stretch properly to prevent any unnecessary injuries and create flexibility and mobility in your body. Make sweating and stretching a part of your daily exercise routine to release stress and do something nurturing for your body and mind.

I have shared so much beneficial and practical information about the fundamentals of health and fitness. I pray you take a few things and start putting them into action. Once you've conquered one health-related task or challenge, add another until it becomes a part of your lifestyle. But, if you don't have a healthy, correct mindset, you will never truly reign over your emotional and physical health. Some of the most beautiful, handsome, fit, or "successful" people in this world think they are ugly, not good enough, and incapable of measuring up. They have the external practice and discipline down but still have a messed-up mindset. Their toxic thinking will inevitably affect areas of their life in a negative and even harmful way.

Mental health has recently been at the forefront of news because we've been living through a global pandemic. We've all been forced to slow down enough to address some really problematic thinking that we've developed as citizens of this world. The negative stigma surrounding mental health is currently being challenged so that people can finally get the help they need and deserve. Pride, egos, comparison, social media, and an unrealistic pace of living has caused the greatest levels of depression, anxiety, sickness, drug overdose, and suicide in our lifetime.

Philippians 2:5-11 says, "Let this mind be in you that was in Christ Jesus." God gave us a mind not to torment us but to create life-giving things around us rather than constant chaos. We live most of our lives in a reactive, not responsive, way. If we think something bad, we often say it without even considering the weight of the consequences of our words. We haven't been trained to reign over our stinking thinking or given the tools to manage the mess that tries to infiltrate our minds. 2 Corinthians 10:5 says, "We demolish arguments and every pretension that sets itself up against the knowledge of God, and we take captive every thought to make it obedient to Christ." This scripture is confirmation that God cares about our mind and the thoughts that we allow ourselves to meditate on and believe about ourselves and others.

A great way to start taking authority over your thinking is to evaluate where and how you are spending your time and energy. Ask yourself, "How much time do I watch the news, scroll through social media, and listen to gossip and the lies the enemy whispers in my ears?" The best way to cancel the lies you've been choosing to believe is to meditate on God's Word, confess His life-giving truth with your mouth, and find a safe place to communicate. When a negative thought comes, stop, take a pause for the cause, and recognize the source of that thought.

Line it up with what God says and put that thought in its rightful place—under your feet.

If you're unable to activate your authority over the enemy, then ask for accountability. It doesn't make you weak or incapable. The strongholds of the enemy are hard to break and take time, intentionality, and consistency. But, the good news is that through the power of what Jesus did on the cross, they are already destroyed, shattered, and obliterated! It's up to us to receive this truth daily and allow it to transform every area of our lives. The Bible talks about how there is safety in wise counsel. Seek out a mentor, friend, or mental health professional who can be a safe sounding board and come alongside you to destroy the toxic thinking patterns in your life. God wants your mind to be at peace and focused on His goodness and mercy.

Lastly, we all need to take a big, deep breath and get some rest. Can you remember the last time you really had a good night's rest? Most people living on this fast-paced planet will tell you, "I will sleep when I'm dead!" That is true, but God didn't create us to be conquering the clock 24/7. He made us with a certain capacity. He even thought it was important to rest on the seventh day of creation and took time to pause, rest, and reflect on His glorious work.

Genesis 2:2-4 says,

> And on the seventh day God ended his work which he had made; and he rested on the seventh day from all his work which he had made. And God blessed the seventh day, and sanctified it: because that in it he had rested from all his work which God created and made. These are the generations of the heavens and of the earth when they were created, in the day that the Lord God made the earth and the heavens.

We can get so focused on creating that we never stop to take in the beauty of the moment. We have to take authority over the spirits of anxiety, worry, greed, and fear by giving ourselves permission to let go and enter into intentional rest. This rest is not just about getting your zzz's. It is a serious way to steward your spiritual health and well-being. It also shows God that you don't idolize your work. God wants us to trust Him by resting in Him in all seasons of life. Hebrews 4:9-10 tells us, "There remains, then, a Sabbath-rest for the people of God; for anyone who enters God's rest also rests from their works, just as God did from his."

At the end of the day, most of us just hit a wall and pass out. We don't really take the time to unwind and prepare our bodies and minds for a good night's rest. Psalm 4:8 says, "I will lie down and sleep, for you alone, Lord, make me dwell in safety." I know it's so tempting to come home, eat, and sit on the couch to "Netflix and chill." I'm not saying it's not good to have those times of straight chillin', but if you know you have to get up to a super busy day, there's nothing worse than passing out on the couch to wake up with a stiff neck at 3:00 a.m., then having to get up and go brush your teeth before crawling into bed. Trust me, I'm speaking from experience. Your sleep gets interrupted, and you wake up wasted and not fully rested the next morning.

Think about how children have their wind-down routine. They eat dinner, get a bath, and put on their jammies, and then mom and dad come to tuck them in for a bedtime story and prayer. We need to emulate this same type of routine. Start by shifting the atmosphere. Turning the lights down low helps the mind start to unwind and prepare to rest. Go take a hot bath or shower, put on some relaxing music, and grab a journal to write down how God was faithful during your day or to release whatever frustration has been weighing heavy on you. Plug in all of your devices in another room so you're not tempted to scroll through emails or social media. There's nothing worse than going to bed with the thoughts of hundreds of "Facebook friends" in your head.

Putting your devices in another room will also help you not to grab them and scroll first thing in the morning. Also, don't forget to set all of your notifications on silent so you can get sweet, uninterrupted sleep.

Over the years, I've heard so many believers talk about how they can't sleep well at night. They lie awake full of worry with their minds racing, trying to figure out how to solve all the world's problems while rehearsing the trauma and drama that went on during the day. This is where prayer comes in. You started your day giving God praise and thanks, and it's truly the best way to end your day as well. Matthew 11:28 says, "Come to me, all you who are weary and burdened, and I will give you rest." Lay all of your worries at the feet of Jesus and know that while you're sleeping, God is fully awake, working on your behalf. Psalm 121:4 states, "He who keeps Israel neither slumbers or sleeps." God is always on watch, guarding and protecting His children. That thought always helps me let go and rest knowing that I am safe and protected.

Scientific facts show us how sleep affects the body. We need proper sleep to ensure that our cortisol levels are balanced. Sleep also helps recalibrate, rejuvenate, restore, and refresh our bodies to wake up reinvigorated to conquer a new day.

From health and fitness tips to proper sleep, perhaps the most important advice is this: Tomorrow is not promised, so make the most of today. Don't live in regret, but keep the main thing the main thing. Travel light. Forgive yourself and others and don't settle for anything less than God's best for you. Don't put off tomorrow what needs to be done today. Make the call, write the letter, hug your loved ones, and breathe in the goodness of God in the land of the living. Amen.

When you choose to Rise, Shine, Reign, Rest, and Repeat, you take God-given authority over your day and create a life-giving routine. Pace yourself and be patient, kind, and encouraging. Take time to be intentional about celebrating along the way and enjoy the journey. I promise you that being consistent in developing healthy habits over time gets you the desired results.

KINGDOM (QUEST)IONS:

1. Do you battle with anxiety, worry, or stress on a daily basis? If so, what do you think is the root cause?

___

2. When was the last time you woke up before the sun rose? If not, challenge yourself to set your alarm clock thirty minutes to an hour before your normal wake-up time.

___

3. Do you read the Bible on a regular basis? If not, start by picking up a daily devotional and downloading the Bible App.

___

4. Who or what can you start praying for today?

_____

_____

_____

5. When was the last time you exercised? How did it make you feel after? What physical activity will you commit to today? Who can hold you accountable?

_____

_____

_____

6. How are your eating habits? What are you struggling with in your body? What healthy foods will you commit to eating?

_____

_____

_____

7. When was the last time you went to see your doctor for an annual checkup?

_____

_____

_____

8. Who do you need to call and encourage today?

_____

_____

_____

9. What distractions can you eliminate from your daily routine to steward your time wisely?

_____

_____

_____

KINGDOM TRUTHS

"This is the day that the Lord has made; let us rejoice and be glad in it."–Psalm 118:24

"The steadfast love of the Lord never ceases; his mercies never come to an end; they are new every morning; great is your faithfulness."–Lamentations 3:22-23

"For this reason He says, 'Awake, sleeper, And arise from the dead, And Christ will shine [as dawn] upon you *and* give you light.'"–Ephesians 5:14

"Then your light will break out like the dawn, And your recovery will speedily spring forth; And your righteousness will go before you; The glory of the Lord will be your rear guard."–Isaiah 58:8

"Every day I will bless You, And I will praise Your name forever and ever."–Psalm 145:2

"Arise, shine; for your light has come, And the glory of the Lord has risen upon you."–Isaiah 60:1

"Jesus Christ is the same yesterday and today and forever."–Hebrews 13:8

"Therefore I tell you, do not worry about your life, what you will eat or drink; or about your body, what you will wear. Is not life more than food, and the body more than clothes? Look at the birds of the air; they do not sow or reap or store away in barns, and yet your heavenly Father feeds them. Are you not much more valuable than they? Can any one of you by worrying add a single hour to your life?" -Matthew 6:25-34

KINGDOM DECLARATION

I decree and declare that this ___ day of _____, 20__, that I will no longer take another day for granted. Today is a gift; that is why it's called the present. I will choose to open this gift with gratitude, surrendering all of my worries, anxiety, and cares to the Lord. I declare peace, grace, and truth to reign over my day. I will commit to starting my day at Your feet and fuel my spirit with Your truth. I will nourish my body—Your temple—with life-giving foods and move it with exercise. I will be kind to myself and posture my day with an attitude of gratitude. I will choose to wake up, dress up, and show up for the battle. I am confident that You are going before me and my steps are ordered to move in confidence and safety. I am loved, protected, and directed down the path of righteousness for Your name's sake. I receive this new day and activate a spirit of expectation for You to meet me through every opposition, obstacle, and setback I might face. Greater is He that is in me than he that is in the world. Today, I rise, shine, and reign with victory!

In Jesus's Name, amen.

Chapter Seven

REIGN IN RELATIONSHIPS

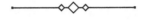

"Therefore, if anyone is in Christ, the new creation has come: The old has gone, the new is here! All this is from God, who reconciled us to himself through Christ and gave us the ministry of reconciliation: that God was reconciling the world to himself in Christ, not counting people's sins against them. And he has committed to us the message of reconciliation. We are therefore Christ's ambassadors, as though God were making his appeal through us. We implore you on Christ's behalf: Be reconciled to God. God made him who had no sin to be sin for us, so that in him we might become the righteousness of God."–2 Corinthians 5:17-21

There's an old saying that goes, "People—you can't live with 'em, you can't live without 'em." At some point in our lives, we've all been tempted to just run from it all, from everyone around us, and go live on an island in the Caribbean all to ourselves. If we could just put our toes in the sand, breathe in the salty ocean air, and immerse ourselves in the warmth of the sun, it would be well with our souls. We would love people from an extremely safe distance and be at peace all the days of our lives. There would be no one to frustrate, irritate, annoy, bother, hurt, challenge, disrespect, or discredit us. It would just be you and yourself, all alone in blessed solitude and silence.

I've lost count over the years how many times I just wanted a moment to myself and a little peace and quiet. To be still with no one yelling, "Mom, come here," or "Court, check this out!" As much as I love serving and nurturing those closest to me and helping others, I get sick and tired of people too. They can be ungrateful, demanding, selfish, arrogant, know-it-alls, and downright raunchy human beings. People are often gross and messy! Their attitudes can stink just as bad as their body odor and breath. Thank God for deodorant and breath mints! Now that I have that off my chest…they are also amazing, loving, creative, kind, inspiring, thoughtful, and genuinely amazing creatures created in God's image!

Now, back to the secluded island to yourself. The reality is, there would come a time when we would begin to miss companionship and human interaction. Remember the movie *Castaway*? Tom Hanks's character is stranded on a deserted island left to fend for himself all alone. It is only a matter of time before he starts missing people so much that he creates a character called Wilson out of a volleyball. The conversing and roleplaying he does on a daily basis help protect his mind and prevent him from going crazy. I know you're probably thinking that there are some people in your life who are literally driving you crazy, but the irony is that God created them to help us stay sane too. I call it the divine balance of humanity.

As tempting as it would be to just live out our days away from people, that is not where God calls the majority of His children. He calls us into the trenches of humanity and moves through the messy moments and relationships of our lives. Relationships are the connections that carry us throughout life, and

> **Relationships are the connections that carry us throughout life, and they teach us many valuable lessons along the way.**

they teach us many valuable lessons along the way. An even greater truth is, without Jesus at the center of our lives, we are all a hot mess. We can spend our days playing the blame game and deflecting our toxic emotions and behaviors onto others.

Here's some "preach talk," as my daughter, Carrington, says. We can all be selfish, self-righteous, arrogant, unkind, rude, fearful, angry, lazy, untruthful, legends in our own minds, and downright draining at times. Maybe this doesn't describe you right now, but at one point in time, we've all had a tendency to lean toward this kind of behavior. This doesn't necessarily make us awful human beings, but when we know there is a better way of life, we're accountable to take responsibility for our behavior and actions. This is all the rotten fruit of our sin nature and is the very reason we *all* need a Savior.

Sometimes we just need to be saved from ourselves and allow God to be the Gardener and do some serious pruning work in our lives. Some of us just need a trim, while others need to be completely uprooted from the toxic soil we're trying to grow in but can't. If we don't allow God to remove the dead places in our lives, then the toxicity of sin can spread, infect, and kill everything around us we want to see grow and thrive.

Today, there is a huge movement of self-help gurus and life coaches telling us that we can create our own destiny, be our own savior, and boss our way through this world to attain success and significance. This false hope and narrative lead many to hopelessness, depression, unfulfillment, abuse, and even suicide. What happens when you fail, cheat, screw up, and don't outperform your latest deal, concert, or sporting event? It all falls on you. What happens when all of the likes and cheers of the crowd go away? The silence can be deafening! The reality is, in this world, you will fail, disappoint, and not measure up to the expectations that others have of you. The world loves to put people on pedestals only to rejoice in their grand fall from grace.

Before we can focus on helping others, we need to receive love and forgiveness for ourselves. John 3:16 says, "God so loved the world that He gave His only begotten Son that whosoever believes in Him will not perish but have everlasting life." Aren't you thankful that we don't have to have it all together before we can go to God and receive His love and forgiveness? This scripture says that He loved the world, which means that He loved and still loves us even in our fallen state. Now, that is what I call unconditional love, and that is the foundation for any and all healthy, life-giving relationships. It's that no-matter-what kind of love, that if-you-do-or-don't kind of love. My love for you is not based on your ability to perform but my desire for you to receive my love and enter into a place of trust, mutual respect, intimacy, safety, and security.

That kind of foundation in a relationship with your Creator and King will give you the confidence to soar above any obstacles that come your way. It allows you to open up, be vulnerable, try new things, and be your true, authentic self without restraint. The ultimate desire within humanity is to be loved and love others in return. God chose us, and love has so much more depth when there is a choice. 1 Corinthians 13:13 says, "And now these three remain: faith, hope and love. But the greatest of these is love."

Our vertical relationship with God will always affect our horizontal relationships with people, hence why He thought it vital to reconcile His creation to Himself through the sacrifice of His Son Jesus on the cross. When we know we are loved, accepted, worth dying for, and adopted into an eternal family, it changes our whole outlook on life and how we see the people He placed in it. Most of the time, people don't come into our lives healed, whole,

> Most of the time, people don't come into our lives healed, whole, and ready to contribute in a life-giving way. They come with baggage, bruises, bitterness, unrealistic expectations, trauma, and drama.

and ready to contribute in a life-giving way. They come with baggage, bruises, bitterness, unrealistic expectations, trauma, and drama. But, underneath all the residue of this journey called life can lie hidden gems and treasures that can bring so much value to your world and the one we live in.

Can you imagine if God gave up on us? What if He just decided not to put a redemption and rescue plan in action? Remember back in the Garden of Eden, when sin entered the world? God had a choice. He could've just said, "I think this human creation 'prototype' is junk and isn't going to work out. Let Me just stick with majestic mountains, breathtaking sunsets, wondrous waterfalls, and amazing animals. Bump this human model! It has too many defects, imperfections, side effects, and a gross, sinful nature." No, God, in His infinite kindness and loving nature, saw something so beautiful, full of potential, and worth redeeming. After all, God is love. It would go completely against His nature to hate and dismiss His creation. He can't help but love us.

God doesn't just cast aside imperfect people. He actually specializes in making them new, whole, and restored by His everlasting love, grace, and goodness. Isaiah 64:8 says, "Yet you, LORD, are our Father. We are the clay, you are the potter; we are all the work of your hand." As we stay on the wheel yielded to His loving and masterful hands, He will mold and make us into something fit and beautiful for His use. He takes the broken and makes it beautiful. 2 Timothy 2:21 tells us, "Therefore if anyone cleanses himself from the latter, he will be a vessel for honor, sanctified and useful for the Master, prepared for every good work." God took Saul, the chiefest of sinners and a murderer of Christians, changed his name to Paul, and turned him into a disciple and soul winner for the kingdom. He went from murderer to martyr because of his encounter with God's unfailing and redeeming love.

God loves us right where we are, but He also loves us enough to not want us to stay the same. His love is supposed to transform us into His likeness and image. The evidence of a true repentant heart is changed behavior. Matthew 7:20 states, "Yes, just as you can identify a tree by its fruit, so you can identify people by their actions." Where there was once anger, there is now peace. Where there was once a mean and abusive nature, there is now kindness, gentleness, and consideration for the safety and well-being of others. Where there was once insecurity, there is now acceptance and confidence. Where there was once intolerance and irritability, there is now patience, compassion, and mercy.

Genesis 1:27 says that God created man in His own image and likeness. Imago Dei is a Latin phrase that means "the image of God" and refers to two things: God's own self actualizations through humankind and God's care for humankind. To say that humans are made in the image of God is to recognize the special qualities of human nature which allow God to be made manifest in humans. Humans differ from all of the creatures because of their rational structure and their capacity for deliberation and free decision making. Striving to bring about the imago Dei in one's life can be seen as the quest for wholeness, as Christ pointed to in His teachings.

God created us with a certain capacity for intimacy in relationships with other human beings. God is the only One who is omniscient, omnipresent, and omnipotent. He can be all things, everywhere, all at once to all of His creation. There is no limit to His love, wisdom, comfort, guidance, mercy, and grace. They never run out or dry up. God's love is ever flowing, ever present, and ever abundant in nature. Philippians 4:19 says, "But my God shall supply all your needs according to his riches in glory by Christ Jesus." So, as we stay connected to the Source of it all, we can become vessels of honor for His love to flow through us into the lives of others. I believe His will for us is to live so fulfilled from His goodness that it flows through our lives. There is no scarcity or lack in His kingdom.

As you release your insecurities, fears, doubts, hurt, reservations, and regrets, you can receive His value, protection, direction, wisdom, provision, peace, and plans for your life. He knows how to make streams in the desert places of our lives when we choose to trust Him wholeheartedly. In Isaiah 43:19, He tells us, "Behold, I will do a new thing; now it shall spring forth; shall ye not know it? I will even make a way in the wilderness and rivers in the desert."

We all know that navigating relationships can feel like travailing through a crazy jungle. We can't have healthy and fruitful ones without boundaries and God at the center. When it comes to relationships and setting boundaries with others, I like to look at the model of how the Israelites built the Tabernacle. This structure was built to carry them through their wilderness journey and create a space for God, Emmanuel, to meet with them. The Tabernacle was the place where God would dwell among men.

Through the power of the Holy Spirit and what Jesus accomplished on the cross for your redemption, you are now God's dwelling place. 1 Corinthians 3:16-17 says, "Know ye not that ye are the temple of God, and that the Spirit of God dwelleth in you?" Christ's ultimate sacrifice made it possible to establish healthy boundaries of protection from His heavenly Father in your life and equip you to parallel those boundaries in your natural relationships. Just as the Tabernacle was constructed to demonstrate the proper protocol to come before the presence of God, there is a proper protocol for how we should approach all relationships during our time here on earth. Establishing healthy boundaries is not a one-time act; it is actually a lifetime's work to reaffirm, reestablish, and refortify those boundaries for your protection and others around you.

In the Tabernacle, there was the outer court, which was where the masses gathered as they made their way to prepare themselves and their sacrifices to go before God. Outer court relationships in our lives represent acquaintances. These are our coworkers, those we see in our community through social events and children's activities, our classmates from high school and college, and more. Thanks to modern-day technology, we all have thousands of "Fakebook," I mean, Facebook friends. These people may think they "know" you, but they don't *know* you...

not on an intimate and personal level. Based on what you post, they feel like they know key details about your life, such as your latest accomplishments, interests, and travels. The reality is, they are only seeing the highlights of your life and are spectators, not participators, in it.

The inner court in the Tabernacle was where the animals were brought to be prepared and given to the priests as a sacrificial offering before they entered into the Holies of Holies. There had to be a blood sacrifice and covenant made between God and His people for the atonement of their sins. This went on for thousands of years before Jesus made the ultimate and final sacrifice on the cross at Calvary.

In your life, your inner court relationships represent people who have "skin in the game." They invest, sacrifice, show up, pray for, nurture, encourage, and commit to do life with you through all seasons. They want God's best for you and hold you accountable to walking in your divine purpose and calling. These individuals have no motive or agenda to be in a relationship with you other than to enjoy, appreciate, and celebrate your presence in their lives. This circle usually consists of close friends, mentors, and extended family. They love you enough to tell you the truth and will go to battle with you and for you any day. They are there when things are going well and when you are at your lowest, reminding you of who you are in Christ. My dad used to always tell me when I was younger that if you can count your true friends on one hand, you are truly blessed. I always thought my dad's words weren't true as I would surround myself with the crowd. It wasn't until I got a little life under my belt that I realized how true of a statement that was and still is today.

Jesus gave the perfect model for inner court relationships by choosing His twelve disciples. He knew what the value of close proximity to Him would give these men. They would see Him move in the miraculous, mundane, and menial moments of everyday life on His journey to the cross, death, burial, and resurrection. Jesus's disciples would get an up-close and personal look at how He would respond to moments of greatness and the onslaught of character assassination, death threats, and accusations. He entrusted them to carry out the most important mission in history: spreading the gospel across the globe. His legacy lived and lives on through His disciples for generations to come. He died for them so that He might live through them for eternity! John 15:13 says, "Greater love has no one than this, than to lay down one's life for his friends." The disciples of Jesus experienced true brotherhood and sacrificial love in Him.

Lastly, the most sacred and intimate place of the Tabernacle was the Holies of Holies. This was sacred space only reserved for those who were worthy to go before the Creator of the Universe. There was a long, thick veil made of very heavy fabric and animal skins which separated the space where the sacrifices were prepared from where they were received. The priests would tie a rope around the ankle of the chosen priest to pull him out of the Holy of Holies just in case he didn't have a pure heart before God and make it out alive.

People had a true fear, awe, and reverence for God's holy presence. The Israelites saw Him bring the plagues on Egypt and part the Red Sea for their safe passage. Exodus 13:21 tells us, "By day the LORD went ahead of them in a pillar of cloud to guide them on their way and by night in a pillar of fire to give them light, so that they could travel by day or night." God fed His people manna from heaven and showed Himself to be a mighty, loving, faithful, and powerful God. Hebrew 12:29 says, "God is a consuming fire." His love is so potent, powerful, and pure that it will incinerate anything that doesn't have the right motives. His love has been referred to as a refiner's fire. Proverbs 17:3 states, "The refining pot *is* for silver and the furnace for gold, But the LORD tests the hearts." 1 John 1:5 says, "God is light and in Him is no darkness at all." His love reveals, exposes, heals, comforts, strengthens, and transforms us into His image. 1 John 4:16 explains, "And we have known and believed the love that God has for us. God is love, and he who abides in love abides in God, and God in him." He is our safe place, refuge, and sanctuary in the midst of a crazy world. He is a strong tower for the righteous to run in and find safety. We all need our safe space from the chaotic pace and battles we face. Acceptance, protection, loving affection, nurturing kindness, and adoration are all found in the presence of our Creator and King.

This space of covenant relationship is reserved for God first and then your spouse. Although, the truth is, no matter how much your husband or wife loves you, their love will never be enough to fill the void in your life that only God can fill. If you expect your spouse to be the source of your joy, peace, and contentment, you will be constantly disappointed and frustrated for expecting them to give you something they were never designed to give all the time.

> We all need our safe space from the chaotic pace and battles we face. Acceptance, protection, loving affection, nurturing kindness, and adoration are all found in the presence of our Creator and King.

When God originally created man, He said that it wasn't good for him to dwell alone, so he put Adam to sleep and took a rib out of his side to create woman. God was so intentional about the physical place he used to create Adam's helpmeet. The word "helpmeet" actually means to come alongside. God never intended for man to reign and lord over woman or vice-versa. Eve was never Adam's lesser but his equal. God's divine purpose was to create a beautiful partnership under His Lordship. In return, He gave man and woman both free will and authority over all of creation. Genesis 1:28 says, "And God blessed them, and God said unto them, Be fruitful, and multiply, and replenish the earth, and subdue it: and have dominion over the fish of the sea, and over the fowl of the air, and over every living thing that moveth upon the earth." There truly is power in partnership when God is at the center and behind the helm of the relationship.

Reigning in Marriage

Jeffrey and I have been married for over eighteen years. In the early years of our marriage, this "power couple" had some serious power struggles. I believe a lot of our challenges had to do with the different ways we were raised and our mutual strong-willed, type-A personalities. Instead of complimenting each other and fully accepting who God created us to be, we were trying to conform one another to what we thought we should be. We were also trying to navigate newlywed life while my in-laws were living with us. Talk about the perfect storm for possible separation and divorce. There were many influences and unrealistic expectations on how I should perform as a new wife.

Jeff grew up in a home where his mom was made to be subservient to his dad and did everything with a demand of perfection. There were a lot of good times in their family, but there was also a lot of verbal and physical abuse, which Jeff's mom endured for many years. My father-in-law made her conform to all the religious churches—and suppressed her physical appearance. At one point, he wouldn't even allow his sons to swim with her in the pool unless she was wearing a long denim skirt and shirt.

One day, Jeff's parents told him that my pants were too tight to wear to church service and that I needed to go shopping to find looser-fitting pants so I wouldn't offend or cause anyone to sin. I was devastated; I felt disgusted and embarrassed at the thought of other people in the "church" looking at me as I was focused on worshipping God. I thought I was in a safe place, not being gawked at and judged. I was made to feel dirty, unclean, and uncomfortable. Whatever happened to "come to Jesus just as you are"? Aren't you supposed to catch a fish before you start trying to clean it up? My heart wasn't to offend anyone or distract them from receiving the Word of God. I so badly wanted to please my new in-laws and honor my husband, so I complied and went out to get a new pair of approved pants.

I even had my mom go shopping with me to help make sure my pants fit more conservatively. I was excited to wear them to church the following Sunday, only to be told that my pants were still too tight! I was beyond embarrassed and felt defeated. For years after that experience, my wardrobe was two to three sizes too big to make sure I didn't offend anyone with my physical beauty. I was slowly losing myself in exchange to be a people pleaser, and what I was brainwashed to think was a God-pleaser too.

I had grown up in a house where my parents exemplified a partnership and were both serving one another and our family. If the dishes needed to be done, my dad would jump in and wash them. If a toilet needed to be scrubbed, he would help get it done. Even though my dad was the main breadwinner, he did most of the cooking because he enjoyed it and was an awesome chef. He loved expressing his love for his family through food. It didn't make my dad less or weak to step in and serve; it was actually the way he expressed love for his wife and family. It wasn't just the woman's job to do everything around the house.

I never saw my dad physically harm my mom or intentionally tear her down. If anything was ever said out of frustration, there would be an immediate apology. My parents didn't agree all the time and would often see things differently, but they would always yoke up and pull together, not apart. My parents would always show affection toward one another and express their love through cards, special gifts, and quality time. My dad was and is passionate about life and his family. By no means was my dad a perfect man, but he always made us feel loved, safe, and cared for. He allowed us to share what was on our hearts and minds without shutting down our perspectives.

For Jeff and me, it took a lot of prayer and "heated fellowship"—aka arguments—to realize there was a better way for our marriage. It also took years of spending time with other couples to see there was a different way. Early on, most of our marital issues were rooted in fear of everything falling apart and "honoring" his parents and our pastors. If everything wasn't perfectly done or handled, then I didn't care, which would lead me to feeling like I never measured up. There was not much room for grace but a strong demand for perfectionism.

As a new Christian, it was so confusing to read about a God who extends mercy, grace, patience, and loving kindness, but that was withheld if I didn't execute with perfection. It hammered at my self-esteem as a young wife, and I felt stuck in a cycle of not being good enough, when I knew in my soul that Christ's love, acceptance, and forgiveness toward me was more than enough. I longed for the freedom to grow in grace and make mistakes while learning, not be defined or paralyzed by them.

It also didn't help that Jeff had his dad in his ear all the time. He would sow seeds of doubt and discord in our marriage so he could influence Jeff and get what he needed or wanted out of him and ensure I was put in my place. If I showed any lack of agreement, then I would be dishonoring Jeff and my in-laws. Jeff's dad used very strategic mind manipulation to shake down his son and make me look like I was out of line and disrespectful. He would make cutting statements and cause Jeff to question my loyalty, commitment, or motives, when I actually never did anything to call any of that into question.

I loved my husband and had a heart to nurture, encourage, and serve him. I took great pride and joy in being his wife and helpmeet. Being a thoughtful, intentional, nurturing, and hospitable person has always been a part of my nature. Jeffrey was the person I chose to support and love all the days of my life. God had shown me his heart, and it was good. He wasn't driven by his ego but by truth and love. He had a genuine, kind, caring, compassionate, and serving nature. I often asked myself how he came from his father. Yes, Jeff is very good looking, smart, creative, and talented, but beyond all of that, he has a pure heart. Despite what he had gone through, there was still tenderness there.

Just like every married couple, we've had many ups, downs, and in-between seasons in our journey. You throw in extended family drama, church drama, financial pressures, raising children, and the endless pursuit of purpose, and you've got a potential recipe for disaster, lots of arguments, and temptations to just give up. We had to make a decision early on that we had something to fight for so we wouldn't tear each other apart. We could allow the enemy to devour our marriage and young family or yoke up and start plowing our way to freedom and wholeness. It felt like we were being torn apart while trying to pull together and break free.

During that season, we knew we couldn't fight alone. We needed the help of the Lord, wise counsel, and a non-negotiable commitment to break generational dysfunctional behavior patterns. Our unified decision to leave the family ministry would forever change the whole trajectory of our family tree. It took courage, commitment, and blessed determination not to get sucked back into the old way of life. We always experienced a pull to return from family members, church members, special occasions, birthdays, holidays, and an overwhelming sense of guilt and responsibility to sound the alarm and save others. However, in that exodus, we devoured life-giving messages, books, and resources that could help equip us for a new way of life.

We had to unbecome everything that was thrown on us. It took years of peeling off old layers of lies, deceit, and discord to re-discover the beautiful treasure we always had in one another underneath the surface of all the insanity. It was there the whole time! I truly believe that Jeff's dad saw early on what Jeff and I had been given in our relationship. In fact, it was so powerful that it would expose, reveal, and disrupt some serious sickness, dysfunction, and toxicity within the family tree. The love of God within our hearts and for each other was piercing through dark spaces and places. We were also told that we thought we were better than Jeff's family. That constant messaging thrown our way was not only frustrating but confusing. That was never the truth. We had just come to fully embrace our priceless value in Christ and one another.

Over the years, as we sought out help, we learned a lot about different personality disorders and mental illnesses to try to gain a better understanding of what we were up against. In our research, we kept coming across the word "narcissistic." Clearly, other people had been dealing with people close to them with similar mental issues. A vital part of our healing journey was finding comfort in the fact that we weren't alone in this battle.

Narcissistic, insecure, and controlling people will project their ill motives and agendas on you and do everything they can to cover up your shine. They are selfish, self-absorbed, and legends in their own minds who can't do any wrong. They love being the center of attention and will take credit for anything good that you do or contribute to this world. They like to use, abuse, and provoke you to anger. They will stick a sword in your side and smile while calling into question your response out of pain and anger. Umm...hello, they just stuck a sharp weapon in your side! What? Are you supposed to respond calmly? Ironically, they make you think you're the one with an anger problem and out of control. Talk about psychological warfare! They don't respect personal boundaries and bully, lie, cheat, steal, and manipulate their way through life. They prey off of the needy, vulnerable, and goodhearted. They are dangerous people to associate yourself with, and they eventually severely damage, if not completely destroy, everything close to them.

The only way you can become free from the chains of someone dealing with narcissism is to accept the fact that changing them is not your responsibility. You will have to set ironclad boundaries in place so you don't continue to position yourself as their victim.

I recently listened to an interview of a holocaust survivor by the name of Dr. Edith Eger. It was the most profound and life-changing hour as I was absorbing the wisdom that flowed from this ninety-three-year-old woman's lips. At sixteen, she was sent to the Auschwitz concentration camp and endured some of the most horrific conditions. She said that she would be sent to shower daily and never knew if water or gas would come out. At the hands of the Nazis, she lost her family, her friends, her boyfriend, and many others she knew. While imprisoned, part of her method for survival was to not let the Nazis get in her head and break her spirit. No matter what they did to her, she had made the decision to remain curious and hopeful. She realized freedom was from within and not just without. God showed her that she wasn't an imprisoned victim; her victimizers were actually the ones imprisoned—in a living cell of hatred.

Dr. Eger said that if a victim doesn't seek out help and address the trauma in their life, they too will one day become a victimizer. This is how toxic behavioral patterns can be passed down for generations. Over the years, Jeff and I learned that all of the abuse we were experiencing wasn't even personal. We weren't being targeted as a couple or a family. We were merely too close in proximity to the toxicity and couldn't gain proper perspective. We had to create space so we could see clearly and reestablish our value, worth, and safety.

My father-in-law would give the same treatment to anyone and everyone who got close to him without letting him control them. Trust me, over time, so many people would share their similar experiences and abuse, whether spiritual, emotional, physical, or financial. This common ground we shared with others didn't make us feel any better about our decision, but it did bring confirmation that we weren't crazy and that we had made the best decision to distance our family from him. Our only regret is that we didn't take that step early on. It was a journey toward freedom, not an instant act. Even years after we physically removed ourselves from the ministry, we were still battling with the effects and damage done in our hearts and minds.

It took my husband and me years of unconditional love, patience, kindness, and de-programming wrong responses to wash one another with the Word of God and give ourselves permission to dream a new dream for our marriage and family. We had to rebuke the lie that when tough situations, trials, or let downs happened, we were being punished or living under a curse. We didn't have an imaginary red letter on us that was causing people to reject us or God to turn His back on us. We had to believe the truth that we were loved, accepted, safe, and protected. We had to decide to trust God with our marriage and family no matter what we faced. We had been conditioned to think that the only way we would be "blessed" was if we were living under the control of my in-laws, attending and supporting their ministry—the only way we could have material wealth, protection, their love, and the favor of God.

Unlearning this distorted way of thinking and acting required many years. True blessing from God has nothing to do with material objects, money, or influence. It doesn't promise us an easy, pain-free life of not having to work or no struggles. A blessed life is a life of hope in Christ and the understanding of what Jesus accomplished on the cross over two thousand years ago. We not only have forgiveness of our sins but a living hope for today and for eternity. Now, that is what I call a blessed life.

As we moved forward and a disagreement came up, we had to decide if it was more important to be right or to get things right. Pride and ego had to take a backseat for humility and unity to reign in our hearts and home. When Jeff and I realized we were on the same team, safe, and going in the same direction, we could take authority over arguments, the spirit of division, and keep the main thing the main thing. A good and godly marriage is not argument free. When you come into a place of identity, intentionality, responsibility, and maturity in your marriage, you can agree to disagree without tearing down each other or the house.

> Pride and ego had to take a backseat for humility and unity to reign in our hearts and home.

Some years ago, I saw an interview in which a reporter asked a couple who was celebrating their seventy-fifth wedding anniversary, "What is the key to longevity in your marriage?" The elderly wife's husband spoke up and said, "We've never had an argument in all of our years of marriage." I laughed out loud and said, "This man is lying through his false teeth!" I thought that he was either a really good liar or deaf and couldn't hear his wife! Listen, marriage takes work. You're not going to agree with one another all the time. How boring would a marriage be if you had a "Yes Sir" or a "Yes Ma'am" around you all the time? That's not a relationship—that's a dictatorship! Spouses like that don't have opinions for themselves, their own interests, or their own perspectives on life. They have zero accountability and no one to give them tough love when they really need it. They don't need a spouse; they just need to live in front of a mirror with themselves!

Have you ever seen the movie *Coming to America*? It's one of my all-time favorite films for many reasons. There is one scene in particular where the prince is meeting potential suitors and asks for a moment alone with the princess. He asks her, "What do you like?" She says, "Whatever you like." He goes on to ask her multiple questions, only to get the same boring response: "Whatever you like." Finally, in frustration and to see how the princess would respond, the prince tells her to bark like a dog and hop on one leg. She does just that in her beautiful gown and heels. In shock, the prince asks her to bark like a big dog, hop on one leg, and she starts to yell, "Woof, woof," in a very deep voice. He then asks her to leave, and off she goes, hopping and barking her way out of the palace with her long, sparkly train following behind her.

As funny as this scene is, it is also sad and very disappointing for the prince. He isn't looking for a slave but a companion and a best friend to experience life with. It is the spark he needs to light a flame within his heart to go on a quest and find his true wife in Queens, New York. Boring is underrated! But, that doesn't mean marriage has to be a constant battlefield either. I believe God ordains a divine balance for marriage that can only be experienced through Jesus's sacrifice on the cross. Ephesians 5:25-33 states very specific details about what God intends for marriage to mirror:

> Husbands, love your wives, as Christ loved the church and gave himself up for her, that he might sanctify her, having cleansed her by the washing of water with the word, so that he might present the church to himself in splendor, without spot or wrinkle or any such thing, that she might be holy and without blemish. In the same way husbands should love their wives as their own bodies. He who loves his wife loves himself. For no one ever hated his own flesh, but nourishes and cherishes it, just as Christ does the church, because we are members of his body. "Therefore a man shall leave his father and mother and hold fast to his wife, and the two shall become one flesh." This mystery is profound, and I am saying that it refers to Christ and the church. However, let each one of you love his wife as himself, and let the wife see that she respects her husband.

Let's break down this scripture in layman's terms. A healthy and godly marriage is not self-serving but serves one another sacrificially. It's supposed to be a joy, not a burden, to serve, support, and help your spouse. Taking care of your spouse is not beneath you but a pleasure. Sharing a unified belief in God and His ways fortifies a married couple's covenant and their family legacy. Speaking the Word of God over your spouse washes their mind of the enemy's lies and infuses them with life-giving truth. It is the greatest form of accountability.

Set boundaries in your marriage by creating a new branch in your family tree. Don't allow outside family members to bring division between you and your spouse. You are combining family traditions and cultures, and one should not be greater or better than the other. Respect is a decision of the heart, not something that your spouse has to earn. When you choose to show respect, you will reap unending benefits in your marriage. Do not—I repeat, do not—vent about your spouse to your family or friends, or on public platforms. You will discredit their reputation over one disagreement. Maybe you have forgiven them and moved on, but it can be hard for others to do the same. If you need counsel, seek it out in private and with a professional. You can visit FocusontheFamily.com and click on their list of counselors. You can place your zip code in the search engine, and counselors in your area will come up. Focus on the Family even offers a free consultation.

Ultimately, your marriage here on earth is to prepare you for the big wedding celebration in heaven. Jesus is the Bridegroom, eagerly awaiting His bride (the church). He is waiting for a spotless, blameless bride to be presented to Him to reign with Him for eternity. We are held accountable to ensure one another hears "Well done, good and faithful servant," as we stand alone before the Lord at the end of our lives here on earth.

Maybe one day Jeff and I will write more on marriage when we have some more experiences under our belt. We are eleven years out of our "previous life," as we like to reference it. It's taken every bit of that time for us to detox, release, forgive, unlearn wrong behavioral patterns, create life-giving memories and new traditions, and accept what we went through together. Every day, we praise God that he brought us out on the other side with our marriage and family fortified. We are living proof that with God at the center, tender hearts, forgiveness, and determination to love, marriage can be a beautiful adventure that develops and grows through all seasons of life.

Here is some marriage wisdom that has brought Jeff and me closer together over the years. The Word says that the two shall become one; this is a process and a lifetime journey of growing together under God's guidance. I truly believe that with intentionality, consistency, and determination, you can enjoy the greatest gift in your spouse. Express your love and gratitude for one another verbally and in written form. Show affection for each other in front of your children, as this gives them a sense of safety, comfort, and well-being, while also showing them how to be affectionate with their future spouses. We are a very affectionate family. We love to hug, kiss, snuggle, and verbally express our appreciation for one another. Our daily mission is to fill each other's tanks to overflowing so we can pour out into the lives of people outside our tribe.

Forgive quickly, keep the main thing the main thing, date one another, and be spontaneous. Embrace and enjoy each other to the fullest. Invest in your marriage daily. This doesn't have to be lavish expressions but small things that can mean so much. I love bringing Jeff his coffee every morning. This is an intentional way to start my day in service to my best friend. Take time to learn your spouse's love language. *The Five Love Languages* by Gary Chapman is a great read and helps you understand how your spouse best receives and gives love.

In marriage, you and your spouse either grow together or grow apart. Find shared interests, listen to messages together, read books together, and try new things together. Take time to go for a walk, talk, and pray together. Get out of your comfort zone, have fun, laugh, let go, and get back to the foundation of why you fell in love in the first place. Create intimacy through intentionality. You will never regret making the effort to pursue your spouse with love and physical touch. No matter what season of life you're in, take the time to connect. Be proactive and don't wait for your spouse to pursue you. Being the initiator will always create positive results for you both. Healthy, consistent connection and respectful communication are keys to a fulfilling and successful partnership.

I love this visual of how when husband and wife keep God first, it draws them closer together, but when God is not at the center of their marriage, they move further apart.

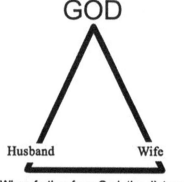

When further from God, the distance between husband and wife is greater.

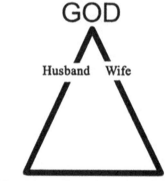

When closer to God, the husband and wife will be closer to each other.

Here are some great resources to help you and your spouse grow in your marriage and in your new life of freedom in Christ:

Love and Respect: The Love She Most Desires; The Respect He So Desperately Needs by Dr. Emerson Eggerichs
Boundaries by Dr. Henry Cloud and John Townsend
Life with a Capital L by Matt Heard

I shared earlier that if you feel like you have something worth fighting for, then you're going to have to dig in and fight with wisdom, prayer, patience, kindness, accountability, and maybe even some longsuffering. I thank God every day that He allowed me to marry my best friend, so I will never settle for anything less than God's best. I just simply enjoy spending quality time together—it doesn't matter if we're snuggling on the couch, sailing across the ocean, or running errands. Jeffrey is the man I choose to spend my days with, and I will keep choosing him until the day I go home to see the Lord.

I'm a one-and-done type of chick. There will only be one man for me in this lifetime on earth. There is no other human on this planet that I would rather spend my days with. I love laughing, crying, building, parenting, and growing through this journey called life with my Jeffrey. His love has helped fortify, strengthen, and establish me into the woman I am today. As his wife, wherever I go, I feel safe, secure, confident, and covered. I guess I'm a little old school and a little new school. I am an empowered woman with my husband by my side and not without. He compliments me, encourages me, and makes sure I'm walking out my calling from our Creator.

My great-grandmother Hannah Rosebrook was quoted before her 104th birthday saying, "Any kind of life is a battle to win. You can't stop. You got to keep going." One thing for sure is that I will go to battle any day for and with my best friend. The battle is ultimately the Lord's, but you have to be committed to do the work daily.

I've also come to understand that divorce happens. God doesn't want it to happen, but the Bible speaks directly about grounds to dissolve a marriage. Not every situation or scenario is created equal. If you're experiencing abuse from your spouse, then you need to find a safe place and set ironclad boundaries. If there are children involved, then their safety and yours should take priority over staying in a hostile environment. You can't become well in the same environment that made you sick. If adultery has occurred in your marriage, there is always a place for forgiveness, but once that covenant has been broken, trust is very hard to restore. God knows how to bring healing and restoration and, in some cases, a completely fresh start. No matter what scenario you're facing in your marriage, I would encourage you to find wise counsel, seek accountability, and surround yourself with a godly support system.

Here are two testimonies of married couples close to us that will encourage you to believe that with two willing hearts and God at the center, all things are possible.

Suzie, my sister in Christ who I was in the Power of a Praying Wife Bible study I joined at eighteen, fought for her husband for eight long years. I couldn't tell you how many times people close to her told her to quit on him, give up, and move on. He was a lost cause and couldn't care about her by the way he was acting. There was even a point when I questioned if it was God's will for her to endure that devastating journey. I couldn't help but respect her commitment, determination, and love for this man and come alongside her in prayer. I vividly remember the day when he left her. We walked in the house, and his hangers in the closet were still swinging from him emptying his side. We got on our knees and prayed for his soul and the restoration of their marriage in that very place. That became her prayer closet and the space she would go to battle before the throne of grace for her husband's soul. If she didn't fight for him, who would?

Suzie's husband, tried to serve her divorce papers, and she would never sign them. She remained in a place of unconditional love, safety, and support for him, no matter how many times he left and turned to drugs, partying, and other women. It wasn't until a major motorcycle accident that his journey to redemption would begin. He finally broke and surrendered his life to Christ. They ended up moving to South Carolina for a fresh start, where God began to restore and heal their marriage.

During that time, Suzie volunteered at an equine therapy ranch and returned to her love of horses, which she had as a child. The couple who owned the farm decided they needed to retire and close the farm. Suzie had bonded with the horses, and her husband gave her the most beautiful gift as a monument of God's faithfulness in their marriage: a horse named Silky. Later, they would end up taking in many more horses and find their way back to Florida to begin New Life Farm. Suzie's husband named their ranch in honor of their new beginning together. Their home and ministry has become a place of refuge and safety for many to learn to lead with love, courage, and grace. You can follow them on @newlifefarmfl on Facebook. Our kids have had the privilege of learning under Suzie's leadership. They've both become confident riders and are learning to lead with love and trust.

The second testimony of restoration is of our brother Jonathan and sister-in-law Valentina. They ended up meeting at the same Gold's gym where Jeff and I met—clearly, a great place to meet a future spouse! Jonathan and Valentina were both young and faced all of the same pressures and toxicity we did in the family ministry. I can't imagine how hard it was for Val to be living away from her family and support system down in South Florida while trying to process everything going on in her life. She had fallen in love with the idea of this awesome family in ministry, just like all the Shaw wives did.

Not too long after they were married, they found out they were going to have a son. All three Shaw daughters-in-law were pregnant at the same time with the next generation of Shaw babies. It was an exciting time dreaming about this new chapter beginning for our families. We couldn't wait to raise our kids together and watch the cousins make memories. However, life would eventually take Jonathan and Val down a different road, which ended up taking them to South Florida. They tried to get away and draw boundaries from all of the craziness of the family ministry, but there was already too much damage done. After trying to fight for their marriage, they kept hitting a wall and ultimately got divorced. At the time, their son was really young, and it was devastating to watch this beautiful family being torn apart.

I'm so thankful that during their time of separation, we were intentional about making memories as a family. We would celebrate birthdays and holidays together. No matter what the future held for their marriage, Valentina and our nephew Alexander would always be our family. Our boys would get matching jammies for Christmas and have dance offs every time they saw each other.

Truth be told, we adored Val and couldn't imagine anyone else for Jonathan. We had so much love and respect for her and enjoyed having her as a sister. She was made of good stuff and was worth fighting for. She didn't have the easiest upbringing, but she never allowed her trials and hardships to make her bitter and hardhearted. Five years later, after much counseling, prayer, brokenness, forgiveness, and healing, Jonathan and Val got married again on the beach in front of their family and friends. Alexander's prayers to have his family restored were answered. I will never forget the overwhelming joy we all had watching God make something beautiful out of dust.

There was a time while they were still divorced when we took a trip to celebrate Alexander's birthday. As we were driving, a song called "Broken Together" came on the radio. It spoke of how God can take two broken individuals and make them whole again as one in His love, forgiveness, and redemption. We shared that song with Val and Jonathan as a seed of restoration sown in their hearts.

Now, five years after their "take two" wedding, God has grown their family tree with two more miracles. Our nephew David Jeremiah was born weeks after our mother-in-law passed, and our niece Sofia Pamela came three years later.

God is able to restore the broken and make it into something more beautiful than the original piece of artwork. There is a Japanese art form called Kintsugi, in which the artist takes something broken, like pottery, and pieces it back together by sealing the cracks with gold where it originally broke. Not only is the piece more beautiful, but it's more valuable and fortified as well. God knows how to turn messes that look shattered beyond repair into masterpieces fit for His use.

Whether you are in a season of singleness longing to be married, dating in frustration, fighting for your marriage, or widowed, God wants to be your all in all, right where you are. Your life is not missing something. You are not damaged goods. When divine timing aligns for you to meet your spouse or for your marriage to be restored, it will be a blessing. In the meantime, heal, rest, serve, and trust while you're waiting. Get the focus off of the mountain in front of you and place it on the Creator of the mountain. You have to allow yourself to feel so you can heal, then God will reveal His greater purpose in your pain. Cherish this time, prepare, and enjoy just being alone with Jesus. Trust me, the shift will happen suddenly.

Reigning in Parenthood

> "I don't know what's more exhausting about parenting: the getting up early, or acting like you know what you're doing."–Jim Gaffigan[8]

Man, there is so much truth to that statement! On our parenting journey, there are countless times when we find ourselves feeling completely inadequate, unqualified, and ill-equipped to raise little humans. We've all heard the old saying that goes, "Fake it until you make it." I say parenting is more like "faith-ing" it until you make it. Parenting is a daily act of surrendering your will and asking for wisdom, strength, sanity, guidance, mercy, and grace from the Lord. It's a never-ending faith journey.

Being entrusted to care for another human being is such a scary and huge responsibility. The last thing we want to do is project our traumas, insecurities, insufficiencies, fears, and unrealistic expectations on them. That is why it's so important to do the necessary healing work and stop the toxic behavior from being passed down to the next generation. I think we all have a strong desire for our children to not only have better than we did growing up but, more importantly, to also be better humans.

Children are a part of your inner circle and your legacy, and they are entrusted in your care for a period of time. They will always be your children, but there will come a time when God will require you to push them out of the nest and spread their wings. Some will even want to jump out on their own. Listen, parenting is not for the faint of heart. It doesn't matter how many blogs or books you read or influencers you follow on social media. There are not enough tips, tricks, hacks, or advice that will prepare you for the joys, sorrows, ups, downs, and disappointments the parenting journey will bring. They send your baby home with you from the hospital with no manual on how to handle everything these tiny creatures will take you through in life. There will be many times when you feel like you're not qualified or that you mess up royally.

Nothing will prepare you for the rollercoaster of emotions, financial investment, and toll children will take on your sanity. It begins with the early stages of sleep deprivation, dirty diapers, feedings, blow outs, and blow ups. If that isn't enough to make someone throw in the towel, then it's time for the terrible twos, tantrums, no's, and endless messes to clean up. I'm getting tired right now just thinking about that stage. Then when you feel like you're finally getting into a rhythm, you become a taxi driver, a tutor, a sports agent, a chef, a maid, a mentor, a teacher, and an events coordinator. Then come the teenage years with raging hormones, an endless desire to be with their friends, and their audacity to start pushing away after all you've done to support them.

Maybe those years are God's way of preparing you for your children to spread their wings and leave the nest.

Every stage comes with its own battles and blessings. My encouragement would be to be present in whatever stage or phase you're in. The old saying goes, "The days are long, but the years are short." There is so much truth to that statement. When your children are little and so demanding, each day can feel like an eternity. As they get into elementary and middle school, they start transforming right before your eyes. It's almost overwhelming and bittersweet. You want them to grow, mature, and develop into independent young adults, but you miss when they were smaller and needed you so much.

> Every stage comes with its own battles and blessings. My encouragement would be to be present in whatever stage or phase you're in.

During the pandemic, our son, Kingston, drastically changed within a two-year span. He doesn't even look like the same kid he was in sixth grade, with his fluffy cheeks and little belly. He's now a lean, mean muscle machine, standing six foot, three inches tall and wearing a size thirteen shoe at thirteen! How I became his little mama at five-nine still blows my mind. He's kind hearted, caring, bright, talented, hardworking, wise beyond his years, a young man with a great sense of humor, and a blessing to all who know him. He plays football and baseball, loves the Lord and the outdoors, and is always up for an adventure. He's also an awesome big brother and super patient with his little sis… well, the majority of the time.

Standing back to back after Kingston's football game

Our daughter, Carrington, is now nine years old and so full of life, passion, humor, tenacity, talent, and creativity, and she has the most caring heart. She's not afraid to stand up for what's right and use her voice to speak the truth. She rocked our world with her vocal chords when she entered this world and hasn't stopped talking, singing, and dancing since.

REIGN IN RELATIONSHIPS

The family at Carrington's dance recital

Our children are both so different yet look so much alike. I adore their big, brown, sparkly eyes and curly hair. Their smiles light up the world, and their presence brings joy everywhere they go. I love how they are not embarrassed to tell us they love us in front of their friends. I pray they will always have each other's backs and be there for one another throughout life. The best parenting advice we've been given is to not live through our children. It's so easy to project our dreams, hopes, desires, and expectations onto them. That is where we have to ask the Lord to show us who He has created them to be and give us wisdom to provide for and guide them, helping them to cultivate those gifts, talents, and abilities for their good and His glory.

As parents, it is important to give our children the freedom to create, laugh, play, explore, try new things, fail forward, and let them be kids for as long as they can. When Care comes home from school, the first thing she does is create some type of art project. I give her that time to decompress and flow in her passion. Kingston loves to be outdoors. It's his therapy and place to let go of the stress and pressures of life. He loves to fish even if he doesn't catch anything. One vital aspect of nurturing a child is to create an environment of rest. We have our kids so overscheduled that they are burnt out before they enter middle school. Resting teaches them to decompress, put their trust in God, and refuel their engines.

Be intentional about making positive memories for your children. Kids don't care as much about money and possessions as they do your quality time and attention. Love is a four-letter word, and it's spelled T. I. M. E. Take your kids on special dates and show them how to be treated. My husband, my parents, and I try to divide and conquer by taking King and Care out for one-on-one time. They always come back with their cups filled full.

Apologize to your kids when you lose your temper. Showing them humility, forgiveness, and that you take responsibility for your actions sets a strong foundation for them. They are growing up in a time of entitlement and convenience. Don't give them everything they want but focus more on their needs, spiritual, emotional, and physical. Be truthful with them, always communicating clearly and openly. Their generation demands information and has access to search it out at their fingertips, so be a safe place for your children to communicate. There's nothing sweeter and more fulfilling than knowing your kids feel confident coming to you no matter what they're going through. Pray with them whenever you get the chance and speak life, blessing, and strength over them.

You can't raise your kids alone. Parenting truly takes a village and can make all the difference in raising a powerful, productive, and purposeful next generation. Our village consists of grandparents, uncles, aunts, cousins, teachers, coaches, youth pastors, and other parents who can fill any gaps, cracks, or crevices in the solid foundation we're trying to establish in our children.

To show the importance of having a village while raising children, a counselor friend of mine used an example of a glass vase. She filled the vase with solid stones that represented unconditional love, food, shelter, and daily support parents give their children throughout their lives. After the glass jar with stones was full, you could still visibly see some spaces that weren't filled. Then she took a cup filled with colored sand and started pouring it over the stones. You could see it start to fill in all of the crevices. It was a beautiful example of how having a solid and diversified village surrounding your children will help fortify and mold them into solid adults.

Andy Stanley wrote, "Always remember that your greatest contribution to the kingdom may not be something you do but someone you raise."$_9$ What an awesome reminder to remember the eternal value of raising a child. Some years back, I was ministering at an event where a prominent woman in the Christian community came up to me and said, "God really has a calling on your life, and I want to share something with you. Your children are young, and you will never get this time back with them. Your calling will never go away, and the ministry will always be there waiting for you." She told me her biggest regret was that she was so busy building her ministry that she missed too many moments while raising her son. In that moment, I knew the fast-paced train we were on had to slow down to prevent me from missing these precious moments with our family.

Between writing our first books, becoming Mrs. Florida, and starting to work in TV and radio, I was getting burnt out. We were always on the go with those ventures, along with the kids' sports and activities. We had a nice, long run, but things had to shift so that I wouldn't miss out on the most important role in my life: being their mom.

During that time, I read a quote from Mother Teresa that gave me the release and peace to be fully present for my family: "If you want to change the world, go home and love your family."[10] It's so crazy to think that this was the message God delivered to me right before the world shut down from the global pandemic. The majority of the events and the rapid pace came to a screeching halt as my full focus became serving my family and keeping them healthy and safe. He had already deposited this in my spirit so that I wouldn't wrestle with this abrupt shift but welcome it as a gift to rest, be fully present, and enjoy the most precious gift in my family.

Community Is King!

Earlier, I shared that part of our outer court relationships will consist of relationships we build in the community. A big part of our personal community surrounds our kids' sports and activities. Coaches have played a huge role in helping mold our children into leaders both on and off the field. Sports provide a great way to connect with people from all different backgrounds, beliefs, and cultures. They are the common equalizer, a universal language, and they can unify children in ways that teach self-discipline, teamwork, camaraderie, respect, trust, and discipline. Both my husband and I grew up playing competitive sports. Although neither of us ended up playing professionally, we've both benefited from all of the valuable life lessons the years of training, discipline, and teamwork taught us. Over the years, we've even stepped in to help coach football and soccer as a way to give back to something that has given us so much.

Our son has played tackle football since he was eight years old. All the kids on his team come from very different walks of life, but over a period of time, an unbreakable brotherhood has formed. In 2020, when the COVID-19 virus was at its peak, we were coming upon football season. I can remember many conversations about how we could keep the kids safe and if there would even be a season for them to play. How do you keep football players six feet apart? It's a contact sport! During this time, all of the players were doing virtual school at home and had very little contact outside of their immediate families.

Not only were we in the middle of a global pandemic, but it was also a very heated election year, and racial injustice was at the forefront with the murder of George Floyd. Fear, anxiety, worry, anger, and every kind of emotion were at an all-time high. But, something really amazing started to happen when we were given the green light to have a season. All of the players and parents were so grateful to return to some sort of normalcy that we all pulled together and set our differences aside to experience the most unforgettable season. We went undefeated in the regular season and won the Mid-Florida Championship, the Southeast Regional Championship, and ultimately the Pop Warner National Championship.

We had no drama, division, injuries, or egos trying to undermine what God was wanting to accomplish in and through these boys and families. We truly became as tight as a family that year and watched what God can do when you come together in the spirit of unity. Gratitude, humility, and coachability always create an atmosphere for the miraculous to manifest. We will cherish the memories we made for a lifetime and always have that experience to reflect back on as a lesson of hard work, dedication, commitment, and how to pull together in times of uncertainty.

> Gratitude, humility, and coachability always create an atmosphere for the miraculous to manifest.

Celebrating Apopka 12U Pop Warner National Championship and undefeated season

REIGNING IN DIVERSITY

Over the years, I get asked, "How can I create diversity in my organization?" This question comes from people with all different types of cultural backgrounds at events I host or speak at. It could be Caucasian people wanting to have more Black, Hispanic, and Asian individuals as part of their business, church, or non-profit, or vice-versa.

Thankfully I've been exposed to many different cultures from growing up playing sports, and also largely because I'm married to a biracial man. I not only embrace diversity but realize how boring my life would be without it. I call our family the United Nations because collectively we cover almost every ethnicity on the planet. Both of my brothers and brothers-in-law married Hispanic women. This gringa will jump in and dance salsa, take advantage of the free Spanish lessons, and throw down some arroz con pollo…and cafe con leche in a minuto. I love all of our traditions, cuisines, and cultures that combine to make an amazing, eclectic, crazy, flavorful, soulful, and beautiful blend.

I will never forget attending my first Shaw Family Christmas reunion right after we were engaged. My father-in-law is the baby of twelve! He would tell you it took his parents twelve tries to get it right and make the perfect child. I think his siblings would probably argue that perspective. Talk about an overwhelming task to learn the names of all of the aunts and uncles and first, second, and third cousins! I was overwhelmed at the idea of that many names to learn and people to get to know.

The Shaw family originated from Kingstree, South Carolina. After doing some research about Kingstree and its roots in slavery, I found a plantation under the name of Shaw. I'm not 100 percent sure that was the original plantation where their ancestors were enslaved and worked, but the chances are pretty good considering the size of that city. Kingstree is ninety-five miles north of Charlestown, South Carolina, which was the port for the largest slave trade in the south. The ancestors who miraculously survived the treacherous, horrific, and terrifying journey from West Africa across the Atlantic Ocean would land in this port only to be sold and distributed all across the south. The Shaw family name was taken on from the slave owners' names and has roots in Scotland.

When slavery was abolished, the family became farmers, business owners, educators, ministers, and very influential people in their community. There is actually a place in Kingstree called Shaw Corner, where they ran their places of business. It's still there today. Eventually,

Jeff's grandfather would make a life-changing decision to start a new life for their family of fourteen in Florida. I'm forever grateful he made that shift, because my family wouldn't be here today if he did not. Isn't it amazing how God can cause life's shifts and disruptions to cross pollinate cultures, lives, and traditions for His greater plans and purposes?

Now, back to the family reunion. For the first time in my life, I was the minority at a family gathering, and I was about to embark on some unknown territory. I would be lying if I didn't say I was a bit overwhelmed. Would they like me? Would I fit in this family? I was immediately embraced with big smiles and warm signature Shaw bear hugs and smooches! I loved their huge, loud, loving family and was in awe of how they could get that many members together to eat a meal. My mom was an only child and my dad came from a family of five; I even thought we had a big family.

Some of the traditions at the Shaw family reunion were to smoke a pig underground (the Shaws are famous for their barbeque), wear matching reunion t-shirts, sing, and sit around the elders to learn all kinds of family history. I've always had a passion to learn about the past and loved listening to all of Jeff's incredible aunts and uncles share stories. Some years ago, they gave us an ancestry book full of old pictures of family members dating back to right after slavery. I cherish that book and will keep it safe to pass down to the next generations.

Our physical differences were obvious, but we all shared our faith in Jesus, pride for our families, the love of good food, and the importance of cultivating and carrying on a meaningful legacy. I am beyond blessed to have so many beautiful, bright, resilient, funny, innovative, accomplished, kind, and loving black men and women in my life I get to call my family. I pray that they will be just as proud of me as I am of them.

I am honored to be Courtney Dawn Shaw and carry a new last name that represents redemption, freedom, perseverance, grit, and grace. The Shaw/Cooper family is the epitome of what it looks like to get better and not bitter despite what life throws your way. Out of the twelve children of my father-in-law's family, many graduated from college and served in the military, and others became business owners, ministers, and influential leaders. To think this family is not that far removed from slavery and there is so much joy, healing, and love is incredible. The evidence of God's faithfulness in their lives is bearing good fruit for generations to come.

When I see a map of the world, my spirit literally leaps with excitement and hears the call to go and answer the great commission, which Jesus clearly states in Matthew 28:19-20: "Therefore go and make disciples of all nations, baptizing them in the name of the Father and of the Son and of the Holy Spirit, and teaching them to obey everything I have commanded you." I love to travel and learn different traditions and cultures, while also seeing how God moves in the hearts of people all over the world. I think it's so important to get out of your cultural bubble and experience the traditions and ways of others. You come home with a broader perspective of humanity and an appreciation of how God sees His incredible creation. You also develop genuine empathy and a deep desire to connect with all people and share the love of the Father.

Faith, family, music, food, and sports are threads that help tie all of creation together to create one race—the human race. If you're unable to jump on a plane and stamp your passport, you can go on YouTube and learn about people and places all over the world. There is no excuse not to listen and learn. You can also connect with people all around you. In your neighborhood, place of work, and your kids' schools, you can meet people literally from all over the world.

The number-one reason most people don't want to step out of their comfort zone and embrace other cultures is because they fear losing their own traditions and beliefs. Racism and hatred are taught and passed down through generations. Children aren't born into this world hating others who don't look like them. They learn it from watching others.

Racism is a result of people looking at diversity as a melting pot instead of a stew. A melting pot is a combination of different ingredients that all cook together into one substance. In this type of dish, you lose the integrity, shape, and form of each individual ingredient. A melting pot of culture is conformity, not diversity. It creates a society of people dressing alike, talking alike, acting alike, and alienating anyone who doesn't conform to the majority's belief systems.

If you are wondering how to create diversity in your organization, you need to ask yourself why you want diversity. Is it just for optics and to increase your profit, or do you really desire to learn from people who come from different cultural backgrounds and in return bring value to people who don't look, act, and think like you? Are you willing to let go of any stereotypes and preconceived notions about someone from a different cultural background who doesn't look like you?

I like to look at creating genuine diversity like making a savory beef stew. Years ago, my Grannie Inez taught me how to make her famous recipe, and it's still a staple in our home today. There is nothing fancy about the ingredients. You need chopped stew meat, onions, carrots, celery, potatoes, diced tomatoes, seasoning, and broth. When you put them all together, then add a little heat, time, and pressure, it turns into the most flavorful, satiating, and nourishing meal. The cool thing about beef stew is that all of the ingredients maintain their original shape and form. Although, when you take a bite of the beef, it takes on the flavor of the onions, carrots, and celery. Each ingredient takes on a little flavor of the others, and it all becomes tender with time.

I believe that is how God wants our hearts to become as we connect with people all over the globe. With

> **With true diversity, His kingdom becomes a beautiful fusion of flavors. That meal of humanity can only be made with love.**

true diversity, His kingdom becomes a beautiful fusion of flavors. That meal of humanity can only be made with love. You can tell the difference between a meal that was thrown together versus one that took time, intentionality, and a lot of TLC. That is one thing we can all agree on. Love is the key ingredient to creating authentic and lasting diversity.

God's love is perfect. 1 John 4:18 says, "There is no fear in love; but perfect love casts out fear, because fear involves torment. But he who fears has not been made perfect in love." The only antidote for annihilating racism and hatred in our generation, which are both rooted in fear, is love. God is very clear in His Word about loving others. In Mark 12:31, Jesus tells us, "And the second, like *it, is* this: 'You shall love your neighbor as yourself.' There is no other commandment greater than these." He's not asking, suggesting, or recommending us to love others but commanding it.

Choosing not to love others is a clear act of disobedience. How could you say you have love for God but withhold it from all of His creation? How could you not believe our Creator loves diversity? Look at the diverse faces of humanity and all of the incredible creatures He so lovingly and thoughtfully created. Beauty is everywhere and in all things, walking and crawling on the earth, swimming in the sea, and soaring through the skies.

Be intentional about pursuing relationships with people who don't look and act like you. Do more listening than talking and let go of any preconceived notions and biases about any culture you might have developed through the media. Over time, consistency builds beautiful, trusting relationships. Don't rush these relationships or place demands on others to think, act, or live like you. Use your voice, influence, and resources to help bring value, awareness, solutions, and spaces for people of all races to be heard, seen, valued, and celebrated.

We're raising multicultural kingdom kids. Because the world likes to put people in categories, children will innocently ask our kids, "What are you?" First, our kids will answer, "A child of God." Next, they will say, "If you're referring to my ethnicity, well, I'm Swedish, African American, German, Irish, English, Cherokee Indian, and Jamaican."

I think our children are a great visual of what heaven will be one day. Revelation 7:9 says, "After this I looked, and behold, a great multitude that no one could number, from every nation, from all tribes and peoples and languages, standing before the throne and before the Lamb, clothed in white robes, with palm branches in their hands."

Jeff and I want our kids to understand, embrace, and appreciate all of their ethnicities, traditions, and ancestries. One is not greater than the other. They would not be here or who they are today without the cross-cultural journey of their ancestors. There are so many miraculous factors, disruptions, and re-directions in their family tree that made it possible for my husband and me to be together and for them to be here on earth for such a time as this. I will dive deeper into the importance of going on that quest to discover your roots in the next chapter, Reigning in Your Legacy.

So, if you desire diversity in your organization, your society, or your life, be intentional about pursuing relationships with people who look, act, or think differently from you. Visit various cultural chambers of commerce, dine at restaurants owned by people from other countries, have tough conversations with others, and listen more than talk. Be open to learn and love and be the kind of friend you would want in your life. Ask God to search your heart and reveal and expose any hidden biases you may have. Trust me, we've all picked them up over our lifetime. Some are very subtle while others are just blatant.

Variety is truly the spice of life. Some of the best food on the planet is infusion cuisine—where two or more cultures are joined together in the kitchen to create culinary masterpieces. One of our friends is Jamaican and Asian. When she puts those two cultures together in the kitchen, magic is made on the plate. Some words of wisdom: don't ever let anyone put you in a box or make you feel pressured to choose a side. My husband grew up as biracial boy in a predominantly white area. He was never white enough or black enough to fit in. The reality is that he was born to stand out as a leader, a student, and an athlete.

Jeff was created by God to become a bridge between both of his cultures and many more. Growing up, he was loved and embraced by the Lord and both sides of his family, and that has helped give him the confidence to own all of his ethnicity and culture. His mom's side of the family, the Barbers, supported Jeff in all of his sports and his talent for art and music, and they embraced our children with that same unconditional love and support. For many years, Jeff felt that being biracial was a curse rather than a blessing, but as he's gotten older, he's been able to appreciate his built-in diversity and the broader perspective on humanity it has given him. It has provided him with tools in business and life to connect with people from all different cultures and backgrounds. He was even asked to be a leader in diversity and inclusion within his company right after there was an uprising in racial injustice.

Based upon Jeff's physical appearance, most people would assume he's Hispanic, and the world would now identify him as ethnically ambiguous. He can move across many different cultures based solely on his physical appearance. Instead of looking at this as a limitation of not belonging, Jeff sees it as a passport to connect with so many more people. Truth be told, the majority of the world will be hard to identify and categorize because of cross-cultural marriages on the rise. The invention of the internet has connected our world and made building relationships with various cultures the norm.

We hate racism and the gross generational effects it has had on families, including ours. We truly believe a lot of the inability of my father-in-law to be in right relationship with others stems from unresolved trauma from racism he faced as a young boy and man. We can't even begin to imagine the pain, rejection, fear, and deep hurt that he went through and still goes through trying to fit in as a black man in society. But, one thing we do know is that he is so loved and not alone.

Millions of other people on this planet have faced gross injustice because of ignorance and racism. We also know that Jesus nailed those sins to the cross and His love is greater than any hate and abuse His sons and daughters have endured. There is safety, healing, and hope for a future to overcome the pain and own the scars inflicted out of pure ignorance and hatred. Healing can happen one conversation at a time, one hug at a time, and one act of kindness at a time. We do everything in our power to speak against racism and live in a way that brings value, unconditional love, and justice in the lives of others.

The Local Church Still Reigns Supreme

A big part of our family's healing journey was finding a local church that could help love our family back to life. We had to make the decision not to believe the lie that all churches are toxic, cult-like, and dangerous places to invest your time, talents, and resources. We also didn't feel called to start a church ourselves no matter how many people would suggest it or say Jeff and I were called to pastor. We experienced a lot of unnecessary pain under leadership that didn't pursue healing and wholeness before taking on a position of power and influence over others. We also truly felt called outside the four walls of the church and had a heart for marketplace ministry and evangelism.

The truth is, there is no perfect church or pastor. But, God does have a beautiful plan for the local church to further His kingdom and spread the gospel around the world. When there are boundaries of accountability and transparency in place for

> When there are boundaries of accountability and transparency in place for the leadership, the local church can be a place of refuge, sanctuary, and strengthening for the body of Christ.

the leadership, the local church can be a place of refuge, sanctuary, and strengthening for the body of Christ.

In our quest to find a local church again, Jeff and I had some non-negotiables based on the Bible and our previous experience. The Word of God had to be preached, and a strong focus on the children's and youth ministry to help pour into our kids had to be in place. There also needed to be an emphasis on baptism, missions, and an atmosphere of worship. We wanted a place where we didn't have to drag our children to go to church but where they would beg us to go back. We also wanted a church where we felt good about inviting others. There was nothing more embarrassing than inviting someone to church to have them left feeling beaten down and drained.

Some key characteristics in a godly leader and pastor should be humility, transparency, and servanthood. A pastor is not in a leadership role to lord over the people but to encourage them, build them up in their faith, and lead them to a fruitful relationship with Jesus Christ. We found that and so much more in Journey Christian Church. The crazy thing was that I was baptized in this church when I was twenty years old. God had brought our family full circle.

Kingston and Carrington loved the children's and youth ministry at Journey Christian. They were excited about their relationship with Jesus and growing in their personal walks. The summer before the pandemic hit, King attended a Student Life Camp and had a powerful encounter with God. His walk became his own that summer. He came home with so much excitement and a new sense of strength. He asked us if he could get baptized in front of the church, his family, and his friends. I will never forget the day Jeff and I stepped in the water with him. King went all in and all under for Jesus! Carrington watched her big brother make that step, and not too long after, she made the same public confession of her faith.

Over the years, we've been washed by timely messages from the leadership, loved back to life, sent on a mission trip to Africa, and shown that a healthy church is possible and vital to serving the surrounding community. Journey's mission statement is: "A place where everybody's welcome, nobody's perfect, and through Jesus, anything's possible." It's a beautiful invitation to be welcomed into the body of Christ without having it all together.

During the darkest days of the pandemic, our local church shined so brightly. Like every other local church across the globe, they had to pivot to online services and find creative ways to serve the surrounding community with overwhelming needs. I'm so proud of how the body of Christ answered the call to be a beacon of hope and the hands and feet of Jesus during uncertain times.

We believe in the importance of the local church and pray that you will find one to get plugged into near you. If you've experienced church hurt, I pray that God will heal your heart and give you wisdom to find a healthy church. We were not meant to walk this Christian walk alone but to forge together with our brothers and sisters around the world to see God's kingdom come on earth as it is in heaven.

Friendships

Don't you remember when you were growing up, how you would be so proud to claim a best friend or be claimed as someone's best friend? It made you feel loved, important, and exclusive. You had other friends, but your best friend was the person you couldn't wait to hang out with, shared so many things in common with, made best friend bracelets with, and would go to battle for at a drop of a dime.

I will never forget my first childhood best friend. My family had just moved from Colorado to Florida, and I was in a completely new space. I was nervous to walk into the first day of second grade until I was greeted by a smiling face. From that point on, Jen and I were inseparable. We were both tomboys and loved riding our bikes around the neighborhood, climbing trees, and diving in ponds to catch giant bullfrogs. Together, we always found ourselves challenging boys to the kicking game after school. By the way, we never lost a match. Over the years, we had many spend-the-nights, adventures, and opportunities to cheer each other on in sports. Jen became an adopted daughter in my family—the sister I always wanted to have. I became a staple around her house as well.

I will never forget our fourth-grade year, when I stayed over at Jen's house and she started crying because her parents were getting a divorce. It broke my heart, and all I could do was hold her and tell her it was going to be okay. As we grew through our middle school years, Jen and I made some of the most amazing memories and our circle of friends grew. We ended up going to different high schools, but our bond would not be separated by a little distance.

Jen would eventually go off to college. While she was home, before heading back to school, she got the most devastating news: her younger sister, Carrie, had passed away in a car wreck right down the street from her house at the young age of fourteen. That moment, it was as if time stood still.

During this season of life, I was newly walking with the Lord and had such a passion in my heart to share the gospel. Carrie's passing was my first real close encounter with the death of someone I cared about. She was like my little sis too. Jen and I would prank her all the time. The day before she was killed, we were at their house getting her ready for her first big day of school. We spent quality time with her and couldn't believe how much she was growing up. Suddenly, the next day, she was gone.

I remember sitting around the table with the priest and nuns at Jen's house, discussing funeral arrangements and her service. I had a moment where I shared my passion for the Lord and comforted the family with the truth that Carrie was safe in our Father's arms. Right then, the nuns perked up and tried to recruit me. I kindly declined and told them I wanted to enjoy being married one day while still serving the Lord. To this day, I'm thankful I didn't take their offer.

Jen's family gave me an opportunity to speak at Carrie's wake. I can remember vividly looking at her body lying in the casket with a Care Bear next to her. "Care Bear" was her nickname. It was just overwhelming to think how fragile life is. None of us know the hour or the day God will call us home. At that moment, I knew that Carrie wasn't there. Her body was literally a shell, but her spirit was with the Lord. That was a pivotal moment in my faith journey, and I knew that I was on a mission to help as many people as I could prepare for eternity. Carrie's death launched me into a deeper purpose and passion for sharing the gospel of Jesus Christ everywhere I went.

Not too long after her passing, the family asked me to join them on an unforgettable journey to the 2000 Olympics in Sydney, Australia. It was bittersweet because Carrie was supposed to be on this epic adventure with her family, not me. I graciously accepted the invitation and was exposed to some of the most beautiful places in the world. I went from recently locking myself in my bedroom, battling depression and contemplating life, to getting my passport stamped in places most people only dream of going. I will cherish those memories and experiences for a lifetime. That trip fanned the flame for travel and global missions within my heart.

As time would move on and Jen was off at college, I would meet Jeff and become a wife at twenty-two. Our lives went down very different paths. We would stay in touch and witness life's major milestones in each other's lives, from weddings to babies and beyond. As young girls, Jen and I always dreamed of living next door to each other and raising our kids together. Although that didn't come into play, no matter the physical distance between us, we always want the best for each other. We both have a new best friend now in our husbands, and that's the way it should be.

It's a very rare thing to have friends in your life who will walk with you through every season of life and ultimately help you cross the finish line from time into eternity. God will bring people in and out of your life for seasons and reasons, but one thing for sure is that there is something to learn from every friendship. Having a variety of friends who all bring different things into your life makes it so rich.

I love my football sisters, Angie and Chris. During game days, we would team up on the sidelines, serving and going to battle for our boys. By nature of spending so much time together, we got to know one another real fast. These two ladies had my back and always reassured me of their support and friendship. I also have incredible sisters in ministry and the women empowerment space as well. Anissa, Tracey, Arlene, Jennifer, Michelle, and Candi all have incredible platforms that give women a voice and value. I love their hearts to celebrate and support other women. They do what they do with excellence and pure hearts, and it's always a joy to serve alongside them on purpose. They all inspire me to keep digging deeper in my purpose and know the value I bring outside of my roles as a wife and a mom.

My most cherished friendships, especially in this season of my life, are the ones that aren't high maintenance. I have a handful of incredible friends who send me messages of encouragement and make sure I know I'm loved and cared about, while fanning the flame of my purpose. They understand the daily demands of being a wife and a super-involved mom. When we talk, we pick up right where we left off. I am beyond appreciative of their support and the value they bring to my life. When it comes to people in my close circle, I will take quality over quantity any day.

I've also been blessed with some great friendships through our kids. Our daughter met her best friend, Gracie, in kindergarten, and they've been buddies ever since. I'm so thankful for their friendship because it brought Gracie's mom, Kelly, into my life. We both have very strong-willed girls with lots of grit, passion, and relentless wills.

At times, it can feel like a war zone, but they've learned over the years to handle one another with TLC. We are always encouraging each other down the path to raise kind, caring, compassionate, and confident girls. I love how Carrington and Gracie always have each other's backs and do special things for one another.

When I was asked to speak at a retreat in St. Thomas and could bring someone with me as a guest, I'm so glad that Kelly gave me a spontaneous yes and joined me for an incredible and meaningful adventure in the Caribbean. We learned so much about each other on this trip, laughed our butts off, cried, and danced like nobody was watching. I think it's so vital to embrace friendships while you're in the trenches of motherhood. It's so easy to lose yourself and feel like you are never good enough or do enough for your children. We need friends to remind ourselves to let go, let God, and have fun!

Lastly, God knew I would need my Shaw Sisters in my life. We all share the same last name and have been entrusted to carry on a new legacy that represents faith, freedom, and unconditional love in Christ. We know that to whom much is given, much is required. Being married to a Shaw man is definitely not for the faint of heart. It's a huge blessing that comes with a big responsibility to guard their hearts. I'm so grateful for the unique things each sister brings to make our family something really special. I cherish the safe place we have in one another and how we support all of our endeavors. They are the most encouraging, present, and loving aunts to King and Care. I love you, Valentina, Diana, and Amaryllis.

2020: The Year We Made It Reign Confetti

I want to end this chapter on relationships with an exclamation point. As I write these words, my heart overflows with deep gratitude for what God has done and is still doing in our Shaw family. We have experienced so much trauma, sadness, loss, heartache, and disappointment. We have suffered years of psychological, emotional, financial, and spiritual abuse, both individually and collectively.

After Jeff's mom passed, everyone in the family was grieving in very different ways and mostly apart from one another. In September 2019, Jeff's birthday was coming up, and we had been on a personal family mission to start infusing our lives with more fun. In the past, when someone's birthday would roll around, it would be dampened by some type of sabotage or a sad reminder of the disenfranchisement of our family, and I was so sick and tired of it. It was enough! We still had life, we had purpose, and God had given us more years here together to give Him praise. Instead of putting our joy on hold, it was time to party with and for a purpose. It was time to start lavishing one another with love, celebration, and appreciation.

Ecclesiastes 3:1-11 says that there is a time and a purpose for every season under heaven. It was finally a time to dance, laugh, and celebrate the goodness of God in the land of the living. So, I decided to plan a fun family night out to drive really fast go karts at Mario Andretti's, followed by stuffing our faces with crazy desserts, singing, and dancing at the Sugar Factory. I sent an invitation for Jeff's second brother, Dominick, and his family to join us. They said yes, and the fun began.

Full hearts and bellies celebrating at the Sugar Factory

After all of the kids raced, the adults decided it was our turn, and off they went to watch their competitive parents safely from behind the glass. There was one point during the race when I caught up to Dominick and was hot on his trail, determined to pass him. We eventually took a sharp turn, and boom! The next thing I knew, I was slammed into the back of his go kart with Diana's on top of mine, tire spinning and smoking. I looked at my right arm, and there was a burnt rubber track from the tire! I still can't figure out how her go kart didn't crush me. We were all in shock at how that crash happened so suddenly. The looks of terror on the faces of the employees and the abrupt stop of the race had us all laughing our butts off. Thankfully, no one was hurt. I picked off the rubber from my arm and slowly drove my go kart back to where the guy was waving the checkered flag.

I couldn't help but think of how that crash wass indicative of all the trauma that had happened to our family through the years. We would all be going so fast through life, and some type of life tragedy would bring us to an immediate halt. Instead of facing the trauma head on and evaluating what had happened and why it had happened, take time to heal, and learn how to prevent it from happening again, we would just back up, get in our race cars, and keep moving. The reality was, we were never racing at full capacity because there was damage from the many collisions that had occurred. Instead of racing as a team, it was every man for himself. We were all conditioned to cover up our wounds and keep the race of life going full speed ahead.

But, this time, instead of there being a falling out and a blaming of who caused what, the crash ended up ushering in a major breakthrough for the four of us. Once we realized no one was hurt, we decided to hightail it out of there before people working there reviewed the security film. We were clearly going way over the speed limit and not following the rules of keeping space between the karts. After the shock wore off, belly laughter broke out. Laughter activates your brain and has been proven to help heal broken connections, and there was no doubt that healing began to flow on that race track. I will never forget the looks on all of the little Shaws' faces. I think they were just as shocked as we were but super relieved to know we were all okay and laughing.

Next, we celebrated our survival with a sweet celebration at the Sugar Factory. We had the server bring out a huge diabetic-coma-sized desert for Jeff with a big sparkling torch on top to usher in a new year of life. He got up and danced like no one was watching, even though the whole restaurant was on their feet cheering him on. It did my heart good to see him smiling, laughing, and feeling so celebrated. Not too long after, Dom and Diana got up and started dancing salsa. The looks of embarrassment on their girls' faces was priceless. I will never forget the joy we all felt that night and the hope for a beautiful restoration of our friendship and family.

Carrington's birthday followed at the end of September, and the whole family was in attendance—even my father-in-law made a surprising appearance. That summer leading up to Care's birthday, Jeff and

I decided to take him out to our favorite sushi place for Father's Day. We wanted to show him unconditional love, grace, and mercy despite how he had mistreated us over the years.

From what we knew at the time, he was all alone after his wife's passing, and we couldn't imagine how he was functioning without her. Pam had done so much for him and the ministry, and she had softened his brashness to society as much as she could. We had ironclad boundaries and zero expectations from him other than to show him kindness and compassion. We always held on to hope that his heart could change but released the weight of trying to aid in his transformation.

During that time, God was allowing us to see him with different eyes. We had done the work to forgive, grieve, accept, and heal. He no longer had the power to make us angry, frustrated, or feel rejected. However, we weren't naive and knew that we could never open certain parts of our lives to him ever again for our protection and his. At Care's party, he was on his best behavior, and we even got a full family photo to commemorate the momentous occasion. This was the first time since Pam passed that her whole family was together under the same roof and being pleasant toward one another.

That Christmas, the three older Shaw brothers and their families took a very spontaneous trip to Asheville, North Carolina, to celebrate Christmas—tWe would soon realize that spontaneous decisions become awesome adventures. It was nice to get away during that time of year because the holiday season brought memories of deep sadness of Pam passing right before Christmas. I think at that point in time, we were all ready to start moving forward, mending our relationships, and creating some incredible memories with the next generation of Shaws.

My parents joined us on the trip as well, and another family we knew, the Ashbys, had rented a cabin in the mountains. We all had a blast exploring the beauty of the Blue Ridge mountains. We went on adventurous, overachieving, and slightly dangerous hikes, ate delicious food, visited the beautiful Biltmore, went to Christmas Eve worship at the Biltmore Church, scaled Chimney Rock, and took all the Shaws skiing.

What went down on that mountain could be a chapter of this book all by itself. Dominick and I were the only ones who knew how to ski, so we were in charge of keeping all the big and little Shaws safe. No pressure there! We started by taking everyone out on the bunny slopes to get skiing 101 down. The most important lesson was teaching them how to stop in a pizza wedge formation (a triangle shape you make with your skis to slow down). It looked promising, based on the fact that everyone was athletic and very determined to conquer the mountain.

Off we went on the ski lifts, wrongly directed to go up the blue slopes instead of the beginner green. It was a scary and dicey ride down the mountain, with Shaws dropping like flies left and right. At one point, we thought our niece Victoria had dropped off the side of the mountain. There were not many barriers set up to protect the skiers. It became pretty clear that there would be little skiing for me that day and more rescue missions. The good news is that we all made it down alive and ready to go back up again to conquer the mountain.

One thing about Shaws is that they don't quit or give up easily. Where there's a will, there's a way! Trust me, there is always a way. I love that relentless, resilient, and determined way of our family. It's helped us to overcome some serious setbacks, disappointments, and losses in life.

Now, it was time for us to return to the ski lift. Diana and her third daughter, Isabela, were in position to get picked up by the lift. All of a sudden, the young man operating the lift sped up the pace of the chairs coming around, and Diana's ski got caught, throwing her down off the lift, with her ski stuck in the chair. Isabela had gotten scooped up in the chair in front of Diana's and went up the mountain by herself. The operator finally hit the button and brought the whole lift to an abrupt stop. Watching this all happen in slow motion was frightening. Thankfully, Diana was okay, but I think that was enough to make her take a break. Not only was this her first time skiing, but she was trying to help her four daughters learn at the same time. The average mom would never take on such a crazy mission. Talk about a scary and exhausting endeavor.

My daughter, Carrington, and her cousin Isabela picked up skiing pretty quickly and wanted to take on the blue slope again. I went skiing with them for a couple runs, and halfway down the mountain, we came across my brother-in-law Jonathan and nephew Alexander. Jonathan came flying past us and threw his ski poles in the air as he was crashing to the ground. A sweet Asian woman skiing nearby dodged one of his poles with an impressive matrix move. Phew, that was a close call! Alexander was like a newborn deer trying to get back up on his skis. He eventually got steady on his skis and was off to the races.

This was also Jeff's first time skiing, and I would be lying if I didn't say that I wasn't a little nervous. He had broken his foot in college while playing football, and the last thing we needed was to drag him down the mountain. At six-two, Jeff is not a petite man.

After all the little Shaws were ready for a break, Jeff, Jonathan, Dominick, and I were ready to conquer the bigger slopes. We got off on the blues and started our way down. Jeff told me to go ahead because he wanted to take his time. Knowing my husband, I realized that he wanted to evaluate every angle, test the winds, and determine the safest path for his run.

When I got about halfway down the mountain, I pulled off to the side and waited for him. I wanted to ski together for the first time and enjoy watching him take it all in. Well, enough time had passed for me to become concerned. I overheard a ski patrol on his radio saying they were looking for someone. I was praying it wasn't Jeff. I started asking if anyone had seen him coming down, describing his appearance, and the ski patrol said that he would check. No sooner than the patrol had gotten on the radio, Jeff came flying down the mountain at ninety miles per hour, like a downhill ski racer in full bent-over position, his poles behind him at a ninety-degree angle. His form was actually quite impressive. I immediately started chasing him, concerned because I knew he was going to have to stop at some point. I was also concerned about how many innocent skiers would be taken out on his way down the mountain.

The next thing I saw was this huge tidal wave of snow and the shocked look on all of the faces of the people waiting at the bottom of the mountain. Jeff was going so fast he couldn't stop with his pizza wedge, so he made the decision to stop by sliding into home plate like he was playing baseball. I was relieved to see he was alive and not fully injured, without hurting any innocent bystanders. We were all laughing so hard that we were crying! Needless to say, Jeff was done skiing after that epic run. Jonathan, Dominick, Kingston, and my nephew Alexander carried on, determined to conquer the black diamonds, and that's exactly what they did. Some of them might've come down halfway on their butts, but they made it down alive and injury free.

That trip, we had many late-night talks over incredible food, played cards, and helped each other process a lot of pain that had gone on over the years. I'm so thankful we said yes and made those unforgettable memories that Christmas of 2019. There wasn't one disagreement, fight, or falling out on that trip. Little did we know that the world would be shutting down in the coming months. That adventure set a new foundation for our family and ushered in a season of restoration. It was a time for peace, unity, and brotherhood and sisterhood to reign for the Shaw Squad like God had always intended it to. You see, we never had a problem having fun together, but there was always a common denominator to bring division and sabotage to that unity. It became very evident that when it was out of the way, we could all clearly see the incredible gifts we had been given in one another.

Making lasting memories

During the year of 2020, in the darkest days of the pandemic, God used the biggest pause of our generation to light a new path of forgiveness, healing, and acceptance in the Shaw family. Every birthday, holiday, and sporting event was an opportunity for us to pursue one another with love. We were the loudest and probably most obnoxious cheering section for all of our nieces and nephews. You always knew my brother-in-law Dominick was present when you heard a loud "Hootie Hoo!" That has become our family call to gather the troops.

We were showing our children a new way of life and establishing a new foundation for generations to come. Trust was being restored through consistently showing up, being present, and always being counted on. Communication became more about listening and not just hearing while thinking about what we wanted to say next. We all had experienced very similar treatment, but each of us processed things differently and at a different pace. We learned to be patient, love, listen, and be that safe space for our family members whenever they were ready.

I lost track of how many confetti cannons and silly string bottles we bought, popped, and sprayed that year. Everyone came to expect this new celebratory way of life and joined right in. Throughout the year, we pulled off some incredible surprises and pranks. We also got the whole Shaw Squad out on the water and introduced them to sailing. It felt so good to infuse our hearts and minds with such fun experiences. Our new reign on life was a big reason to celebrate the victory over the enemy's plans to divide and conquer our family. All of the beautiful new memories we were making helped us release the trauma of the past and embrace the healing gift of the now. The reality of our losses never went away, but it was no longer paralyzing or preventing us from receiving the precious gift we had in one another in the present.

I can't help but think of the joy Mama Shaw must be feeling as she is cheering on her legacy among the great cloud of witnesses. Her greatest legacy and contribution to the kingdom lives on powerfully through the lives of her four sons, daughters-in-love, grandchildren, and all of the people she poured into during her years here on earth. Throughout our family time in 2020, much listening and many genuine apologies were expressed and received. Healing words flowed around the Thanksgiving table as we shared the things we appreciate about one another. We cried, laughed, released a lot of anger and confusion, and poured out unconditional love and respect toward one another. I'm so incredibly thankful that once we decided to take down our walls and preconceived notions of each other, that choice actually ended up giving us permission to love, accept, and enjoy one another right where we are.

God was restoring so many years we had sowed in tears. We grieved the loss of quality time together that we had missed for so long, and we embraced every opportunity to bake, play, laugh, be creative, and cook, all while lavishing our brothers, sisters, nephews, and nieces with TLC. Our family is so dynamic and gifted, and everyone brings so many beautiful, different, unique, and valuable things to our lives. Kingston and Carrington couldn't wait to spend more time with their Shaw uncles, aunts, and cousins. We've all settled into our roles in the family and appreciate what we add to fortify our family tree. I'm excited for the future of our family and to see what God will do in and through our lives as we continue to keep Him at the center and love unconditionally. There are countless milestones to look forward to and be present for in each other's lives.

My encouragement to you is if your family is disenfranchised, broken, toxic, or completely uprooted, surrender it to the Master Gardener. Ask the Lord to give you wisdom and courage to take the first step toward reconciliation. Someone is going to have to take that first step, and it may just need to start with you. When you know to do better, then you should do better. That's how you reign in maturity, humility, and wisdom. Pride can block you from your biggest blessings right in front of your face. Yes, putting yourself out there again after being hurt so badly can feel extremely scary and risky, but when you've taken the time to heal and forgive with boundaries, you enter a safe space to love with acceptance and realistic expectations.

> Pride can block you from your biggest blessings right in front of your face.

Romans 12:18 says, "If possible be at peace with all men." I've come to understand why that concept is expressed that way in the Bible. God knows the stubbornness of His creation, and He also gave us free will. Not everyone will be open to receiving your love, kindness, generosity, and presence in their lives. That leaves you with a decision to make. You either accept it or not. You can allow someone's rejection of your love to make you bitter, angry, and sad, or you can redirect your time, efforts, energy, and heart into a new direction where your love is received with deep appreciation and reciprocated.

Your journey toward healing and forgiveness in your own life might look totally different from that of someone else. You might be in a position where you have to start completely new, and that's okay. Your new reign to change begins with you and your willing heart in the Master's capable hands. Maybe you have a family tree that just needs some pruning and re-shaping. Taking baby steps gives you the courage and confidence to take the next one in repairing your relationships.

You will need to water your family tree with a lot of prayer, patience, kindness, and some spontaneous fun sprinkled in with no agenda. When we get our egos, pride, and hurt out of the way, the Holy Spirit knows how to divinely orchestrate the impossible. He will nourish your roots with joy, laughter, and divine healing to repair what was broken. In 2020, God used intentional fun to heal our family in the most life-giving, spontaneous, and unexpected way, and He can do the same for your family.

Ephesians 3:20 has been one of my favorite scriptures since first walking with the Lord. The meaning of it in my life has manifested in many different facets. "Now, unto Him that is able to do exceedingly, abundantly, above all we can ask or even think according to the power that works in us." Never in a million years would I believe the things that I'm now writing. We never gave up hope on the restoration of our family.

Trusting in the Lord's process rather than our own was truly a faith walk. How God has done it blows my mind and is above and beyond anything I could've ever dreamed of. The best part is that He's just getting started! When we choose to get our hand off the steering wheel and let Jesus take the wheel, He will take us on a road trip of a lifetime. There might be some unexpected roadblocks, pit stops, and breakdowns along the way. But, one thing you can count on is that the journey will make the destination even sweeter. God wants to take you to new spaces and places and show you how much sweeter it is to share all of His beauty with some really special faces.

Family can mean something different to everyone. For us, it means coming home to a safe space where we can take off our armor and be accepted, loved, protected, nurtured, and built back up. Our new Shaw family core values are built on God's unconditional love, trust, humility, kindness, respect, fun, and accountability to fulfill the call on all of our lives to hear the words "Well done, good and faithful servant." It's a new dawn, a new day, and a new reign in the Shaw family.

Reigning in Acceptance

So, whatever became of my father-in-law? That's a great question. That year, our family continued to meet for meals with him and do a lot of listening. It was becoming very clear to us that he was on a diligent search for someone to take care of him. He was extremely vulnerable, lonely, and lost without my mother-in-law. Many crazy things were happening to him, such as getting in a major car accident, falling off a ladder, and having a tree almost fall on him. God was obviously trying to get his attention but to no avail.

He would speak about the many different women he would meet and how he was weighing his options, openly sharing this in front of our children, which was upsetting to them. He showed little focus or interest in their lives and well-being. It got to the point where our children dreaded having dinner with their grandad and listening to his antics.

He had given himself some timeline based upon when his father had remarried after his mom passed. It was like he was trying to mirror his dad's life path in more ways than one. He even got to the point where he started to introduce us to some of these women.

For his birthday that year, the family took him out to dinner to celebrate. We all sat around the table, extending kindness toward him and presenting him with gifts. It was a pretty monumental moment, considering all of the devastation that had taken place over the years.

All of the grandchildren gathered around him and shared their hearts, telling him how much they missed Meemaw and how he would have to bring this potential new wife to meet all of the family so we could help him in this decision-making process. Ultimately, everyone knew it was his decision to make, but it would not be an easy transition for anyone to fully embrace. No one could ever replace Pam and take her place in our hearts and lives. I remember Carrington telling her grandad that whoever he chose would have to show their social security number and get a thorough background check and thumbs up or down from all of the cousins. She was very protective of Meemaw and extended that same sense of protection toward her grandfather.

You have to understand that all of the kids were so young when their Meemaw passed. They all had made special memories with her, baking, playing dress up, snuggling, and receiving her TLC. She was in their lives one day and suddenly gone the next. They all had vivid memories from her wake and funeral. It was a devastating loss for them. They watched their parents grieve and go through much family trauma and drama over the years. That experience will forever be ingrained in their memories. They all miss her and have done their best to keep her memory alive by talking about her.

My father-in-law's decision to bring a new woman into the family was so much more than their grandad choosing a new companion; it was about honoring the life and legacy of their Meemaw, the guys' mom, and his wife of forty-plus years. It was an opportunity for him to finally do things as right as he could.

That summer, it was time to celebrate the youngest Shaw brother and his wife's baby shower. They were having their first child, and it was a boy. Due to COVID-19 restrictions, the location of the shower had to be moved, and the only place available that would accommodate it was our father-in-law's church building. We hadn't been back there since Pam's funeral, and it was not something we were looking forward to. We were excited to celebrate the upcoming arrival of our nephew, but we had so many bad memories attached to that place. The exciting part was that all of the Shaw brothers, sisters, and cousins were going to be in attendance to support. The baby of the Shaw family was now having a baby of his own, and we were all happy about the family growing.

The baby shower was beautiful, and we were having a wonderful time. However, we did notice a woman in attendance who had caused a lot of dissension in the church because of her "interactions" with my father-in-law. Jeff and I had never met this woman before, but we knew that she and her fiancé were at one point being counseled by my in-laws when Pam was still alive. After some crazy things went down between my father-in-law and her, it was strongly encouraged for him not to engage with this woman any longer. It not only put his life in jeopardy (literally), but it wasn't honoring God or the family at all. He had overstepped his boundaries as both a pastor and a counselor to this couple. He knew this woman's vulnerabilities and took advantage of the situation. She obviously had developed a sick infatuation with my father-in-law during these sessions. Her fiancé found them in a car together and about took them out and himself! This man felt betrayed by someone he had trusted with his soul and relationship.

We found out about this incident through a mutual friend and knew that if my father-in-law valued his life, then he had to dissolve this relationship. He was vulnerable and loved the attention he was getting from women in the church. Not only did this woman have some serious issues, but she was also much younger than him and had children of her own. Knowing how he handled his first family, it was scary to think how he would treat those children.

Not one point during the shower did my father-in-law introduce this woman to the family. Some knew her and of her because they had been a part of the church more recently.

Another woman came up to Jeff and me to introduce herself to us, and she was very friendly and kind. We appreciated the fact that she took the initiative to come and say hello. After the fact, we found out that she was another woman our father-in-law was leading on. The other lady didn't even make eye contact with us.

When the baby shower was coming to an end, my father-in-law went up to say some words over the parents-to-be. He ended his message by saying, "Be at the church tomorrow for some exciting things that are going to take place." My mother-in law's portrait was still hanging in the entryway of the church where the baby shower was held. My nephew leaned over at the table and said, "Memaw is watching and doesn't like this!"

Not too long after, my father-in-law walked toward the back of the building to his office, and the woman he didn't introduce us to followed after him. He invited all of the grandkids back and handed each of them gifts. It was like he was trying to win them over in front of her and show this woman what a doting grandfather he was. They all came running back to us to share that they saw this lady interacting with their grandad and they were not happy about it. They even called themselves the CSI: Cousins Spy Investigators. Clearly, my father-in-law still had something going on with the woman everyone had strongly advised him to stay far away from.

God always has a way of exposing things. We soon came to find out that this woman was renting a place nearby the home of one of our family members. There were plenty of sightings of my father-in-law's car over at her place and leaving behind the alley after spending the night.

Only a couple months before, he had introduced us to a really nice woman who was a singer and an evangelist. All he ever did was talk about this lady and how amazing she was. We all met her and really liked her. Although, I think we came to the conclusion that she was not going to be his subordinate, stay home, do the laundry, take care of him, and put up with his controlling ways. She was confident in Christ, was known all over the globe, and had a passion to empower women to use their voices in the kingdom. From the outside, it looked like a no-brainer choice for him because they could do ministry together and travel the world. He could finally step away from the role of a pastor and let that weight go. But, if she ever got the chance to really know my father-in-law, she wouldn't tolerate his treatment for one second.

Somehow, he had charmed her and put on a good show for her to actually entertain the idea of moving to the states and marrying him.

We went out to eat with them, and he was very flirtatious with her, yet she was being very classy and respectful in front of us. You could tell it pumped his ego to have a woman of her caliber interested in him. After he walked her to the car, he made sure to let us all know that she wasn't the one. But, that didn't stop him from continuing to lead her on and making her think she was his only focus.

Not only was it deceptive and dangerous to lead on multiple women at once, but it wasn't godly behavior for a pastor. Who did this guy think he was? I pitied these women who had fallen under his spell. I knew on the other side of marriage was a prison cell waiting for them. To them, he came across doting, caring, and thoughtful. He even paraded these women in front of us like we were all one big, happy family to join in on. Little did they know that we were in the infancy stage of trying to find some type of reconciliation after all of the years of damage he had done with his abusive actions. His behavior was nothing short of a facade that he was using to leverage his buy in power from these women.

Now, back to the baby shower. My father-in-law and this woman ended up leaving out the back door, and the rest of us all stayed to help clean up. The next day, all of the Shaw siblings got together to spend time before the family went out of town. Our sister-in-law who still attended the church with the youngest Shaw brother pulled all of the Shaw sisters aside and said that she needed to tell us something. She explained that during the service that morning, our father-in-law randomly proposed to this woman in front of the church before they collected the tithe and offering. She didn't want us to find out from someone else because it was on a Facebook Live recording.

I wouldn't even call what he did a proper proposal. It was very matter of fact and nonchalant, lacking any ounce of genuine romance or expression of love. We were all shocked and so saddened by his irrational decision, as he did not even have the decency to communicate or introduce this woman when he had his whole family in the room! In that moment, all the meals we had shared together and any ounce of trust we were trying to restore disintegrated. He had been lying to us the whole time.

He had been running around with so many other women but keeping this one his dirty secret behind closed doors. How embarrassing for this woman. He didn't love her; he was just using her to take care of him. He made this choice out of an act of defiance to others who were trying to help him—not out of devotion, love, and adoration for this woman. He hadn't sought wise counsel and didn't have the decency to share his intentions with the family he was trying to reconnect with. If anyone knew of the precarious beginnings of their relationship, they would never encourage him to marry this woman.

Yet, it was done, and we were once again left with the sobering reminder that he hadn't changed at all. He was a liar and a deceiver who would ultimately do whatever he wanted without taking anyone around him into consideration. The family was once again disappointed and saddened by his sabotaging ways and pathological lying.

Within a couple days after this so-called proposal, all of the Shaw sons received a text message with an invitation to their wedding ceremony! What? The majority of us had never even met her, so why would we ever endorse, support, or sanction what God hadn't ordained? God does everything decently and in order. It was now time to share what was on all of our hearts. We were deeply concerned about my father-in-law's irrational decision. How could he think that this union would be blessed and celebrated? God doesn't bless mess! We all expressed our concerns out of genuine care for his soul, well-being, and right motives for getting remarried.

In return, he, in text-book fashion, began trying to put all of us in our places and saying how he and the Shaw guys' mother didn't raise them to be so disrespectful. What did their mother have to do with this selfish, childish, and ungodly decision? Nothing! It was as if he had convinced himself that he had her blessing of this corrupted union. He even went so far as to say that Pam had been preparing this woman to be his wife during these "counseling sessions" they had been having with this woman and her fiancé!

He was no longer talking to children but grown men of God who had a genuine concern for his irrational behavior. That "respect and honor" card was always his go-to power play to try to get some type of submission to his twisted will. Well, it no longer had power over any of us. He then proceeded to let all of us know that this woman was a six-digit earner and would take care of him. Wow! What a great reason to enter into a covenant of marriage before God and your family—not! He wasn't marrying this woman out of love but usury and convenience. It became clear to all of us that he felt justified in his actions and was going to move forward without the blessing of any of us.

Jeff and I received a personal text from his dad imploring us to go out to dinner to meet this woman and decide for ourselves how wonderful she was. Well, it was a little too late for that. We weren't going to be bullied into dismissing his lying and overlook the fact that he had been in a relationship with this woman the whole time without telling us. Not too long after, we received the nastiest, weirdest letter in the mail from Jeff's dad. Enough was enough! He was moving on with his life and didn't care or appreciate any efforts we had made to build a bridge of reconciliation. The bomb had been detonated, and we all had to clean up the aftermath and accept the fact that he wasn't ever going to change.

We had come to understand that you can still love and forgive someone without having them as a part of your life. That past year, we had pursued him, not the other way around. In reality, we had always pursued him from the beginning. Proof of genuine desire is always in the pursuit. In any relationship, to build a solid and safe bridge of reconciliation, two strong footers are needed. In this situation with Jeff's dad, that bridge was always one-sided and unstable. It didn't matter how many times we tried to meet him in the middle. It was always us and everyone else making the sacrificial effort. There was never safe passage because instead of him choosing humility and genuine repentance and taking responsibility, he willfully chose pride, justification, self-pity, and sabotage.

Healthy relationships are win, win, win. They aren't one-sided but should be like a healthy river, free flowing, ever abundant, and life giving. There is often a possessive spirit of ownership over people and relationships. Let's just call it what it really is—modern-day slavery. Human trafficking is on the rise, and it sadly starts within family relationships. In any journey to reconciling a relationship, there comes a point when you know that to do better, you just have to do it. If not, the damage that will be done to you and those close to you could become devastating.

In order to walk and live in your new reign, you have to receive what Jesus Christ already did for you on the cross. He nailed rejection, abuse, hatred, envy, strife, codependency, generational curses, and bondage to the cross. He took *all* of the sin of the world and became it so that we might truly know acceptance, unconditional love, and safety in His presence. You can't just believe that truth; you must receive it, conceive it, embrace it, and ultimately live in it. It's one thing to accept Jesus Christ as your Savior. It's another level in your relationship to make Him Lord over your life and everything in it.

In order to receive this new reign in Christ, He needs to be in control, not you. He guides, orders, and directs your steps on a safe path. When we ask God to direct our path, we have to accept the closed doors as part of His will too. We can sometimes find ourselves trying to play God in other people's lives. In actuality, we're not helping them get their deliverance; we are really enabling them and empowering them to think they are in control and justified in their wrong behavior. Narcissists have a sick, powerful, and convincing way to make you feel sorry for them. That is why so many people stay in toxic relationships much longer than when God originally told them to run.

Trust me, I speak from experience. It took Jeff and me years to finally break free physically, emotionally, and spiritually. We felt guilty and thought God was holding us responsible to help my father-in-law change. We thought we were the chosen ones to bear this cross and suffer in this abusive relationship that God willed for us. Instead of stepping out in obedience and running to our heavenly Father, we ended up running right back into the unsafe arms of our abuser. Some eventually fight their way to freedom, but so many don't make it out and suffer years of psychological, spiritual, emotional, physical, and financial abuse. They slowly fade away and lose their hope and will to fight for freedom.

Psalm 51:6 says, "Behold, thou desirest truth in the inward parts: and in the hidden part thou shall make me know wisdom." There is no celebration in this outcome. Ecclesiastes 1:18 tells us, "For in much wisdom is much grief: and he that increaseth knowledge increaseth sorrow." We can either find ourselves living willfully ignorant of Satan's devices or embrace wisdom and accept the loss of that relationship.

Once you create healthy boundaries and enter into a place of safety, it's much easier to evaluate what that relationship brings to your life. The truth is, we didn't miss the anger, disappointment, devaluing, dissension, and discord. There was now a new place of peace, joy, and security in Christ. It didn't happen all at once, but little by little, we came into a place of acceptance and chose to love my father-in-law from a distance. "Sad" is the word that resonates throughout the Shaw siblings when we think of the outcome. No one wants to feel that way about their natural father. If you willfully choose denial or turn a blind eye, you will continually end up hurt, disappointed, angry, resentful, and bitter, and you will risk setting yourself up to become a victimizer just like them. In order to break this generational curse and reign in newfound freedom, peace, and joy, you actually have to accept the truth, no matter how sad, ugly, and disheartening it is. You also have to release the responsibility and the idea that God is holding you personally responsible to change your abuser.

2 Corinthians 6:10 says, "As sorrowful, yet always rejoicing; as poor yet enriching many; as having nothing and yet possessing all things." I call that the divine balance of life. Our deepest sorrows, sadness, and tragic situations can lead us into the greatest safety net in our Savior's arms. We can be sad yet still hopeful and joyful. From the outside, it may appear that you don't care, are calloused, and have given up on that relationship. However, it just means that you've chosen to accept your value in Christ and abide in the grips of His never-ending grace.

You see, God had answered our prayers for healing and reconciliation in the Shaw family. Everyone who genuinely desired and invested in that new beginning was present and accounted for. In grieving the loss of a relationship, you go through stages of anger, resentment, unforgiveness, bitterness, and regret, and you finally arrive at the stage of acceptance.

Jeff's dad never wanted to love us the way we all deserved and desired to be loved. In fact, he was actually incapable of expressing unconditional love. He chose the path of selfishness, hardheartedness, and pride—not us. He wasn't well but mentally sick and deranged in his own toxic thinking. The truth is, he hadn't been well for a very long time. He had needed serious professional help but didn't want it or didn't think he needed it. No one was capable of speaking truth in love into his life. He was convinced that everyone was the enemy and that no one really wanted to help him. We weren't some professed and labeled prodigal sons and daughters. The reality was, we were finally at home, safe and accepted in our heavenly Father's arms.

Through the years, any time we would reaffirm our boundaries with Jeff's dad, he would ask Jeff, "Why don't you just change your last name to Phillips?" That was my maiden name. We always thought that was such a childish and foolish statement. This situation was never about

Jeff forsaking his family heritage for mine. Our marriage was a joining and blending of two family trees, traditions, and legacies. I loved my new last name and the man I married who had carried it his whole life. Our last names are bigger than our first names. My first name, Courtney, is about me. My new last name is about us, Jeff and I, and the legacy we're creating for our children, family, and others.

However, when I got married, my deep family roots didn't go away; they came with me. They helped mold and shape me into the person I am today, and they became engrafted to Jeff's the day we signed our marriage covenant. God brought us together to break generational curses on both sides of our families, along with anything toxic attached to the last name. God's unconditional love now reigns, and it waters the roots of our family tree to create a new living legacy.

The Shaw last name originally belonged to a slave owner and caused generations of family members to suffer unimaginable abuse, bondage, and trauma at the hands of greedy and wicked victimizers. It could be justifiable to take that pain, rejection, and torment and project it onto others for generations to come. But, in order to reverse the curse, the buck had to stop with us! Would the legacy attached to the Shaw name continue to be one of hatred, oppression, and abuse? Would we allow the toxic reminiscence of slavery and racism to seep down into the roots of the family tree and poison future generations? Where there was once rejection, there is now acceptance, safety, and a new standard of life.

The final stage of forgiveness is acceptance. This stage doesn't mean you've lost hope or faith, or that you've quit on that person in your life. Rather, you've finally come to accept that it is not your responsibility to change that person. However, it is your responsibility to guard your heart and your family. I didn't say harden your heart or become cynical, jaded, or mean. No, I said guard it—and with ironclad boundaries. It is your responsibility to show others how you deserve to be treated. Boundaries do not end relationships. Boundaries create more sustainable and meaningful relationships. When you understand this key concept, setting and enforcing boundaries becomes so much easier.

Abusive relationships are not okay in any way, shape, or fashion—physical, emotional, psychological, spiritual, or financial. Walking in truth is not just about what God says of you but about the reality of your life's circumstances. Admit, own, and accept what you went through. You don't have to be ashamed, embarrassed, or regretful. God allowed those experiences to make you better and a more-polished version of who God intended you to be. Perspective is everything. My prayer for many years was, "Lord, change my circumstances or change me." Truth be told, most of the time, God ends up changing us through trials and tribulations, hardships, and relationships. He will make a way of escape or give us hinds feet to leap over the treacherous terrain of our trauma and empower us to roam freely in a new, broad land of endless opportunities in Him.

> Boundaries do not end relationships. Boundaries create more sustainable and meaningful relationships. When you understand this key concept, setting and enforcing boundaries becomes so much easier.

Relationships are the currency of the kingdom and so worth investing your time, talents, and treasures in. Don't buy into the idea that all people are dangerous, not trustworthy, or out to hurt you. You will soon realize that on the other side of your bondage is a world full of people who have gone through similar or worse circumstances than you. There are countless others who have chosen to surrender to Jesus the debilitating pain from their toxic relationships and receive a beautiful new beginning with greater wisdom, compassion, realistic expectations, and healthy boundaries.

If you are currently in a relationship that is abusive and you feel unsafe, please reach out for help by calling a counselor, a local church, or friends you can trust. The number for the National Domestic Violence Hotline is 1-800-799-7233. By reaching out to your local church or community center for resources, you can receive help in a safe place, find wise counsel, and start your journey to healing.

KINGDOM (QUEST)IONS:

1. Are you currently in a relationship that makes you feel unsafe, devalued, disrespected, or demoralized? If so, how long have you been in this relationship?

_____

_____

_____

2. If you have broken free from this relationship, are you still dealing with unresolved trauma? Do you need healing?

_____

_____

_____

3. How is your relationship with your immediate family?

_____

_____

_____

4. What are some major issues you need to address and work on in your close relationships?

_____

_____

_____

5. Who do you consider to be your close friends who can you count on to help you walk out your deliverance and healing from toxic relationships?

_____

_____

_____

6. In what relationships do you still need to establish healthy boundaries?

_____

_____

_____

7. What are some toxic family traits that you want to be free from so that you do not have to carry them on to the next generation?

_____

_____

_____

8. If you are in a place of wholeness, who around you needs help, prayer, and support to become free from unhealthy, abusive, or toxic relationships?

_____

_____

_____

9. How is your personal relationship with God? Do you trust Him and believe in His promises for your life? If not, are you angry with God?

_____

_____

_____

10. What are your non-negotiables in a relationship? Write them down and share them with someone who will hold you accountable to walk them out.

_____

_____

_____

11. Is there anyone in your life that you are holding unforgiveness toward? Remember, forgiving is not forgetting but releasing your anger toward the person who hurt you.

_____

_____

_____

KINGDOM TRUTHS

"If possible be at peace with all men."–Romans 12:18

"Mark the perfect man for the end is always peace."–Psalm 37:37

"Though one may be overpowered, two can defend themselves. A cord of three strands is not quickly broken."–Ecclesiastes 4:12

"So in everything, do to others what you would have them do to you, for this sums up the Law and the Prophets."–Matthew 7:12

"May the Lord make your love increase and overflow for each other and for everyone else, just as ours does for you."–1 Thessalonians 3:12

"As iron sharpens iron, so one person sharpens another."–Proverbs 27:17

"Am I now trying to win the approval of human beings, or of God? Or am I trying to please people? If I were still trying to please people, I would not be a servant of Christ."–Galatians 1:10

"How good and pleasant it is when God's people live together in unity!"—Psalm 133:1

"Dear friends, let us love one another, for love comes from God. Everyone who loves has been born of God and knows God."—1 John 4:7

"Do not be misled: 'Bad company corrupts good character.'"—1 Corinthians 15:33

KINGDOM DECLARATION

On this ____ day of _____, I, _____, choose to receive my priceless value and worth in Christ. I acknowledge that I am worthy of being in a place of safety, love, wholeness, and freedom. I choose to fix my eyes on Jesus and focus on growing my vertical relationship with Him, understanding that this will affect my horizontal relationships with others in my life. I will commit to embark on the healing journey to address, accept, and release any unresolved relational trauma. I will walk in discernment, wisdom, respect, humility, and kindness toward others. I will establish healthy boundaries and realistic expectations in all of my relationships. I will open myself up to be loved and love again. It's a new dawn, a new day, and a new reign in my relationships at home, in the workplace, in my community, and in my church.

In Jesus's name, amen.

Chapter Eight

REIGN IN LEGACY

◦◊◦

"Know your roots so you can bear much fruit." – Courtney Dawn Shaw

"You did not choose me, but I chose you and appointed you that you should go and bear fruit and that your fruit should abide, so that whatever you ask the Father in my name, he may give it to you." –John 15:16

Other than having a past, another thing we all have in common in this life is the surety of death. We will all die one day, but will we choose to really wake up and live? Will we choose to selfishly get all we can get for ourselves, or will we choose to live intentionally with our legacy in mind? Everyone is leaving a legacy, whether they realize it or not.

Let's define and break down the meaning of a legacy so we can get a better understanding of how to live daily with ours in mind. A legacy is:

1. A gift by will, especially of money or other personal property.
2. Something transmitted by or received from an ancestor or predecessor or from the past.
3. Something carried over from an earlier time, such as your life's work, gifts, and talents.

Legacy focuses on what will endure. It's about passing on things of lasting value to those who will live on after us. Your legacy can be your faith, your wisdom, your life experiences, your business, or even your family traditions around the holidays. It can also be your gifts or passions, such as your gift for serving others, your creativity, your education, your craftsmanship, your cooking skills, or your love for music or writing or travel.

Will your legacy be one of regret, bitterness, excuses, pain, and blame on what previous generations did or didn't do? Or, will it be one founded on God's truth, healing love, forgiveness, acceptance, and freedom in His Son Jesus? Will you allow change to begin with you? The very fact that you are reading this book shows that you are ready for a new reign and to intentionally bring new meaning to your family name.

> **Will your legacy be one of regret, bitterness, excuses, pain, and blame on what previous generations did or didn't do? Or, will it be one founded on God's truth, healing love, forgiveness, acceptance, and freedom in His Son Jesus?**

Like Esther in the Bible, maybe you were chosen to break generational curses and change the trajectory and future of your family tree. Esther 4:14 says, "For if you remain silent at this time, relief and deliverance for the Jews will arise from another place, but you and your father's family will perish. And who knows but that you have come to your royal position for such a time as this?" God has called you out, chosen you, and anointed you for such a time as this, as a son or daughter, to surrender fear and step out in faith to attain a new reign and way of life. Esther was so focused on the survival of her people's future generations that she was willing to perish if it meant the guarantee of their safety and succession.

When the pain to stay the same becomes greater than the pain to change, then and only then will you commit to change. When we truly surrender the pain of the past and present and lay it at the feet of Jesus, we can rise up, reign, and shine in His strength to conquer the prison of past generations. We can leave the bad, learn from it, take the good, and forge ahead into a beautiful future where there is grace, truth, and meaning in our moments.

I think it's so important to remember how you started. God forbid we ever forget the pain, disappointments, failures, setbacks, and rejections we have endured in the past. If we do, we are in jeopardy of repeating this kind of demoralizing behavior. But, there comes a time, which I believe is right now, to start focusing on how you finish. Philippians 3:12 says, "But one thing I do, forgetting those things which are behind and reaching forward to those things which are ahead. I press toward the goal for the prize of the upward call of God in Christ Jesus."

I don't know about you, but when I stand before the Lord alone and time has become a thing of the past, I long to hear the words "Well done, good and faithful servant; you have been faithful over a few things, I will make you ruler over many things. Enter into the joy of your lord." That is when our eternal reign with Jesus begins and all sorrow, sadness, grief, and pain grow strangely dim in the light of His glory and grace. It's time to wake up and dream new dreams and take the limits off what God wants to do in and through your life that can live on for generations after you've gone to reign with the King of kings. That is called a living legacy. What will you allow to live on?

Years ago, when I first started walking with the Lord, this song by Nichole Nordeman was circulating on the radio. It sowed some serious seeds of intentionality and helped me realize life is about living for so much more than myself.

I don't mind if you've got something nice to say about me
And I enjoy an accolade like the rest
And you could take my picture and hang it in a gallery
Of all the who's-who's and so-and-so's
That used to be the best at such and such
It wouldn't matter much
I won't lie, it feels alright to see your name in lights
We all need an "atta boy" or "atta girl"
But in the end I'd like to hang my hat on more besides
The temporary trappings of this world
I want to leave a legacy
How will they remember me?
Did I choose to love?
Did I point to you enough?
To make a mark on things
I want to leave an offering
A child of mercy and grace
Who blessed your name unapologetically
And leave that kind of legacy
I don't have to look too far or too long awhile
To make a lengthy list of all that I enjoy
It's an accumulating trinket and a treasure pile
Where moth and rust, thieves and such
Will soon enough destroy
I want to leave a legacy
Not well-traveled, not well-read
Not well-to-do, or well-bred
Just want to hear instead
"Well done, good and faithful one"
I want to leave a legacy
I don't mind if you've got something nice to say about me

Do I want accolades, accomplishments, titles, degrees, and affluence to take precedence over the power of salvation, service, and a life surrendered to my Lord and Savior? The blood of Jesus that was shed on Calvary over two thousand years ago still washes sin as white as snow. It was the perfect sacrifice for the atonement of mankind's sinful nature. There is blessing in the blood—DNA is a roadmap to reveal deeper purpose and meaning of life.

It's also important to understand our natural bloodline and how that affects the legacy we're carrying on and leaving on this earth. In order to bear much good fruit moving forward, you must take time to get to know your family roots. Our family history has keys to unlock our present and give us a deeper purpose as we reframe and build a beautiful future.

When I had my first meeting with my publishing team, my editor, who happens to have the name of Courtney as well, shared something so simple yet profound. I felt led to bring to our meeting my great-grandmother Hannah's handwritten journal from over seventy-nine years ago and a book of poems written by my maternal grandmother, Mimi. Courtney looked at me and said, "There is so much power in the blood." At first, I thought she was just referring to power in the blood of Jesus, and I said, "Amen!" But, she added to that by saying, "Courtney, it's in your blood to be a writer." This is part of the generational blessing passed down from previous generations. It really brought a sense of coming full circle in my purpose.

Never dismiss certain inclinations, desires, skills, talents, and tendencies you may feel. My writing journey really began when my mom gave me a blank journal years ago, and here I am thirty-plus years later, flowing in my calling to document the goodness and faithfulness of God for future generations. The legacy lives on and is like a golden thread that ties one generation to the next. Words help create a living tapestry that will tell a story of redemption, restoration, and resilience of our family lineage for many generations to come.

Your roots help ground you during life's storms and act as an anchor to hold you when the winds of adversity come to try and tear you down. Your roots nurture an internal fortitude that holds you together when it seems like everything and everyone around you is falling apart.

Taking time to learn your family history is such an important part of the healing journey. When we go to doctor appointments, we are given a questionnaire that asks about our family health history. Why do doctors care about health issues or diseases our parents and grandparents dealt with? They are looking for genetic diseases; diabetes, heart disease, cancer, and other forms of sickness can be passed down in the blood. When we know there is a history of disease, it can help our doctors put a preventative course of treatment in place before the disease takes over in our bodies.

For example, if you had a parent who suffered from heart disease, then maybe you would be more cautious with how you manage stress in life. You would become more intentional about what you eat, exercise more consistently, and be faithful in getting your heart checked annually for any issues. You wouldn't be taken by surprise or left in the dark but enlightened to take proactive measures to care for your heart.

It is not only important to know our physical health history; we should be aware of our spiritual, mental, emotional, relational, and financial health history as well. God doesn't want us ignorant concerning Satan's devices. There are generational curses He wants to expose, reveal, and break in our family tree in order for us to thrive and bear life-giving fruit for generations to come.

So, what are generational curses, and how do we break them in our lives? According to The Gospel Coalition, a "generational curse describes the cumulative effect on a person of things that their ancestors did, believed, or practiced in the past, and a consequence of an ancestor's actions, beliefs, and sins being passed down."[11] Our family history and baggage impacts who we are as people, whether we like it or not. You may consider your family a blessing or a burden because of the long history of negative traits they've passed down. Examples of generational curses are divorce, domestic violence, abuse, mental and physical sickness, money problems, religiosity, incarceration, and more.

The good news is that while your family history can affect you, you are not bound by these generational curses. God gave you free will. Therefore, you have the choice to either continue to follow in the footsteps of your ancestors and pass on these curses to your children or, with great intentionality and diligence, end these curses over your life and future. You get to decide if the generational curses continue or end with you.

There is so much freedom in breaking a generational curse and creating a healthier relationship for yourself, the people you love, and the generations to follow. You can be a trailblazer by stepping out in faith and giving yourself grace to forge a new path for your family. Everything will be different and you will face some challenges, but you can keep pressing forward knowing you will make the path clear for future generations. Generations from now, you could be traced in your family tree as the one who decided to be a way maker, risk taker, door buster, chain breaker, shift maker, and curse destroyer. Do you want future generations to thank you, or say to you, "I can't believe you did that," or "Why did you allow that to continue?"

> Do you want future generations to thank you, or say to you, "I can't believe you did that," or "Why did you allow that to continue?"

I watched one of the most powerful messages on legacy by Brian Bullock, and I suggest you watch it too. It was named the best motivational message of 2020 on YouTube. In the message, Bullock shares a story about a time when he rented a car while on a business trip. There were only two choices from the car rental center, and he chose an SUV. As soon as he got in the vehicle, he could tell the person who rented it before him had smoked in it. However, because he was in a rush, he chose to just take the vehicle and deal with the smell. There were no other issues with the car, so he went on his way. At the end of his trip, he returned the vehicle, and a week after he got home, he was sent a bill for over $300.00, stating that the SUV smelled like cigarette smoke when he returned it. He picked up the phone and spoke with the manager and explained that it had smelled like smoke when he got the car. The people at the company didn't care about his story and told him, "All we know is that when you turned it in, it reeked of cigarette smoke, and you had to pay the fine."[12]

Isn't that so much like some of our lives? We often find ourselves paying the price for what someone else did! Somebody didn't care about legacy when they took your social security number and started purchasing things that now show up on your credit report and prevent you from buying your first home or vehicle. Now, you are responsible for cleaning up a mess that you didn't even make! Some of us are living in the stench of what was passed down to us from previous generations. Thank God Jesus paid it all on the cross and we are no longer slaves and debtors to the poor choices of someone else. That is the living hope we have to break free.

What are you passing down to your future generations? Blessings or curses? Are you living with the next generation in mind, or are you living carelessly and selfishly? Don't hoard information. Don't be the only one in your family tree who knows how to invest in real estate, cook your famous recipes, or have a godly and successful marriage. Information should be passed down for succession. Legacies are built now but experienced later, so we must either make excuses or make changes!

Consider becoming an investigator for your family. There is one in every family who takes the time to go on a quest to learn about previous ancestors, who they were, how they lived, where they came from, how they treated others, what they did for a living, and what they believed. On the Phillips side of our family, my Aunt Sue did some extensive ancestral research and documented her findings in binders for all of the family members to have. I've learned some really interesting things from our ancestors, and that knowledge has helped give me clarity.

I come from a strong lineage of pioneers and trailblazers, and many came from Ireland, Sweden, Germany, and England and lived under religious oppression, longing for a life of freedom in America. Jeff's aunts on his father's side documented their family history in a book with pictures, and we have learned that Jeff's ancestors survived slavery, oppression, and abuse for generations but eventually broke free and started a new reign in their family tree. Do you see a running theme here? In both of our families, there was a deep longing and fight for freedom. Perhaps that is why Jeff and I would go on to write a curriculum called *FIT 2B FREE*.

Today, there are so many informational websites and tools in place to help you do your own research. Ancestry.com actually takes your DNA sample and provides you with a report of your genetic mapping and where your ancestors came from. They've built a database of people from all over the world to connect family members and relatives. A friend of ours named Patrice even found her biological father after living her whole life without knowing the man who gave her life. They were reunited and now have a beautiful relationship. There is no questioning their relation. She is a spitting image of her dad, and so is her son. Patrice had always felt a huge void in her life that only her father could fill. Now, she's a self-professed daddy's girl in her fifties. It's never too late to seek out the answers to questions you've had your whole life.

Let's start your own ancestral quest by doing a genogram of your family history. Try going back at least four generations. This will include your parents, grandparents, and great-grandparents. If you can go beyond that, great. The key is to get started with your biological parents. Recognizing a generational curse is the first step in the fight to end it. Genograms can be freeing because they show that you're not the only one in your family who has struggles with specific issues. They are designed to bring light to the darkness of generational curses and help you walk forward in the light of hope and healing. Making your own genogram will help you understand how your family's behavior impacts your own relationships with your significant others, friends, or relatives.

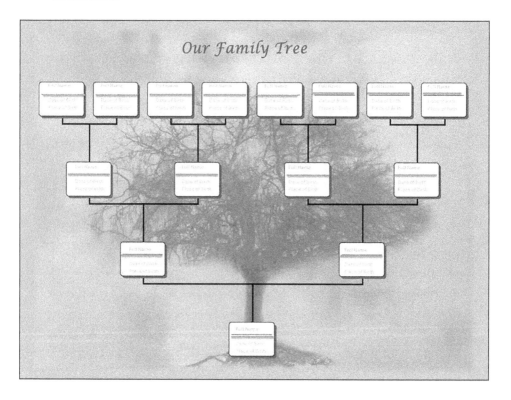

Next, create a list of questions to ask your family members. These can be any questions that help you understand more about your spiritual, physical, mental, and financial history. Here are some examples: Did you have cancer? Did you battle with depression? Did you have an anger problem? Were you ever molested? Were you abused mentally or physically? Did you struggle with finances? Did you go through a divorce? Did you lose a child? Did you attend church faithfully? Did you have a good relationship with your parents and grandparents?

Were you addicted to drugs, alcohol, or pornography? Was there adultery in your marriage?

While asking these questions, be prepared to be met with some resistance. Some previous generations consider asking personal questions about family members offensive, rude, out of order, disrespectful, or dishonorable. This is usually because the answers to your questions will expose shame, guilt, regret, embarrassment, pain, trauma, and more. Some people literally block out certain traumas for survival, and it's often not until something triggers that memory or someone asks about it that it will get unearthed, exposed, and brought to the surface. When your heart is in the right place, God will make a way and move on the heart of someone to share the truth concerning your family history. Sometimes a person is just waiting to be asked. Your questions may not be about just your own freedom but your ability to help another family member release years of held-in secrets. Lies and secrets are like cancers in the soul. They eat away what is good and leave behind only destruction.

> **Lies and secrets are like cancers in the soul. They eat away what is good and leave behind only destruction.**

Before and during this journey, pray for peace, clarity, healing, comfort, and closure in your family. Be patient and keep in mind that many more things may come to light than you expected. This process can be healing, but before the curses can be broken, you may endure a period of grief or anger because of brokenness in your family. This is all a part of the process. There is no perfect family, no matter how much it may appear like it on the outside. It takes courage to confront, expose, have the hard conversations, and come to a point of acceptance of what happened in the lives of our loved ones.

Throughout this process, I would recommend speaking with as many family members as you can. Everyone has a different perspective of what happened in the past, and each person can give you a different angle to reveal a more realistic view of the generational dysfunctional behavior. Remember, you are seeking out *the* truth. Some people can lie to themselves so much that the lie can become their truth.

During the pandemic, one of our cousins on the Shaw side set up a family Zoom call. A bunch of aunts, uncles, and cousins jumped on. The younger generation began to ask questions, and we learned a lot in that short period of time about the health history of the family and much more. You could tell certain family members were starting to feel uncomfortable and thought the questions were too invasive, but that's to be expected. The intent was never to bring shame or blame but to get a better understanding of the family history so that our generation could make informed decisions and changes for the better.

That is healthy succession. Each generation should get better with time. Lessons should be learned, traditions should be passed down, lies should be exposed, and toxic behaviors should be changed for the better. Previous generations were never allowed to ask questions because it was considered disrespectful. Our generation has been on a quest to break curses, often being met with great opposition to blaze new trails, but the next generation will demand truth. They have access to so much information in the palm of their hand. Not only will they find the truth and verify it, but they will be forced to prove previous generations liars. There is no greater accountability than having to look your children in the eyes and give answers to their questions and give an account for what you chose not to confront.

Now that you've been able to identify, address, and break generational curses, it's time to replace them with truth, life, and blessing.

LET BLESSINGS REIGN

Let's talk about activating generational blessings in your life. There is so much power within spoken blessings. Proverbs 18:21 tells us, "Death and life *are* in the power of the tongue: and they that love it shall eat the fruit thereof." Our words have great influence in the lives of those around us, and spoken blessings can bring hope, healing, affirmation, encouragement, and direction to our families, friends, and others. Many people begin experiencing deepening relationships, healing, and spiritual encouragement when they discover the power of spoken blessings.

On the other hand, there is nothing more destroying than a family member or someone we look up to using words as weapons in our lives. I can remember for years being tormented by the spirit of fear attached to curses spoken over our family. It took time, daily effort, and intentionality to reverse those curses. Although we knew in our hearts and minds those words of death weren't true, they still sowed seeds of doubt, rejection, and fear.

2 Corinthians 10:5 says, "Casting down imaginations, and every high thing that exalteth itself against the knowledge of God, and bringing into captivity every thought to the obedience of Christ." Continually taking the lies and curses spoken over you and lining them up to the truth of what God says about you can be an overwhelming and exhausting effort at times. Yet, the seeds of doubt, fear, rejection, worthlessness, and anxiety can take root and hold you hostage the rest of your life if you don't pick up your weapons and fight back.

John 8:32 says, "You shall know the truth, and the truth shall make you free." Your breakthrough may not come in an instant or overnight, but the truth of God's Word always prevails. You can find hope, strength, and comfort knowing that there is light at the end of the tunnel of family curses. As you raise up a new standard and way of life, the reign of deceit, lies, wickedness, dissension, and division will be dethroned. Unity, peace, provision, and divine purpose will prevail in your family tree for generations to come. Despite how real the lies can feel, you have the authority to activate faith in God's Word over your life.

Conquering family curses is a battle that ultimately belongs to the Lord. Remember, He goes before you, and in the end, you win! Declare with your mouth out loud that Jehovah Nissi—our God of Victory—waves His banner over the battlefield of your family drama and trauma.

When we're addressing sickness in our family tree, we can't just uproot, run, and replant the whole tree and think that the past toxicity and pain will just disappear. We have to get down to the seed of the situation and bring it into the light to be dealt with.

I will never forget a story my mother-in-law shared during a message she ministered called "No Greater Love" when I first started going to their church. She shared her journey about getting to the root of why her dad would always hide presents and not open and receive gifts given to him on special occasions. He ended up with a closet full of unopened presents from years of celebrations. During a visit to the hospital when her dad was dying, she crawled into bed next to him and asked him why he had never opened the presents. Her whole life, she had battled with the feelings of rejection because he never received the gestures of love she had given him. He finally began to share with her about something that had tormented him his whole life. When he was younger, he was left in charge of caring for his siblings. One of them tragically passed away under his supervision. He never forgave himself and went his whole life feeling unworthy of any love. In that moment, my mother-in-law began to minister to him about the greatest love of all in Jesus. He accepted Christ as his Lord and Savior and finally received the most precious gift of all—forgiveness and salvation for his soul.

> When we're addressing sickness in our family tree, we can't just uproot, run, and replant the whole tree and think that the past toxicity and pain will just disappear. We have to get down to the seed of the situation and bring it into the light to be dealt with.

Pam always loved roses and had a rosebush in the front of their home. At one point, the rosebush was thriving and flourishing with many roses budding forth. Suddenly, it started getting sick and choked by weeds. She kept pulling the weeds up by the roots, but they kept coming back with vengeance. It wasn't until she treated the soil with pesticides that the seeds of the roots actually died, allowing her beloved rosebush to thrive once again. What a clear visual to seek out, search out, and destroy the cause of the sickness and toxicity in our lives.

Recently, my husband, Jeff, bought a rosebush and planted it by our front door to honor his mom's living legacy. To this day, it's thriving and blooming. That rosebush serves as a beautiful reminder that we must continually allow our lives to be pruned by the Master Gardener so that future generations can bloom beautifully in the midst of the thorns of life. Pam is laid to rest in the Garden of Hope, and it serves as a powerful visual that God still turns the graves in our lives into flourishing gardens.

Deuteronomy 7:9 shares God's faithfulness toward us living in the present and toward future generations in our family tree. It says, "Know therefore that the Lord thy God, He is God, the faithful God, who keepeth covenant and mercy with them that love Him and keep His commandments to a thousand generations." On this quest to bring healing, unity, and wholeness in your family tree, you will need to take time to reflect, investigate, identify, track change, pray, seek support, and celebrate a new reign in your family. Surrender your time clock to your Savior and allow Him to make everything beautiful in His time, as Ecclesiastes 3:11 declares

Reigning in Gratitude

So, in summary, there is power in the spoken blessings over your life, family, and others. Be intentional in every way and in every day to make it your business to be a blesser. Pray over others; speak blessings out loud for others to hear; write them in cards, texts, emails; and show blessing by embracing one another with kindness, tenderness, and love. People don't know how much you care until you show them how much you care. Never assume that those around you know that you appreciate them.

A very simple yet powerful way to bless others is by expressing your gratitude. Let people in your life know how much you appreciate them, how special they are, and how valuable they are in the eyes of God. To me, there is nothing more genuine and sentimental than receiving a handwritten note from someone. In the day of texting, emailing, and social media, a handwritten expression shows extra effort of care. I treasure, cherish, and keep all of my handwritten notes of encouragement and appreciation. What a beautiful way to declare blessing over someone's life. I love going to the mailbox and receiving a special handwritten note from certain people in my life. We even have a special lady on the Shaw side of the family, Aunt Hattie, who has made it her business to send all of the Shaws a handwritten birthday card through the years. Aunt Hattie has never missed a birthday and always made beautiful crocheted blankets for all of the babies. I pray I can take on that same level of love, care, and expression toward others as she has.

Never ever forget how powerful and healing your words can be. Proverbs 16:24 says, "Pleasant words are as a honeycomb, sweet to the soul, and health to the bones." Reigning in gratitude is a daily decision to receive the gift of grace and extend it toward others. Numbers 6:24-26 offers us a powerful, life-giving promise to speak over others: "The Lord bless you and keep you; The LORD make His face shine upon you; the Lord turn His face towards you and give you peace." The song called The Blessing written by Cody Carnes and Kari Jobe declares these simple yet powerful words over your family. May His favor be upon you and a thousand

> **Never ever forget how powerful and healing your words can be.**

generations, and your family and your children and their children, and their children. Amen.

It is our royal, rightful duty as children of the King to declare and speak blessing over our lives, spouses, children, family, friends, co-workers, church, community, and world. How would the atmosphere shift in our hearts, homes, and world around us if we chose to reverse the curse and activate blessing?

REIGN WITH THE END IN MIND

Another big way to live legacy minded is to take the time to get your house in order. There is something so powerful and freeing about living backwards. How will you reign? That was the question that came to mind as I was staring at my mother-in-law's rose-gold casket being lowered into the ground.

Not too long after my mother-in-law passed, my parents went on a personal mission to get all of their final wishes in place. They chose their final resting places and paid for everything in advance. Jeff, the kids, and I went over to the cemetery with them to see where they would be laid to rest. They both chose to be cremated and have their remains placed in a beautiful outdoor mausoleum in the Garden of the Apostles.

I remember Carrington looking at the space where their urns were to be placed, and she said, "How are Pa and Ma Bear going to fit in those tiny boxes?" Wow! Out of the mouth of babes. Her question led to us educating her on the process of cremation versus being laid to rest in a casket and buried. It was a pretty intense conversation to have with a six-year-old. It really made me realize that we need to wake up and live outside of the box before we ultimately end up in one. There's nothing more sobering than knowing where your earthly remains will be. That moment really awakened us all to start living and appreciating one another even more. It brought a humbling sense of the fragility of life, yet also a huge sense of relief knowing what they wanted.

I know life can get busy and the thought of addressing your final wishes, arrangements, will, investments, and life insurance policies can be overwhelming and daunting. Thankfully, my parents also spent a lot of time putting all of their documentation and their financial house in order so that if anything happened to them, we would know where to find everything. They witnessed firsthand how stressful it was for the family to make such tough decisions in the face of extreme grief and tragic circumstances. When you suddenly lose a loved one and are faced with making all of their final arrangements without even knowing their wishes, it makes the process even more overwhelming. It can also become a cause for family arguments, when the focus should be on celebrating the life of your loved one. When your family doesn't know your desires, it puts a huge burden on them to try to make decisions that would honor you.

Proverbs 13:22 says, "A good man leaves an inheritance to his children's children, but the sinner's wealth is laid up for the righteous." Do you want to leave an inheritance of frustration and anger, or one of deep appreciation and celebration? You might not be in a financial position to put all of your arrangements in place, but you can start by creating a legacy drawer. What is a legacy drawer? Basically, a legacy drawer is where you house all of your family's important information so it can be easily found in the event that something happens to you. I know it's not a pleasant subject to talk about, but when you look at it as a tool, you realize how incredibly valuable it will be in helping your family in a difficult situation.

No matter what your age or the size of your family, you should really make it a point to set up a legacy drawer. Having a drawer with all of your important papers in a central location will help ensure everything necessary remains intact. You might even want to invest in a fireproof safe to protect your documents. Creating a legacy drawer is honestly an easy decision to make and can be done as soon as possible. Whether you are single or married, with or without children, you should prepare for your future to ensure vital documents remains with your family. DaveRamsey.com has some great information on how to set up a legacy drawer for your family.

Here are three important steps to establishing your legacy drawer:

Step #1: Decide on a safe location for the legacy drawer. You can place it in a closet, designated piece of furniture, or store it in a safety deposit box at your local bank.

Step #2: Have a family meeting in which you share your heart behind creating your legacy drawer, and reveal its location. During this meeting, you should also review the documentation, as this will help to prepare your family members and give them a chance to ask questions.

Step #3: Decide what to include in the drawer. Make a cover letter addressing all of your family members and your final wishes. Be specific about your medical wishes as well. Do you want to donate your organs in case of an accident? Do you want to be taken off life support? These are important details for your family to know. Include your will and estate plans. Be sure to include the name(s) of your executor and the Power of Attorney if one is assigned. All of your insurance policies for life, health, home, and car insurance should also be included. Additionally, you can create a cover sheet with explanations for quicker access. List contact names, phone numbers, and addresses as well. You will also want to have all information regarding your checking, savings, CD, investments, 401K, loans, mortgage, credit cards, memberships, etc. Anything that involves money that is in your name and/or your spouse's name should be included. In addition, place all legal documents including deeds, social security cards, birth certificates, passports, and titles in the drawer. If you can't include the originals, make sure to have a copy along with the location of the original. Make a list of passwords for all of your major accounts. There is nothing more stressful than trying to become an investigator and crack the code to log into your accounts. You can also get a safety deposit box at your bank to place back up information. Include your monthly budget so that your loved ones will know exactly what bills are paid and need to be paid each month. Keep a copy of two to three years of tax returns. You don't need to include everything, but the main return can be helpful. List exactly what you want for your funeral arrangements. You can get as detailed as you desire. Lastly, the most meaningful part of your legacy drawer will include specific items to be passed down, such as a handwritten letter with your words of blessing and comfort to your loved ones, heirloom pieces, family recipes, jewelry, etc.

A legacy drawer is a gift—a gift for you knowing that important things are covered the way you want them to be and a gift for those who need to handle your estate in the future.

Now that you have your legacy drawer in place, let's start getting your house in order by cleaning out your personal items. Start by going through your closet. If you haven't worn a piece of clothing within the past year, you might need to consider donating it. Next, go through your paperwork. Over the years, we tend to collect a lot of unnecessary mail, outdated documents, and clutter. If you take a walk through neighborhoods across America, you might find that most people can't even park their cars in their garages because they have too much stuff where their cars should be. The reality is, you can't take any of it with you. Having an organized, simplified home creates space for peace, joy, creativity, and productivity. In Matthew 6:19-20, Jesus states, "Store up for yourselves treasures in heaven where moths, rust, and thieves can't destroy." Travel light by letting go of unnecessary weight, objects, and items that no longer hold any value in your life.

As you get older, and maybe even a little wiser too, you realize that material things fade, go out of style, become irrelevant, and just don't have the same value in your life. Over time, you begin to understand the value of people and invest in making memories with them that will live on way beyond your time here on earth. Stuff fades, but memories remain. That is a motto the Shaw household has been living by for the past couple of years, and it has made a huge difference. It has brought us greater peace and joy, along with a deeper appreciation of what really matters most.

A friend of mine named Don, who is super passionate about preserving and perpetuating his family legacy, said, "If you want to live on forever, go spend time with your grandkids because they will pass down stories about you for generations to come." Proverbs 17:6 tells us, "Grandchildren are the crown of the aged, and the glory of children is their fathers." For some reason, many people have a messed-up mentality that children should pursue their parents and grandparents, but I personally believe it should be the other way around. Think about mirroring our heavenly Father's love for us toward our family members. Jesus left the ninety-nine to go after the one. He was and still is pursuing us with an everlasting love. I want to be that kind of parent now and grandparent one day. I don't want to miss a moment. Not wanting to spend time with your children and grandchildren is a sad sentence of self-induced isolation, self-deprivation, and punishment. Living legacy minded is about pursuing and planning the next adventure, experience, and cherished moment together. I am forever grateful for the unconditional love and daily phone calls, texts, and efforts my parents made to support all of our crazy endeavors, sporting events, holidays, and spontaneous meals together.

Another meaningful and unforgettable way to make memories with your family is to plan a legacy trip. During COVID-19, many families were separated for long periods of time and were reminded of how important it is to spend quality time with their loved ones while they can. A family legacy trip is any trip you take with your multigenerational family members to build a stronger bond and memories that will live on forever. You can take historical trips where you and your family can learn about your past or take new adventures to places that will propel you all into an exciting future. You can even take a trip down memory lane by looking at old photo albums or making a family recipe together.

> A family legacy trip is any trip you take with your multigenerational family members to build a stronger bond and memories that will live on forever.

A friend of mine named Michelle had a legacy trip for multiple generations of her family when her dad arranged for them all to go visit the Holy Land together. They had matching t-shirts made and created unforgettable and transcendent moments together in the place where Jesus walked, preached, died, and rose again. Little did they know that a year later they would lose their father to the pandemic and hold on to those priceless memories together. Talk about living on purpose and for a purpose bigger than yourself. That is leaving a living legacy! Living life with intentionality and action leaves no room for regrets.

Reigning on the High Seas

Earlier in the book, I shared about some of our family sailing adventures as a crew of six. As I explained, sailing is something in our family that ties previous generations with the present and will carry on in the future. Yet, I would be remiss if I didn't share the epic tale of Crunch's Crew surviving Christmas in the Keys at the end of 2020. This was a legacy sailing trip down to the Dry Tortugas, which is ninety miles from Cuba.

This destination is a bucket-list item for a lot of adventurers. Sitting on a mass of land called the Dry Tortugas is a city that rises up out of the sea called Fort Jefferson, named after President Thomas Jefferson. It was erected in 1846 and is made of over sixteen million beautiful red bricks, and the contrast of those bricks against the blues of the ocean is absolutely breathtaking. The original intent was for it to be a naval station to help suppress piracy in the Caribbean. It served as a military post to guard the United States and also housed some pretty notorious prisoners. It's now a national park where people can tour, camp overnight under the stars in the middle of the ocean, and take the ferry and a seaplane from Key West.

Unless you are willing to brave the high seas, I would recommend taking the ferry or seaplane, which will get you there in under two hours—unlike our trek that took a total of two days and almost thirteen hours of enduring scary seas. It has some incredible snorkeling around coral reefs and shipwrecks, and it is surrounded by shallow reefs that have caused many vessels to sink due to lack of knowledge of the area.

That was by far the most challenging, terrifying, and unforgettable venture across some seriously treacherous seas. This was the first time for Crunch's Crew sailing with no land in sight. We would be solely dependent on our navigation and satellite to keep us on course, sailing completely off the grid and away from contact with anyone back home. Along the way, we would encounter waves the size of houses that would drop out like we were on a never-ending roller coaster with winds up to thirty-five knots! We would also get hit from side to side by waves and tossed around like a wet noodle. It was like being thrown in a huge washing machine with no end in sight. Every time you tried to come up for air, you would be hit by another wave.

Nothing could have prepared us for this trip. I can remember after hours into the first leg of the trip that time began to fade, nerves were shot, hope for an end became more distant, and there was nothing but a deep, bellowing groan and roar from the ocean. I remember asking my husband and dad if that sound was coming from the engine, and they both looked at me and said, "No, that is coming from the ocean!"

Psalm 29:3 says, "The voice of the LORD is over the waters; the God of glory thunders, the LORD thunders over the mighty waters. The voice of the LORD is powerful; the voice of the LORD is majestic. The voice of the LORD breaks the cedars; the LORD breaks in pieces the cedars of Lebanon." In that moment, all I could feel was a deep sense of fear and awe of God and how powerful He is! I was also praying, "Dear God, please don't break this vessel into pieces with Your powerful voice!"

Up until this point, we all had survived a global pandemic and didn't want to go down with this ship in the middle of the ocean. We were sailing in controlled chaos! There was a rhythm, cadence, and pace of the waves, and God was the orchestrator of this mad symphony on the high seas. All I could do was focus on the hope that this messy masterpiece of music would eventually calm down and come to an end. Have you ever listened to a song that was so intense, it induced anxiety and panic, putting you into a full-body sweat, and you couldn't change the dial fast enough to just make it stop? Yeah, that's what it felt like on this sail, except we were in the middle of the ocean with no other humans in sight.

We would eventually arrive at Grand Marquesa Keys, about five hours away from Key West, to anchor overnight. This particular land mass was created by an underground volcano erupting, making it one of the top fishing destinations in the world. This was our first time staying on anchor overnight. The interesting aspect of anchoring is that the anchor can drift no matter how well you set it. We have an app that will start barking when our anchor drifts outside the circle of safety. Trust me, except for the kids, everyone sleeps really lightly when we are on anchor. There is always a fear of hitting the bottom, a neighboring vessel, or worse, drifting out to the ocean in the middle of the night. God knew we had no desire to experience what we had earlier that day in the dark.

The other enemies we were up against were crab pots everywhere! We were sailing in the middle of crab season, and trying to avoid them was like dodging landmines. If we got one of them wrapped in our propeller, we would be in serious trouble. Our engines could be shot, and we would be sitting ducks with no power other than our sails.

Once the anchor was set, Jeff, King, Care, and I took the dinghy out to explore the uninhabited island. It was absolutely beautiful experiencing the solitude and serenity of this safe haven in the sea. We walked the beaches, collected purple sea fans and unique shells, and admired the sun setting as we glanced back at the catamaran anchored off shore. This moment made the crazy sail there all worth it.

The next morning, we rose super early to start off on our second leg of the trip, which would consist of a five-to-seven-hour sail to Fort Jefferson. We somehow ended up going through naval training waters, and this leg was much longer and even more treacherous than the first. At one point, the whole ceiling in the main cabin fell down, and everything that wasn't secured became a flying projectile to dodge. When we first started off, we could see the ferry behind us, but it soon blasted by us, leaving us all alone as we made our way to explore the city on the sea.

When we originally planned this sail, the weather was set to be calm. But, as we all know, the weather is always subject to sudden change. It doesn't consult you before you secure your plans and lock in your float plan. Winds came down from up north, and we sailed waters that not even a seasoned sailor would take on. After seven long hours, some very seasick sailors, and a very windblown captain and co-captain, we spotted land! I think we all couldn't help but feel overwhelmed with gratitude, excitement, and deep appreciation for some relief in sight. It was absolutely magical laying eyes on this massive fortress that seemed to be floating out in the middle of the ocean! We slowly made our way to a cove on the leeward side of the island to find anchor and protection from the wild winds through which we had just sailed.

To our surprise, there were multiple other vessels that had made that same trek, and a mega yacht anchored in front of us. It felt so good to take a huge, deep breath, knowing that we could rest, explore, and take in the beauty of this bucket-list destination. We had made it by the grace of God, our two determined captains, and a lot of prayer. None of us even wanted to think about having to turn around in a couple days and making that same trip back across those scary seas.

Exploring Fort Jefferson

The next day, we took the dinghy to shore and explored the massive fort and every nook and cranny of that place. We couldn't help but be in awe of the courage it had taken for the people to build, live in, and preserve this huge fort. There was no fresh water on the island, so they had designed an aqueduct system to collect rainwater. We climbed to the top of the fort and took in the most epic views of the Atlantic Ocean. There was nothing but blue as far as the eye could see. I will never forget the feeling of accomplishment of what we conquered as a crew. Later, we spent time on the beach, snorkeled around the fort, and took in the most amazing views. It really felt like we were on the set of a James Bond movie.

It was soon time for us to pack up, batten down the hatches, and make our way back to Key West in time to celebrate New Year's Eve with our brother Jonathan, our sister Valentina, and our nephews. Incredibly, the way back was even worse than our sail there. The weather took a turn for the worse, and the winds, waves, and rain created scary conditions. We were now going against the wind, and it was too gusty and dangerous to put up the sails. We were motoring our way back, and it took double the time. It was only by the grace of God that we made it to our halfway point at Grand Marquesas Key to anchor overnight. I will never forget the faces of my dad and Jeff when we finally set the anchor. They were soaked, windblown, shocked, and pretty beaten up by that leg of the journey. My dad ended up going to the front of the boat to breathe a huge sigh of relief and shed some tears of joy. Jeff immediately went into the kitchen and started making chicken noodle soup for everyone. I don't think any of us had eaten anything all day, in fear that it would come right up and out all over the boat. That soup was the best meal I've ever had in my life.

There's something about almost dying that makes you really appreciate and savor the simple things in life. As we all bowed our heads and gave God thanks and praise for keeping us safe, it started pouring outside. The Lord had allowed us to get to safety before a big storm rolled through. We all passed out and felt confident that our anchor was secure in the sea bed. By this point in the journey, I think we had become more confident with our skills.

The next morning, we rose early with anticipation to get back to Key West and ring in the new year on solid ground. We had no phone connection with anyone back home, and I'm sure they were wondering how Crunch's Crew was still alive.

Not too long after we lifted anchor, we caught hold of a crab pot and got it wrapped around our propeller. There was just no avoiding them. They were literally everywhere, and with the waves so high, it was difficult to spot them. We figured this out because Kingston started to see smoke coming from one of the engines. *No!* We had already made it through the hardest part of the sail, and we had a timeline to get back. Now we only had the power of one engine, and this would significantly slow our time back—not to mention we needed to get back to Key West before it was dark. We all had zero desire to try navigating those waters in the night sky.

We finally came upon Boca Grande Key and decided to drop anchor and see if we could cut the rope loose and free up the prop. We came upon a bunch of day boaters hanging out on this island and saw the bluest milky-colored water we had ever seen. Although it was beautiful, that water would make it really hard to see clearly under the boat. My dad jumped in with his snorkel mask to see if it was even possible to cut the rope. After a couple of minutes, Jeff decided to jump in with a kitchen knife. It was the sharpest thing we had on board, and he was determined to cut us loose. Of course, we looked into the water to find the boat surrounded by these weird-looking neon-blue jelly objects that looked like aliens.

In all of our time in the ocean, we had never seen anything like these creepy creatures. We looked them up, and sure enough, Jeff was surrounded by Portuguese man-of-wars, one of the deadliest jellyfish in the sea! *Really? Can we just get a break, God?*

Jeff was already in and hacking away at the rope. One thing I know about my husband is that he is determined. Once he starts something, he will see it all the way through. We kept a close watch and made sure he wasn't getting stung by any of his surrounding alien-like friends. The scariest thing was that we couldn't see underneath him. We were just praying there were no sharks lurking below. Little by little, we saw more rope float to the surface, and we were free!

Jeff did it, and we were on our way back to ring in the new year. I can't even begin to tell you how relieved we all were to make it back to harbor before it got dark. We had just enough time to get dressed and meet our family to celebrate our survival with an incredible meal at the resort.

New Years Day Brunch with the crew

The next morning, we invited our family over to celebrate on board with a Cap'n Crunch New Year's Day brunch. We had a delicious breakfast, toasted to another year of life, shed some tears, and stayed closer to shore. We had originally planned to take our family out for a day sail, but we couldn't bear the thought of taking them out on the water we had just sailed through. We loved them too much to expose them to that much chaos. We will never forget that crazy Christmas sail and forever thank God for faithfully helping us navigate through some of the scariest seas. Those stories will live on for many generations to come and be a part of our family's legacy as sailors.

Reigning in Identity

Legacy trips can also come in the form of a personal quest to discover your roots. We all have this deep longing to go home embedded in our souls. We all want to have a place where we can be seen, accepted, loved, safe, protected, and affirmed. We all desire a sense of belonging to someone or something bigger than ourselves. Ultimately, we will all find our home in heaven and come full circle in our journey through life here on earth into our eternal home. After all, we are all just sojourners passing through on our way to one day reign with the King of kings.

My grandmother wrote this poem called "Home," and I think it's a perfect description of our universal longing to go home, which ties humanity together as one race—the human race.

HOME

> Wherever we go, there's always a desire to get home.
> We must leave behind security when we roam.
> Traveling and visiting gives satisfaction and pleasure,
> But don't underestimate the peace you left to treasure.

The longing to be at home is as natural as can be
Because your familiar belongings and people you like to see.
Your own domain allows you to simply just live
By your standards, flexible, without principles to give.

Memories of things that you have loved and collected
Make you sensitive to your roots, so you get connected.
Recollections of furnishings you have assembled now,
As your past experiences have taught you how.

Each generation's lifestyle varies so very much,
As everyone's home had a real spiritual touch.
The comfort of your home is regulated by you
And meets your needs like a well-worn shoe.

Self-inspired touches give warmth to a home
And put you at ease under your own dome.
The ability to create a home, not following a trend,
Certainly gives your trademark a happy end.
The reality is, we're all just passing through,
Until one day we release this earthly home for a beautiful place
called heaven prepared specifically for you.

One year before the world got shut down from a global pandemic, Jeff had a once-in-a-lifetime opportunity to take a legacy mission trip to Africa. When we first got married, we were making plans to go to Ghana, but the trip got cancelled. It was disappointing, but we never let go of the dream of going one day.

There was a message series our pastor was preaching called "The Year of Yes!" During the series, this question was presented to the congregation: what would happen in our lives and those surrounding us if we would just say yes to the Lord and what He wants to accomplish in and through us and stop overthinking or questioning His leading? I remember this being a time where our faith was activated and God was fanning the flame in our hearts to trust Him again and let go of limitations in our lives.

That following week, I went to celebrate my cousin's baby shower at a place called Board and Brush. There, you get to pick out a project that involves wood, nails, sanding, hammers, stain, and some creativity under supervision. I was presented with so many choices, but I kept being drawn to this map of the world that you can stencil and include your family name and the words "Enjoy the Journey." Some years back, I went to a Christmas party of someone on the board of the television station I worked for. On the wall in their beautiful library hung a framed map of the world with pushpins placed in all of the countries they had travelled during their lifetime. I loved that idea and knew I would one day create that for our family. Travel is a gift that keeps on giving memories, new perspectives, and a broader appreciation of God's incredible creation. I presented this gift to Jeff and immediately hung it on the wall of our home.

> Travel is a gift that keeps on giving memories, new perspectives, and a broader appreciation of God's incredible creation.

A week later, we were invited to dinner with the executive pastor of our church and his wife. We sat down to eat at one of our favorite sushi spots, and the pastor looked at Jeff and said, "Just say yes!" We knew exactly where he had gotten those challenging words. Without any hesitation, Jeff said, "Okay, then...yes!"

Then the pastor told us, "Well, that settles it. We're going to Africa!" Jeff and I looked at each other and laughed, then we began to listen.

They would be going to Burkina Faso to help support a ministry of an incredible couple that left their life of comfort behind in the US to serve people in a foreign land. The husband ended up losing his life in a terrorist attack, but his wife carried on their work serving the people in Burkina. The ministry is called Sheltering Wings, and it helps orphans, trains and equips women through their crisis center, and finds solutions to farming through experimental agricultural projects. The second leg of the journey would lead them to Ghana to partner alongside the International Justice Mission. They have a full operation set up to help rescue young trafficked children who have been forced to work on fishing boats on Lake Volta.

I'm sure Jeff could write a book about all of his adventures back in the motherland. All I know is, as his wife, I spent almost two full weeks on my face in prayer for his and the team's safety. I also knew this was something so personal for him to experience and that God would show Himself specifically to Jeff throughout his time in Africa. It would be a full circle journey for him to walk where his ancestors did before they were taken from their home and sold into slavery.

One of the cool ways we stayed in touch with the team was through WhatsApp. It was always encouraging to get a message saying that they were well and had made it to their next destination safely. The team also sent us pictures of some of the incredible God moments that happened along the way. Of course, the day that they landed, there was a terrorist attack reported on the world news that was not too far from where they were staying in Burkina Faso. A pastor who had served there for over thirty years had been murdered. Just north is Mali, which is a hotbed for terrorists. I will never forget hearing Jeff's voice for the first time, knowing he was okay.

On one of their stops in Burkina, Amy, their host, made sure to bring them to a local tailor to pick out a custom handmade suit. As they walked up, there was a mural painted on the front of the store, and Jeff realized the man in the painting looked so similar to him. The face, skin color, bone structure, facial hair, stature, and even the outfit he was wearing was identical to Jeff! Talk about staring your ancestors in the face! There was no doubt there was someone living in that very place that resembled my husband. Jeff took a picture standing next to the man in the mural, and it was a full circle moment of coming home.

Jeff in Burkina Faso, Africa

I truly believe God loves us so much that He will move heaven and earth to show His love for us. Sometimes He speaks in mysteries and enigmas, and other times He is so literal in the ways He speaks to us. This was one of those literal moments for Jeffrey. I knew God was with Him and had gone before him on this epic trip.

Another powerful moment was when the team visited the slave castles along the gold coast of Ghana. There was something so haunting about how much horror could happen in a place of such beauty. The contrast of the white castles lining the shores against the beautiful blue ocean was breathtaking. This would be a very sobering and transcendent experience for Jeff on this journey. He was literally walking the ground where his ancestors were imprisoned, stripped from their identities and family names, and shipped across the Atlantic Ocean to eventually arrive in South Carolina. Jeff was the only person on the team who had direct ties to this horrific place.

After the trip, he showed me a picture of a hallway that led out of the castle into the slave ships. This was called the point of no return. Many who walked down that hall would not make it across the ocean alive, and none of them would ever return to their homeland again. I can't even begin to imagine the fear, shame, hopelessness, and terror they faced on the high seas, stacked like animals only to arrive in a foreign land where they didn't know the language and no one looked like them. Everything would forever change. They would be separated from their families and sold off to different places.

Standing there, Jeff said he had an overwhelming feeling of gratitude for what his ancestors endured and overcame so that he could experience the freedoms he has today as a biracial man in America. It was a healing moment between him and God. He realized even more what strong roots he has and the awesome privilege he has to be alive in Christ and continue to help set the captives free for future generations. Freedom truly isn't free but paid for by the precious blood of Jesus and our ancestors who went before us to pave a smoother path for us.

There's No Place like Home

That famous line comes from the classic film *The Wizard of Oz*. When most people ask me where I'm originally from and I tell them Kansas, they always bring up Dorothy and her dog, Toto, from the movie.

Over the summer, I had an opportunity to travel back to Kansas with King, Care, and my parents to visit our sweet Mimi. She is my only living grandparent and an absolute treasure in our family. Her poetry is shared throughout this book, and I pray it has blessed you like it has me. She lived independently and managed all of her personal affairs into her nineties. Like many elderly people, COVID-19 wreaked havoc on her physical state, mental health, and well-being. We were finally all cleared to travel and come on a mission to surround her with love and bring her joy.

Visiting my grandparents' home is like stepping back in time. Nothing has changed from my childhood other than my Papa is no longer living there. After he passed away, my Mimi continued to manage their rental properties, write, and paint. I couldn't wait for King and Care to meet her and spend some time with this remarkable woman. It felt so good to see her in person and give her a big hug, look her in the eyes, and tell her how much we loved her.

When we arrived at her home, the kids wanted to take a tour of the house. Together, we looked at old photos, went down in the basement, and explored Mimi's art studio, which Carrington loved because she is passionate about art. We also learned more about our family history. At one point, Mimi handed me a tablet full of her poetry that hadn't been published yet. It was like she was passing the baton off to me to help her finish the next leg of the race. I knew at that moment that my mom and I would take on the mission to get Mimi's second book published.

Visiting Mimi in June 2021

Mimi's work was always full of wisdom, wit, humor, and seeing God in every detail of life. Her second book of poetry is called *Whimsical Poems: Seeing God in the Serious, Silly, and Seemingly Insignificant.* Any time I have had the opportunity to speak, I always find one of her poems to fit the specific occasion and share it with the audience.

As we were sitting there with Mimi, I noticed the big family Bible resting on a shelf, and I asked her if I could look through it. She said yes, and as soon as I opened the first page, a piece of paper fell out. It was a beautiful poem my Papa had handwritten for her on their forty-seventh wedding anniversary. The last line of the poem said, "Then we will walk into the glorious sunset still holding hands as we enter the gates of heaven. Your loving husband, Jack Amburgey. " I pulled up a small stool and sat by my Mimi as she read the poem . She then told me that she had never read it before. What a sweet message from heaven that had been hidden in plain sight.

Mimi hadn't gotten out much during the pandemic other than to doctors' visits and getting her hair washed weekly. We were all on a mission, with her permission, of course, to get her out and about and help lift her spirits. I asked her when the last time she picked up a paintbrush was. She then said, "Courtney, some things you just let go of when you get older." That broke my heart because I knew how much joy painting had brought her over the years.

For decades, Mimi had worked with oil-based paints and had given that up because it took a lot of effort to clean up. Later that day, we went to the store and found a Bob Ross watercolor painting book. The pages were pre-loaded with color, and all she had to do was dip her paintbrush in water and paint away. It was the perfect way for Mimi to become creative again without making a huge mess. She was very inspired by Bob Ross's work and loved painting landscapes.

Carrington was determined to paint with her great-grandmother before we left Kansas. So, boldly yet gently, she asked Mimi if she wanted to paint with her. She sat down by Mimi and showed her how it was done. Not a moment sooner, Care said, "It's your turn." Mimi picked up the brush and started bringing the scene to life. It was like she knew exactly what to do. She loved it so much that she never gave the brush back to Care. She wanted to finish the whole painting. That was one of my favorite moments where four generations collaborated on a painting.

My other favorite moment was when the kids wanted to go to the Sedgwick County Zoo and asked Mimi to come along. To all of our surprise, she said yes! The weather was perfect, and we wheeled Mimi all around that zoo, looking at all of the amazing animals and making special memories together. That day, there was a time where Care asked if she could push Mimi in the wheelchair. We all looked at her and told her to take it easy. We didn't want her to take her great-grandmother on a rollercoaster ride.

Six months after that trip, Mimi turned ninety-two years old, and I'm so thankful we had that time together. Dementia has taken a toll on her mind and body, but her spirit thrives on through her family. Watching a loved one suffer with mental disease is like watching someone walk through a house and shut off the lights in each room one at a time. It's a slow and devastating process. It's even harder on the loved ones and caregivers to watch someone so remarkable and full of life, love, and humor start to crumble before their eyes.

During our time in Kansas, we also spent time strolling down my parents' memory lane and saw the houses where our family began their journey. We also took a trip out to Lake Cheney, where my dad proposed to my mom on his sailboat at the lake house. It had been hard for me to imagine how sailing in Kansas would be possible, but after seeing how big the lake was and knowing how high the winds can get, it all made sense. We even walked the trails my parents did as a young engaged couple and appreciated the beauty of the place where they fell in love. The kids stood along the shore next to their Pa and Ma Bear and skipped stones across the lake.

Next, we took a long road trip out to Lakin, Kansas, to see the Phillips family farm where my dad grew up. This was the land that our ancestors homesteaded on as pioneers from Sweden. The original house they lived in was made out of sod. The grass kept things cool during the summer and warm during the cold winters. We had heard so many stories about this special place.

Today, we carry on a lot of family traditions that began at the family farm. One of my favorites is making Aunt Ellen's homemade ice cream. My dad still has the original recipe in her handwriting. When our ancestors would gather at the farm on special occasions, a family member would go to town and purchase a big block of ice and hand crank the ice cream churn so everyone could enjoy this special treat. My dad even made this ice cream for my parents' rehearsal dinner before their wedding. We now enjoy it on birthdays and special occasions.

On the road, we could see and smell nothing but stockyards and see wheat fields for miles and miles. There was something so simple and breathtaking about the landscape. I could just imagine our ancestors making the trek across the prairies to eventually stake their claim on the land that would have generations care for it.

In the book written on my great-grandmother's life called *Hannah A. Rosebrook: Community Journalist/Local Historian*, it mentions the trip that she and my great-grandfather Charles took to "get rich" out in western Kansas on a covered wagon in 1907. Her brother-in-law coaxed her husband to make the trek that ushered in the most unsettling time of her life. She said that she hated to leave that home in Lincoln, which was so warm and comfortable. Along their way, they came across a man whose covered wagon was "shredded like carpet strings." He asked them where they were headed. They told him that they were going to western Kansas. He replied, "Hell! Turn back! There's nothing out there but wind!"

As pioneers and farmers there, they endured a lot of hardships. At one point, they had lost everything when their crops were wiped out by hail storms and their cattle died to black leg disease. In these situations, my great-grandfather would beg his wife to return east, but she firmly reminded him, "You forced me to come out here against my will in the first place. We are going to stay and stick it out."

Hannah shared all of the hardships of pioneer life in her writings. She found her voice in turbulent times as a writer for the *Lakin Independent* from 1918-1980. Prior to her death at age 104, she was cited by various sources as the oldest living reporter in America and perhaps the world. She passed away one year before I was born, so I never met this remarkable matriarch of our family.

I was determined to make a quick stop through the single-street "downtown," which had no stoplight, to see where it all began. There was a police department, a post office, a couple other small stores, and the *Lakin Independent* newspaper. It was still running long after my great-grandmother Hannah wrote her last article at 104 years old, one month before she passed away in 1980. The newspaper had hired her to write a weekly social column. I love how she inserted her beliefs and thoughts on events taking place in the world at that time. As a woman, she found her voice through her writing and became very well respected by both men and women for her perspectives. She wrote about everything from the weather and the hardships of farming to social events, World War II, her hatred for Hitler, the political climate, and the struggles of being a pioneer. Her writings are a detailed time capsule that eventually became published in the book about her life.

One of the things I cherish the most from my great-grandmother is her handwritten journal from 1949, the year my dad was born. It's something that ties me to her and will be passed down to my children one day, along with all of my own journals and books. Inside the journal are pressed wildflowers, pictures, and very transparent accounts of her daily life. She was truly a woman beyond her time. Although she had very traditional values as a woman of great faith, she was also a forward thinker and a risk taker. I like to think of myself in the same manner.

Standing in front of the Lakin Independant

Upon my arrival, I got out of the car and stood in front of the place where my great-grandmother Hannah had found her voice in writing. I tried to peek in, but the newspaper office was closed on Sunday. It was incredible to think I was standing in front of the door she would walk in every week for sixty-seven years to turn in her column. It was said that she never missed a deadline.

Now, it was time to head out to the Phillips Family farm. As we pulled up to the property and saw several of the original structures still standing, I got chills. That's pretty amazing, considering the weather in Kansas can be extreme. There are tornadoes, intense heat, and extremely brutal winters. As we drove down the dirt road that led to the property, I rolled down the window and took in the fresh air. When I was a child, I had visited this place with my family, and now I was back, just recently turning forty, and with my son and daughter. Something about having the privilege of growing older makes you appreciate these experiences even more.

As an adult, I've taken the time to learn more about our family history and hear all of the family members share their stories about their humble beginnings on the farm, which helped me really take in this time. I could just imagine my dad and his siblings running around this land, working the wheat fields, and growing up in a place so isolated from the rest of the world. It didn't appear that anyone was there, but we all encouraged my dad to go knock on the door to make sure. We didn't want to get shot for trespassing on the property.

After my grandfather passed, the family tried to keep the farm going, but it wasn't ideal with the older siblings away at college and the conditions too rough to keep it profitable. My grandfather died from cancer when my dad was seventeen years old. His ashes were spread over the land their family had stewarded for years harvesting wheat. They ended up making the tough decision to sell the farm.

Phillips Family Farm

My grandmother Inez had to start all over in her fifties. She went from being a full-time farm wife and a mom of five to becoming a very successful female commodities broker in a male-dominated industry. She didn't just spend her time on the farm cooking, cleaning, and serving her family and the farmhands, but she also handled all of the books and finances. That prepared her for her take two. She received many accolades and had an opportunity to speak at a major commodities convention among her male peers. As she finished her speech, a man stood up in the audience and began to clap, saying out loud, "That was the best speech I've ever heard." That man just so happened to be Les Brown, the world-renowned motivational speaker. That is one of my favorite stories about my Grannie Inez.

She was truly a force to be reckoned with and had the courage to start a whole new life after her husband passed. She even bought a hot air balloon and raced it with a team. She never remarried, although she had many men interested in her. It's crazy to think who Inez would have become if she stayed on that farm.

Grannie Inez had a lot of grit but was always loving, kind, supportive, and gracious to all who knew her. I miss her so much, and I pray that I will carry on her legacy by finishing my race strong just like she did. She beat breast cancer at eighty-nine and lived to be ninety-five years old.

At her retirement, a newspaper in Garden City interviewed her. She was quoted saying, "A lot of people want to connect me to the feminist movement because of what I accomplished in a male-dominated industry. I was never a feminist but a product of my tough circumstances." Losing her husband and the family farm catapulted her into a deeper purpose. She still had a family to care for, and to provide for them, she had to make it happen herself.

When we were visiting the farm, the wheat was about to be harvested. It was so beautiful to stand in the fields and watch the amber waves of grain flow like waves in the wind. The original family house was standing, as well as the barns, the outhouse, and old farming equipment. I became emotional walking behind my dad, who is now in his seventies, as he revisited his childhood roots. Time really does fly by, and there is nothing more grounding than taking time to go back and stand in the place where your story began.

The grand finale of our time there was letting Kingston take the wheel and drive us down the same dirt roads his Pa Bear did as a kid. He kept the car in the middle of the road and did a great job. It was something so simple yet so profound in that moment. I had Kingston pull to the side of the road so I could glance back at the farm and snap a picture while grabbing some wheat to take with me. I wanted a tangible reminder of our family's humble beginnings. Everywhere I looked, there was nothing but fields ready to be harvested. It made me think of Matthew 9:37-38, which says, "Then he said to his disciples, The harvest is plentiful, but the laborers are few; therefore pray earnestly to the Lord of the harvest to send out laborers into his harvest."

Looking out into the fields, an overwhelming sense of calling and responsibility came over me to keep sharing the gospel of Jesus Christ everywhere and in every way I can with everyone I can. I knew without a shadow of a doubt that is what I'm supposed to spend my days here on earth doing.

I got back in the car, and we soon began to talk about Kingston's big dream. One day, he wants to have land and call it King's Ranch: Where Freedom Reigns. It's amazing how things really come full circle. At age thirteen, there is a longing in him for a simpler way of life and to get back to the family roots. I have no doubt that dream will come to pass in his lifetime.

On this trip, we all talked so much and were able to share the incredible journey that began with our pioneering ancestors and led to my parents forging a new path that took them to Colorado and eventually Florida. I'm so thankful my family had the courage to move forward and create a new legacy and traditions for the next generations. Life's disappointments, devastations, and redirections can be looked at as divine interruptions that ultimately lead us to our destiny. So many little things had to occur in order for my family of four to be together today. You can see God's hand through it all in your own journey when you take the time to go down memory lane and bring Jesus along the road trip of your life.

Reign in the Finish

How we finish our race in life is so much more important than how we started. This truth reminds me of when I was running cross country in the Junior Olympics. The first team I ran for was ironically called Alpha and Omega (the beginning and the end). My strategy at the starting line was always to sprint out ahead of the pack to set the pace and not get lost in the crowd. This strategy had worked for me for some time because I had the speed. However, when I got older and the distance grew longer, this started working against me. I found myself gassing out halfway through the race and didn't have enough reserve in me to finish strong.

I eventually learned the lesson and decided to slow my roll. I didn't have to be the one out front setting the pace. I actually found it more motivating and fun to chase down the runner who was in first place. Maybe it looked like I was behind, but I knew that if I paced myself, I would have enough energy at the end to sprint across the finish line with everything I had and could possibly capture first place. This gave me permission to be fully present for the whole race, rather than just focusing on how I started and finished. I was able to actually enjoy the journey and not just endure the race.

This showed me that I had become so focused on winning that I forgot why I started running at all. Running always came naturally to me. God had given me a gift, and with it came many expectations to perform at a high level all the time. I had originally fallen in love with running because it gave me a quiet place and space to escape the pressures of life. It was just me, my sneakers, the road, and the sound of my breathing. When you first start running, there can be pain and some discomfort, but when you become conditioned and in shape, you feel like you can run for miles. There is something called a "runner's high" that you can get when your endorphins kick in. It's like getting a second wind that allows you to run on high-octane fuel. After your run, you feel energized, empowered, refreshed, and like you could conquer the world.

You might be reading this right now and saying, "But I can barely even walk! How am I supposed to run?" Ecclesiastes 9:11 says, "I returned and saw under the sun that—The race is not to the swift, Nor the battle to the strong, Nor bread to the wise, Nor riches to men of understanding, Nor favor to men of skill; But time and chance happen to them all." In life, the circumstances you've been dealt don't really matter. Life and chance happen to us all. You can plan, prepare, strategize, save, invest, tuck away, have the best looks, come from a wealthy family, and have countless possessions—a beautiful house, a nice car, a successful career, a huge following on social media—and then things just happen.

Have you recently failed at something? Did you tragically lose a loved one? Did you make a huge mistake? Did you lose your home or file for bankruptcy? Did you lose your job? Perhaps everything inside of you is screaming to just throw in the towel and quit. You have the power to decide whether you are going to take that towel as a sign of defeat or use it to wipe your brow and get back in the race of life. It's your choice, your race, your reign, and your move.

Just know that you've never been running just for yourself or by yourself. There is someone waiting at the finish line to celebrate with you. That someone is Jesus. I'm not sure where you are in your race. Maybe you've already given it all you have to get to this point in the race. Maybe you can't fathom mustering up another ounce of courage and energy to lace your sneakers back up and get back on course. I get it. I've been there, tired, worn down, exhausted, hopeless, depressed, downhearted, and feeling completely defeated. I'm too old, too wrinkled, not smart enough, washed out, a "has been." But, that is the moment when God steps in as your coach in this race to remind you who you are and whose you are. You are His son or daughter, called to rise, shine, and reign for such a time as this.

Now, get up and get back on track! After healing the leper, in Mark 1:40-45 God told him to get up. There comes a time when self-pity has to take a backseat and you have to rise in your royal identity. It's not too late to start right now. Tomorrow is not promised. Seize the day before it's too late. Finish that degree, go to that counseling session, eat that healthy meal, pick up those weights, draw that boundary, extend forgiveness, take that step to building your credit, write your book, fight for your marriage, and receive your reign!

The good news is that we're not running this race alone. We have Jesus on our team running alongside us. He gives us a supernatural advantage to finish our race strong with both hands in the air, crossing the finish line in victory. There is genuine strength that is found only in surrender. That is the great exchange to activate your reign.

> There comes a time when self-pity has to take a backseat and you have to rise in your royal identity.

In order to receive that surge of supernatural strength, you need to release the unnecessary weight in your life. Hebrews 12:1 says, "Wherefore seeing we also are compassed about with so great a cloud of witnesses, let us lay aside every weight, and the sin which doth so easily beset us, and let us run with patience the race that is set before us." You have a heavenly audience cheering you on to finish your race with courage and faith. Everyone who has gone on before you has a front row seat to witness your epic finish.

> Don't look at this present time in your life like you're starting completely over. You are getting back in the race with greater wisdom, compassion, and insight, along with an internal and eternal fortitude that can't be defeated.

Your story can be one of a glorious comeback told for generations to come. One day, you will tell your story about how you overcame what you went through, and it'll be someone else's survival guide. I pray this book has been that for you. There is always a second wind, fresh fire, and new grace for a new beginning. Don't look at this present time in your life like you're starting completely over. You are getting back in the race with greater wisdom, compassion, and insight, along with an internal and eternal fortitude that can't be defeated. You have breath in your lungs, clarity of mind, and a heart beating with divine purpose in your chest. You are fully alive and more than a conqueror in Christ Jesus!

Throughout this life, your "why" has to be something so much bigger than yourself. You will have opposition along the path to the fulfillment of God's promises in your life. You can let yourself down, lie to yourself, disqualify yourself, and take yourself out of the race. But, when you really get a vision for the race of your life, you won't give in, give up, or quit. You may need to crawl, walk, and get fueled back up, but you will keep moving forward boldly and confidently toward the finish line.

In a relay race, a team has members that each cover a specified portion of the entire course. Each leg of the race is just as important as the next. Cadence, pace, and timing are all required to synchronize a smooth and successful transition. The person you are passing the baton to is already in motion and in position to receive it. There has to be a clean exchange so the baton won't be dropped. 1 Corinthians 9:24-30 says, "Do you not know that in a race all the runners run, but only one gets the prize? Run in such a way as to get the prize." Everyone who competes in the games goes into strict training. They do it to get a crown that will not last, but we do it to get a crown that will last forever. "Therefore, I do not run like someone running aimlessly; I do not fight like a boxer beating the air."

How you choose to run your race and pass off the baton of divine purpose will absolutely affect how the next generation runs the next leg. When you live a life surrendered to Christ and allow Him to bring healing and wholeness into your family, you will be able to transition to the next generation with peace and joy, creating momentum for a bright future ahead.

LEGACY OF FAITH

In a blog called *Rock This Revival,* Abby Rike shares about the legacy of the Graham family. There is no better example of leaving a legacy of faith than that of Billy and Ruth Graham. Billy was quoted saying, "My home is heaven. I'm just traveling through this world."[13] Billy is finally home. He and his wife, Ruth, left an immeasurable impact on the world for the kingdom of God.

Legacies like theirs don't happen by accident. They are intentional. They both lived lives of humility all the way to the grave. Both Billy and Ruth opted for pine caskets made by prisoners from the Angola Prison in Louisiana. They knew that one day they would be wearing their crowns in heaven and didn't want an extravagant funeral. They both honored their marriage vows and made sure to have safeguards in place out of the utmost respect for one another and the covenant they made before God and their families. They were the definition of a team on a kingdom mission to fulfill the highest calling as servants of the king.

There is something to be said about the legacy of integrity Billy and Ruth Graham guarded while on earth and after they left. There were no known scandals attached to their ministry. Although, when being interviewed by a reporter, Billy was asked what his biggest regret was. He said, "I wish I would've spent more time with my family." That was the biggest exchange and sacrifice of his life. For decades, he had kept such a rigorous schedule and knew he would never get that time with his family back.

In today's world of superstar preachers, mega ministries, and Christian social media influencers, there always seems to be another headline of infidelity, misuse of church funds, falling away from the faith, or some type of sinful scandal. It's sad to think that this has become the norm. Christian culture has almost been forced to support and celebrate the sinful lives of our leaders. Maybe, in some sick way, it helps us feel like we are off the hook from having to truly repent of our own wicked ways. We may be thinking, *If it's okay for them, then it's okay for me.*

The problem with this diluted version of deliverance is that it leaves a gaping hole in the hearts of humanity for the enemy to take residence and ruin the lives of believers everywhere. For some reason, living an upright life of humility, kindness, responsibility, and servanthood is not rewarding, flashy, or glamorous. The Christian life is so much more than wearing a faith-inspired t-shirt, going to a trendy worship gathering, or finding the perfect "holier than thou" crew to hang with. There's nothing wrong with modern-day expressions of faith, but these should never be used in place of a genuine and personal relationship with your Lord and Savior.

I think there is a deep longing to get back to the teaching and preaching of the gospel of Jesus Christ and for us to not make ourselves of any reputation. There is no me, myself, and I in God's kingdom. That is the very mentality that got Lucifer kicked out of heaven. He wanted to be worshiped and receive all of the adoration. He wanted a fan club and followers and didn't like the fact that God was getting all of the attention. The modern church has been seduced by the smoke and lights of showmanship versus the desire of genuine servanthood and longing for salvation, discipleship, and freedom for our souls. God doesn't need or want us to perform for Him or others. Stages, microphones, speakers, social media, television, podcasts, and books are merely tools to further His kingdom here on earth, and they should be used as such.

God wants us to live a life of surrender and total dependence on His never-ending love for us. He wants us to be vessels for His kingdom to reign here on earth. We've found ourselves using the wrong measuring tools for success. Instead of focusing on souls being saved and lives being transformed by the power of the Holy Spirit, we are often measuring the number of attendees at programs and events or how many followers we have. We are to lead people to the Source, not to become their source. There is so much freedom found when we choose to continually get out of the way and receive God's mercy and grace.

I pray that this generation develops an insatiable hunger for God's living Word, along with a strong desire to activate their prayers and reign in total faith. May we inspire those to come after us to trust in God's unchanging plan to redeem, restore, and reign through humanity. Let our legacy of faith be ignited in this simple prayer Jesus taught His disciples to pray in Matthew 6:9-13: "This, then, is how you should pray: 'Our Father in heaven, hallowed be your name, your kingdom come, your will be done, on earth as it is in heaven. Give us today our daily bread. And forgive us our debts, as we also have forgiven our debtors, And lead us not into temptation, but deliver us from the evil one.'"

Take this time to communicate with your family members and come up with your own vision and mission for a new reign. Habakkuk 2:2-3 says, "Then the Lord answered me and said: 'Write the vision. And make *it* plain on tablets, That he may run who reads it. For the vision *is* yet for an appointed time; But at the end it will speak, and it will not lie. Though it tarries, wait for it; Because it will surely come, It will not tarry.'" Habakkuk 2:4-14 says,"Behold the proud, His soul is not upright in him; But the just shall live by his faith." Your vision is the big picture and the end goal in mind, and your mission is how you will accomplish it.

For example, this is our Shaw family vision:

> *The Shaw family will be founded on the truth of the living Word of God, be a light to this world wherever they go, and express the Father's unfailing love to the hearts of His creation.*

In addition to this vision, we also have a mission that will help us make that vision a reality:

We will be committed daily to study and live out the Word of God, and choose to be vessels of hope and service to others. We will walk in humility, kindness, wisdom, care, and consideration for others. We will be quick to extend and receive forgiveness, take responsibility for our actions, and have a lot of fun along the way. We will glorify God in our bodies and spirits, which are His, and let God's kingdom reign in our lives daily. We will see the goodness of God in the land of the living!

Receive Your Reign

So, now that you've been on this journey to reign in your royal identity, take authority over your past, activate your faith, stand on the truth of God's Word, claim new territory, be present in your day, maximize your relationships, and live with your legacy in mind, it is time to answer one question: how will you reign?

The season of regret, blame, and shame has come to an end. Let that end be now, while you have breath in your lungs and not on your deathbed. Today can be the day where you say, "Enough is enough! I'm sick and tired of being sick. I'm not going to do crazy anymore. I refuse to be defined by the circumstances, traumas, and tragedies that I have faced up until this very moment. I break agreement with every lie that has been spoken over my life and my family. I will not feel sorry for myself any longer. I am not a victim; I am a victor!"

We all need someone in our lives who will love us enough to tell us the truth and not let us settle for anything less than God's best. I pray that I have been that channel of God's love and voice of hope in your life throughout these pages. I'm sure at times the journey has been uncomfortable and unsettling, and it may have even stirred up some serious mess that was lying under the surface of your smile. But, change never happens without a true shaking and awakening to the reality of life that Jesus died for us to live. We need to know that His unconditional love reigns over the ruins of our lives. He wants to be a solid fortress around you with fortified walls of protection from the attacks of the enemy. Proverbs 18:10 says, "The name of the LORD is a strong fortress; the godly run to him and are safe." There is safety and shelter in your surrender. With God's protection, you will get better, wiser, and stronger and shine more brilliantly than ever before!

> But, change never happens without a true shaking and awakening to the reality of life that Jesus died for us to live. We need to know that His unconditional love reigns over the ruins of our lives.

Today is the day your life can forever change! It's a new dawn, a new day, and a new reign in your life! You are no longer in the dark or ignorant concerning the enemy's devices. Daniel 2:22 tells us, "He reveals deep and hidden things; he knows what lies in darkness, and light dwells with him." Quite frankly, the enemy is pretty predictable in how he likes to attack our lives. He is not a creator but an imitator. Once we become fully aware, awake, and alive in Christ, we pose a threat to his kingdom of darkness. He wants you to forget that you are the light of the world, a city set on a hill that cannot be hidden, according to Matthew 5:14. Will you spend the rest of your days dimming your light and existing in the darkness of the devil's lies, or will you wake up from your sleep and take your rightful reign in the kingdom of God as a son or daughter of the living God?

Ephesians 5:12-15 says,

> But all things become visible when they are exposed by the light, for everything that becomes visible is light. For this reason it says, "Awake, sleeper, And arise from the dead, And Christ will shine on you." Therefore be careful how you walk, not as unwise men but as wise,

making the most of your time, because the days are evil. So then do not be foolish, but understand what the will of the Lord is.

When reading that verse, insert your name where it says "sleeper," because God is talking directly to you, as one of His children, in this passage. It is time to awake and arise from the dead, letting the light of Christ shine on you, in you, and through you.

Your new reign starts right now, one moment at a time, one day at a time, and one decision at a time. You have to make the choice not to sleep on this pivotal divine appointment in time. Don't miss this moment where time and eternity collide. The King of kings and Lord of lords is ready to hand you the keys to the kingdom and give you authority over your life under His lordship.

In order for His piercing light to break forth through the dark shadows of your situation, you are required to do only one thing. That one thing is surrender! You can only receive this great awakening by letting go and letting God have His way with every aspect of your life. You must get vulnerable and give Him complete access to all of the places and spaces of your soul. However, know that He will never force Himself on you. God is a perfect gentleman and is standing at the door of your soul, gently knocking to come in. Once you open the door, your life will never be the same. Old things will pass away, and all things will become new.

When you say yes to His Word, will, and way, there is a divine transformation awaiting you. John 14:6 says, "Jesus answered, 'I am the way and the truth and the life. No one comes to the Father except through me.'" The way out of the darkness and into His marvelous light is only found by receiving something you could never earn or afford. This gift is priceless, and no earthly value could ever be placed on it.

1 Peter 1:19 tells us,

> For you know that it was not with perishable things such as silver or gold that you were redeemed from the empty way of life you inherited from your forefathers, but with the precious blood of Christ, a lamb without blemish or spot. He was known before the foundation of the world, but was revealed in the last times for your sake.

Don't be afraid to allow God to do a new thing in your life. Get used to being comfortably uncomfortable. You need to step out of your comfort zone to create genuine, lasting, and permanent change for a new legacy to reign for generations to come. Take the limits off of what and how He wants to move in your life. Your new reign, new beginning, and fresh start might not look like anything in your past. We are human beings, not human doings. You are not what you do to pay the bills or what's happened to you in your past. You are a child of the King, called to rise, shine, and reign over everything. After all, life is just a series of new beginnings. Reinvent yourself, try new things, and don't be bound to one thing your whole life. Most people evolve, change, and redirect with time, and life-altering circumstances have a way of shifting things into divine alignment.

Don't be like an oak tree that uproots itself when the storms hit, but be like a palm tree and learn to bend and sway in the seasons of struggle and uncertainty. Maybe that's why God made me a Florida girl—so I could learn to be flexible and sway during life's storms. After a hurricane, one of the first things people notice here in Florida are that the palm trees are still standing. Your roots have to be dug down deep, but you have to be pliable to bend in the direction of the winds and waves. When the stormy, dark skies clear, God will let the Son shine again over the wreckage of your life. Psalm 119:30 says, "Commit your way to the Lord; trust in him and he will do this: He will make your righteous reward shine like the dawn, your vindication like the noonday sun." God knows how to redeem, restore, and reward those who diligently trust Him.

James 1:17 declares, "Every good gift and every perfect gift is from above, coming down from the Father of lights with whom there is no variation or shadow due to change." Now, as you believe that truth and receive it with every fiber of your being, your reign will resound through heaven and earth with shouts of praise! Genesis 1:3 states, "And God said, 'Let there be light,' and there was light." May His truth and never-ending love for you pave your path with peace and purpose.

In Psalm 119:105, we read this powerful truth: "Your word is a lamp unto your feet and a light unto my path." Ultimately, all paths lead us home to streets paved with gold, where we will reign for eternity with our heavenly Father. The things of the world will grow strangely dim in the light of His glory and grace.

Psalm 23 gives us a blessed reassurance that we will one day reign over death and enter our eternal reign with King Jesus.

> The Lord is my shepherd; I shall not want. He maketh me to lie down in green pastures: he leadeth me beside the still waters. He restoreth my soul: he leadeth me in the paths of righteousness for his name's sake. Yea,

> though I walk through the valley of the shadow of death, I will fear no evil: for thou art with me; thy rod and thy staff they comfort me. Thou preparest a table before me in the presence of mine enemies: thou anointest my head with oil; my cup runneth over. Surely goodness and mercy shall follow me all the days of my life: and I will dwell in the house of the Lord for ever.

In the meantime, we are not here just to buy time, check out, or rush Christ's return. God has given us too much for us to keep it all to ourselves. In Mark 13:32, Jesus tells us, "Heaven and earth will pass away, but My words will never pass away. No one knows about that day or hour, not even the angels in heaven, nor the Son, but only the Father." We know that Jesus will one day return, so be on your guard and stay alert! He wants to occupy the throne of your life and empower you by the Holy Spirit to awaken the kingdom within and take new territory for His glory.

Hebrews 12:2 says, "Looking unto Jesus, the author and finisher of *our* faith, who for the joy that was set before Him endured the cross, despising the shame, and has sat down at the right hand of the throne of God." Let your tongue be the pen of a ready writer and declare that your story is just being written.

I will leave you with the powerful words of my great-grandmother Hannah: "When we left a book, we knew it." I pray that every word you read waters the roots of your spirit and soul with life-giving nourishment. May this book always be a reminder that you were called and created to rise, shine, and reign for such a time as this!

_____ (insert your name), your reign begins now...

                Reigning in gratitude,
                Courtney Dawn Shaw

KINGDOM (QUEST)IONS:

1. What do you want your legacy to be?

   _____

   _____

   _____

2. Have you created a legacy drawer? If not, what is the first thing you will do to get it started?

   _____

   _____

   _____

3. Have you written your final wishes? If not, give yourself a timeline to get it done and place them in your legacy drawer.

   _____

   _____

   _____

4. Have you documented your family history? If not, start with your biological parents.

   _____

   _____

   _____

5. What are your new family core values?

6. Have you spoken a blessing over your life and family? If not, write a blessing to speak aloud. Speak things that are not as though they are. Take the limits off what God wants to do in and through your life and those surrounding you.

7. What is your family vision/mission statement?

KINGDOM TRUTHS

"One generation shall commend your works to another, and shall declare your mighty acts."–Psalm 145:4

"But lay up for yourselves treasures in heaven, where neither moth nor rust destroys and where thieves do not break in and steal. For where your treasure is, there your heart will be also."–Matthew 6:20-21

"I have no greater joy than to hear that my children are walking in truth."–3 John 1:4

"I press toward the goal for the prize of the high calling of God in Christ Jesus."–Philippians 3:14

"Praise the Lord! Blessed is the man who fears the Lord, who greatly delights in his commandments. His offspring will be mighty in the land; the generation of the upright will be blessed. Wealth and riches are in his house, and his righteousness endures forever."–Psalm 112:1-3

"I call heaven and earth to witness against you today, that I have set before you life and death, blessing, and curse. Therefore choose life, that you and your offspring may live, loving the Lord God, obeying His voice and holding fast to Him for He is your life and length of days, that you may dwell in the land that the Lord swore to your fathers, to Abraham, to Isaac, and to Jacob to give them."–Deuteronomy 30:19-20

"We will not hide them from their children but tell to the coming generation the glorious deeds of the Lord, and his might, and the wonders that He has done."–Psalm 78:4

KINGDOM DECLARATION

New Dawn, New Day, New Reign
Declaration

On this ___ day of ____, 20____,

I, _____, declare and decree that my family tree changes with me. I will be intentional about how I live daily with my legacy in mind. I will choose to speak life and blessing over my family and those around me. I will choose to rise up in the resurrection power of Jesus Christ and reign over past generational curses and dysfunctional behavioral patterns, and I will let go of any limitations that have been spoken over me and my family. I choose to take on the belief system of a son/daughter in Christ and know that I am safe, confident, and fully equipped in my heavenly Father's love for me. As for me and my house, we shall serve the Lord. It's a new dawn, a new day, and a new reign in my life.

ABOUT THE AUTHOR

Courtney Dawn Shaw is married to her best friend, Jeffrey, of eighteen years. She is mom to Kingston (thirteen) and Carrington (nine). She is an author, a speaker, a television and radio host, a certified personal trainer, and Mrs. Florida America 2014-2015. You can view her show *Authentic Living* on 24 Flix. She is a lifetime health advocate and a member of the President's Council on Sports, Fitness, and Nutrition. You can always catch Courtney in the community supporting her children's sports and hosting charitable events.

BIBLIOGRAPHY NOTES

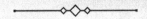

1. Definition of new dawn, new day, new reign, accessed February 25, 2022 http://www.dictionary.com,

2. Footprints Poem, Footprints in the Sand poem, accessed February 25, 2022 http://www.praywithme.com

3. Dr. Caroline Leaf, Cleaning Up Your Mental Mess, http:www.drleaf.com, article accessed February 25, 2022

4. Come to the Edge Poem by Christopher Logue, poem accessed February 25, 2022 http://www.goodreads.com/quotes

5. Dr. Caroline Leaf, Cleaning Up Your Mental Mess, http:www.drleaf.com, article accessed February 25, 2022

6. Handy Manny, One Step at a Time Official Music Video, Disney Junior, accessed February 25, 2022 http://www.youtube.com/watch?v=RXHLIZo3DWg

7. Fish Oil, article on Fish Oil by Mayo Clinic Staff, Overview of benefits, accessed February 25, 2022 http://www.mayoclinic.org

8. Jim Gaffigan, Parenting quote, accessed February 25, 2022 http://facebook.com/lifeafterbirthAZ

9. Andy Stanley, quotes about raising children, accessed February 25, 2022 https://www.azquotes.com

10. Mother Teresa, quote accessed February 25, 2022 https://www.azquotes.com/motherteresa

11. Gospel Coalition, definition of generational curses, accessed February 25, 2022 http://gospelcoalition.com

12. Legacy Message by Brian Bullock, accessed February 25, 2022 http://www.youtube.com/BrianBullock

13. Billy Graham quote, Article on Rock this Revival Legacy, Accessed February 25, 2022 http://www.rockthis.org